W9-CNQ-056

ENCYCLOPEDIA OF

FAMILY HEALTH

ENCYCLOPEDIA OF

FAMILY HEALTH

CONSULTANT

DAVID B. JACOBY, MD

JOHNS HOPKINS SCHOOL OF MEDICINE

VOLUME
7

INFERTILITY–LIQUID DIET

MARSHALL CAVENDISH
NEW YORK · LONDON · TORONTO · SYDNEY

Marshall Cavendish Corporation

99 White Plains Road

Tarrytown, New York 10591-9001

© Marshall Cavendish Corporation, 1998

© Marshall Cavendish Limited 1998, 1991, 1988, 1986, 1983, 1982, 1971

Update by Brown Partworks

The material in this set was first published in the English language by

Marshall Cavendish Limited of 119 Wardour Street, London W1V 3TD, England.

Printed and bound in Italy

Library of Congress Cataloging-in-Publication Data

Encyclopedia of family health

17v. cm.

Includes index

1. Medicine, Popular–Encyclopedias. 2. Health–Encyclopedias. I. Marshall Cavendish Corporation.

RC81.A2M336 1998   96–49537

610'. 3–dc21   CIP

ISBN 0-7614-0625-5 (set)

ISBN 0-7614-0632-8 (v.7)

This encyclopedia is not intended for use as a
substitute for advice, consultation, or treatment by a
licensed medical practitioner. The reader is advised
that no action of a medical nature should be taken
without consultation with a licensed medical
practitioner, including action that may seem to be
indicated by the contents of this work, as individual
circumstances vary and medical standards,
knowledge, and practices change with time. The
publishers, authors, and medical consultants disclaim
all liability and cannot be held responsible for any
problems that may arise from its use.

INTRODUCTION

We Americans live under a constant bombardment of information (and misinformation) about the latest supposed threats to our health. We are taught to believe that disease is the result of not taking care of ourselves. Death becomes optional. Preventive medicine becomes a moral crusade, illness the punishment for the foolish excesses of the American lifestyle. It is not the intent of the authors of this encyclopedia to contribute to this atmosphere. While it is undoubtedly true that Americans could improve their health by smoking less, exercising more, and controlling their weight, this is already widely understood.

As Mencken put it, "It is not the aim of medicine to make men virtuous. The physician should not preach salvation, he should offer absolution." The aims of this encyclopedia are to present a summary of human biology, anatomy, and physiology, to outline the more common diseases, and to discuss, in a general way, the diagnosis and treatment of these diseases. This is not a do-it-yourself book. It will not be possible to treat most conditions based on the information presented here. But it will be possible to understand most diseases and their treatments. Informed in this way, you will be able to discuss your condition and its treatment with your physician. It is also hoped that this will alleviate some of the fears associated with diseases, doctors, and hospitals.

The authors of this encyclopedia have also attempted to present, in an open-minded way, alternative therapies. There is undoubtedly value to some of these. However, when dealing with serious diseases, they should not be viewed as a substitute for conventional treatment. The reason that conventional treatment is accepted is that it has been systematically tested, and because scientific evidence backs it up. It would be a tragedy to miss the opportunity for effective treatment while pursuing an ineffective alternative therapy.

Finally, it should be remembered that the word *doctor* is originally from the Latin word for "teacher." Applied to medicine, this should remind us that the doctor's duty is not only to diagnose and treat disease, but to help the patient to understand. If this encyclopedia can aid in this process, its authors will be gratified.

DAVID B. JACOBY, MD
JOHNS HOPKINS SCHOOL OF MEDICINE

CONTENTS

Infertility

Q My husband and I have been trying for a year to have a baby. A friend told me that she conceived when her doctor told her husband to wear loose underpants! Can this really work?

A Tight underpants or trousers can cause the temperature of the scrotal sac to be much higher than sperm can tolerate, thus killing them off. However, this is only one of several possibilities. Go to your doctor to discuss the problem.

Q You often read of people who thought they were infertile adopting a child and almost immediately having a child of their own. Why should this be?

A A couple who are eager to have a child and then become very anxious when they don't conceive may be infertile for this very reason. Once they adopt a child the pressure is off them, and this may be all that is necessary to restore fertility.

Q My doctor has suggested I take a fertility drug, but what if I couldn't cope with a large number of children at once?

A Fertility drugs do not always cause multiple births. There is a slightly increased chance of twins being conceived, but more babies than that is rare if the medication has been properly monitored.

Q My doctor is recommending me for AID (artificial insemination by donor). My husband agrees that I should do this since he is infertile and we both want a child. What does it involve and will it work?

A With AID the vagina is gently opened with a speculum (a gynecological instrument) and a plastic tube moves donor sperm from a syringe to the cervix (neck of the uterus). It is usually done on three consecutive days around the time of ovulation (when the woman is fertile) and is continued for six months to a year. About two-thirds of the women who have AID conceive within three months.

Failure to produce a much-wanted child can cause great psychological stress in both the man and the woman. Fortunately treatment for infertility is improving all the time as new advances are made.

It can come as a severe blow to a couple to find that they cannot have children. Many of the cases of infertility have no accompanying symptoms, so it is only when the couple try to conceive that they realize they have a problem.

Possible infertility is indicated when a couple fail to achieve conception after a year or more of having intercourse without contraception. Some doctors prefer a couple to try for two years before they begin tests and treatment for infertility, but this will depend to some extent on the age of the woman.

Between 10 and 15 percent of couples are infertile and the numbers seem to be rising gradually, possibly due to the increasing incidence of sexually transmitted diseases (STD). Sex becomes a strain, focused as it is on the fertile time of the month, and many couples experience a loss of desire if they feel that each time they are trying (and failing) to make a baby, rather than making love.

It is important that both partners go to see their doctor, because the problem is just as likely to affect the man as the woman.

If the reason for infertility is not immediately obvious then tests are performed to find the cause.

Causes
There are many different causes of infertility and it is a subject that is constantly under review, with new discoveries causes and treatments being made all the time. Infertility is just as likely to be caused by a problem in the man as in the woman, and in 30 percent of cases it is a combination of factors on both sides.

The most common cause in women failure to ovulate (release an egg from the ovary each month) due to a hormone failure. Sometimes hormone imbalance can produce hostile mucus in the vagina that actually repels the male sperm or stops the fertilized egg from attaching itself the lining of the uterus.

In some women the problem may be physical one, such as a hymen or a vagina that is too tight for intercourse or a malformation of the vulva (external genitalia the vagina, or any reproductive organ.

Other disorders that can lead to infertility may happen at any time, such as

Reasons for infertility

Problems	Possible causes	Symptoms and diagnosis	Treatment
IN MEN			
No sperm or low sperm production	Mumps after puberty; marijuana; exposure to X rays (e.g., chemotherapy); high temperature of scrotal sac; excessive alcohol	Semen analysis will show sperm count. Less than 20 million per cubic centimeter is below average	Male hormones may increase sperm count temporarily. Where the sperm count is low, women may be artificially inseminated
Inability of sperm to swim	Chronic prostatis (inflammation of the prostate gland); surgical removal of the prostate; hormonal imbalance	Semen analysis will show whether the sperm can swim actively	Steroid treatment may be prescribed
Inability to deposit sperm in vagina near the cervix	Impotence; premature ejaculation; obesity	Physical examination and case history will diagnose the problem	Sexual therapy for impotence and premature ejaculation
Blockage of tubes carrying sperm	Untreated STD; varicocele (varicose veins in scrotum)	Same as above	Drugs to treat STD. Surgery to tie off varicocele
IN WOMEN			
Pelvic inflammatory disease such as parametritis (which affects the uterus); salpingitis (which affects fallopian tubes); or salpingoophoritis (which affects the tubes and ovaries)	Gonorrhea; certain bacteria; viruses; irritation from IUD	Pelvic pain; pain with intercourse; pain with menstruation; irregular bleeding	Occasionally surgery is suggested to clean out scar tissue formed during long-term infection
Endometriosis (tissue that normally lines the uterus found in abnormal places)	Tissue forms in response to abnormal hormonal stimulation; cells from the uterus travel up fallopian tubes and implant themselves elsewhere	Menstrual pain; pain with intercourse	Surgical removal at an early stage may halt the problem, accompanied by hormone treatment
Sexually transmitted disease (untreated)	Intercourse with an infected person	Routine tests will show gonorrhea	Drug treatment of any infection; possible tubal surgery
Failure to ovulate (release eggs)	Malfunction of pituitary, thyroid, or adrenal glands that influence the menstrual cycle	Endometrial biopsy (biopsy of uterus) may be performed; also hormone tests	Treatment with fertility drugs
Cervical problems	Cervical infection; mucus that repels sperm; polyps	General examination; possible scrape of cervix	Treatment with drugs or possibly surgery depending on cause
Inflammation or blocked fallopian tubes	Could be caused by peritonitis; infection; tuberculosis	Rubin's and hysterosalpingography tests and laparoscopy inspection	Treatment will depend on results of tests. May need surgery

infection from bacteria or viruses; sexually transmitted diseases; or the growth of fibroids, polyps, or cysts.

Emotional stress is another common cause. Psychological factors can stop ovulation or cause spasms in the fallopian tubes that inhibit the passage of the egg to the uterus.

Infertility in men can be due to no sperm, low sperm production, or sluggish sperm that do not swim as they should. High numbers of abnormally shaped sperm can also cause infertility.

A blockage of one of the tubes that carries the sperm is another cause of male infertility. This may be the result of varicocele (varicose veins inside the scrotum; see Varicose veins), a tuberculous infection of the prostate gland, or untreated sexually transmitted disease. Alcohol can reduce fertility. Impotence and pre-

mature ejaculation also cause infertility, and these may have a psychological basis.

Diagnosing the problem

An infertile couple will be referred by their doctor to their local hospital or infertility clinic, and they should go together since it is just as likely for the man to be infertile as it is for the woman or for there to be a joint problem.

Diagnosing the trouble can take a long time. To start with, both partners will have a general physical examination and medical histories will be taken. The doctor will want to know when the woman's periods started, whether she has a regular menstrual cycle (regular periods), in addition to details about both partners' past and present health and their sex life.

The man will have a semen count, since there would be no point in per-

forming tests on the woman if the man has a very low sperm count. He produces a sperm sample by masturbating into a clean, preferably sterile, glass or plastic container. The couple should not have intercourse for at least two days before the test, because the number of sperm in the semen should be as high as possible.

It will be assumed that the man has no fertility problem if his sperm count is no lower than 330 million sperm per cubic inch (20 million per cubic centimeter) of semen, that at least 40 percent of the sperm are active, and 60 percent are of normal shape.

If no abnormality is found then tests will continue on the woman. She will be shown how to prepare a basal temperature chart to indicate when she is ovulating. The basal body temperature (the temperature of the body at rest) rises when a woman ovulates, but because it varies with many factors, such as the time of day, it should be taken at the same time each morning, before getting out of bed or having anything to drink.

Ovulation is indicated by a rise of about 0.4°F (0.2°C) or more. Sperm can live for three to five days in a woman's fallopian tubes; the egg only lives for about 12 hours after it is released from the ovary, so the couple must make sure they have intercourse at that time.

Physicians often recommend that the woman keeps a basal chart for several months so that they can establish her ovulation pattern (see Menstruation).

However, not all doctors consider this method of pinpointing ovulation reliable. Other tests may be used, among them the serum progesterone test. Using the woman's temperature chart as a guide or, alternatively, by giving her a blood test about six days before her next period, the rise in the level of the hormone progesterone, which happens immediately after ovulation, can be measured.

An endometrial biopsy is another test. By taking a sample of the endometrium

The ovulation pattern
The basal chart below shows the hormone and temperature changes during a woman's menstrual cycle.
Day 1: first day of period—low estrogen level makes the pituitary gland produce FSH (follicle stimulating hormone). BBT (basal body temperature) is normal.
Day 4: FSH stimulates egg follicles. Estrogen is produced, stimulating growth of uterus lining as pituitary produces LH (luteinizing hormone) instead of FSH. BBT is normal. Period finishes. Increased estrogen causes production of thick mucus.
Days 10–13: progesterone produced, softening uterus lining for an egg.
Day 14: LH causes egg follicle to burst—ovulation. Peak mucus occurs and progesterone raises BBT.
From Day 15: if no pregnancy estrogen and progesterone levels fall. BBT remains high. On Day 28 low progesterone level causes shedding of uterus lining. BBT is back to normal.

(lining of the uterus) and examining it under a microscope, the doctor can tell whether or not ovulation has occurred and approximately when it has taken place. This is a reliable test and is usually done under general anesthetic.

Postcoital test
An abnormality of the cervix or the mucus in the cervical canal can be diagnosed by a simple, painless test called the postcoital test. This involves taking some of the mucus from the cervix to see what is happening to sperm in the vagina after intercourse and whether the sperm are still active after several hours. The test is best performed around the time of ovulation. The woman will be asked to have intercourse the night before or on the morning of the test. The mucus should be clear and still contain moving sperm.

Rubin's test
This is one of the tests that is done to see if the fallopian tubes are blocked. Gas is passed through a special applicator into the uterus, sometimes under a general anesthetic, and the doctor listens to the

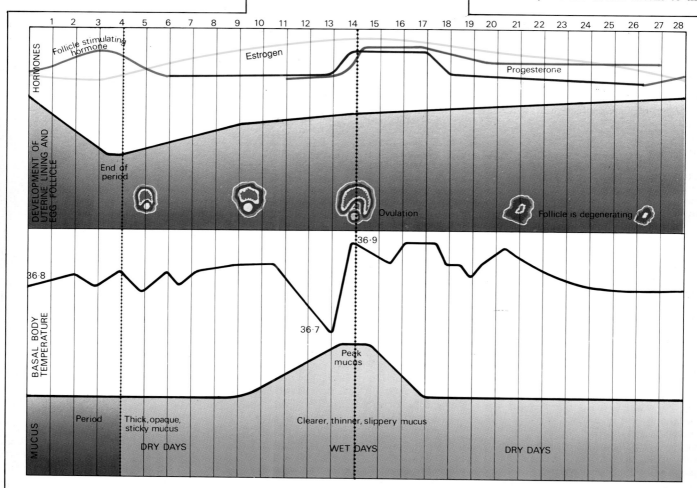

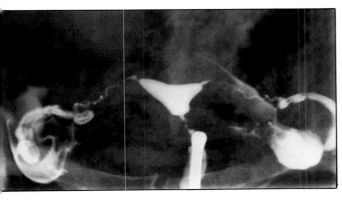

Dye has been injected through the cervix and can be seen flowing along the fallopian tubes (left). The dye cannot get through the blocked right-hand tube (right).

gas passing through each fallopian tube with a stethoscope. The pressure of the gas is measured, and if both tubes are blocked the pressure gauge will show a steep rise almost immediately.

Hysterosalpingography

A more accurate test, called a hysterosalpingography, involves injecting a colored dye through the cervix and up each fallopian tube. X rays are then taken to reveal any blockage of the tubes, the shape of the uterus, and to show whether the cervix is functioning properly. The test is usually performed during the first 10 days of the menstrual cycle. An anesthetic is not usually necessary.

Laparoscopy

A relatively new test, the laparoscopy, allows a direct view of the uterus, fallopian tubes, and ovaries. It is done under a general anesthetic since it involves piercing the abdominal wall with a thin needle through which gas is passed to distend the abdominal cavity. Then an optical instrument called a laparoscope is passed through a slightly larger incision just below the navel. The ovaries and uterus can be biopsied if necessary. It is possible to perform minor surgery through the laparoscope (see Laparoscopy).

Treatment

In over 10 percent of all infertile couples, no reason for infertility is found but, taking all the cases into account, a five percent spontaneous cure results before any treatment is started. The very fact that a couple is in the care of an infertility specialist can ease tensions when the problem is based on emotional factors.

Treatment varies according to the diagnosis. Failure to ovulate may be treated with fertility drugs with a very high success rate.

Surgery is sometimes needed to: clear blocked tubes; scrape the uterus; correct

Most women cope well with twins after they are born. Fertility drugs can result in two babies, and sometimes more than that.

congenital (since birth) abnormalities; and to remove fibroids, polyps, or cysts.

The man may be treated with hormones or steroids. If his sperm count is low, then his partner has a greater chance of conceiving if she is artificially inseminated with his sperm. This is known as AIH (artificial insemination by husband) and the technique is exactly the same as AID (artificial insemination by donor; see Artificial insemination). It may be possible to clear blocked seminal tubes and tie off varicocele by surgery.

When there is no effective treatment, artificial insemination by donor (AID) may be recommended.

Any infection that may affect the fertility of either partner will be treated with the appropriate drugs.

In both men and women, psychotherapy or couples counseling may be more helpful than physical treatment when the problem seems to have an emotional or psychological basis.

Outlook

Some fertility problems respond well to treatment. On the whole male problems do not respond as well as do female fertility problems to the types of treatment that are available currently.

Couples who have not found a treatment that works for them should not give up hope entirely. It is worth their while to keep in touch with their hospital or infertility clinic in case their problem is solved by research at some future date.

Spectrum

Inflammation

Q Are there any areas of the body where inflammation is especially dangerous? What about the heart and the brain?

A Inflammation of the heart lining is dangerous, as are brain inflammation and inflammation of the brain coverings. These need urgent medical management. However, the most critically dangerous form of inflammation involves the inner lining of the voice box. Inflammatory swelling of the laryngeal lining can sever the airway, leading to asphyxiation and death. In such cases an emergency tracheostomy (where a cut is made at the front of the neck into the windpipe below the larynx) may be necessary to save the patient's life.

Q How do the white blood cells know that they are required at a particular site of tissue damage?

A Messages are sent around the body in the form of chemical substances released at the site of damage. These substances (called cytokines) are produced by both damaged and undamaged cells; white blood cells move toward the highest concentration of the chemicals by a process called chemotaxis. The white blood cells also produce cytokines to attract more white blood cells so that the number at the damage site quickly builds up.

Q If white blood cells work by producing oxygen free radicals, why do experts recommend the use of antioxidants as a health aid?

A White blood cells kill germs by releasing megadoses of free radicals in localized areas of the body; these concentrations do not affect the rest of the body. Antioxidant vitamins such as C and E work in very low concentrations, so they do not adversely affect the white blood cells. If free radicals are present in large amounts (from cigarette smoke, for example), antioxidants may mop up the excess.

When the body is damaged in any way, whether by physical or chemical injury or by infection with bacteria, viruses, or other organisms, it responds by the process of inflammation. This makes inflammation the most common indication that a disease is developing.

Inflammation is the response of living tissue to injury, and its features are so obvious that they must have been recognized from the earliest times. In the first century A.D. the Roman medical writer Aurelius Cornelius Celsus, whose book *De Medicina* was finally printed in 1478, recorded a remarkably accurate account of the inflammatory process and described its four cardinal signs: redness, heat, swelling, and pain.

Inflammation is the most common of all the disease processes included in the general term *pathology*. This is demonstrated by the enormous number of disorders whose names end in *-itis,* a suffix meaning "inflammation of." Thus tonsillitis is an inflammation of the tonsils, gastritis an inflammation of the stomach, dermatitis an inflammation of the skin, neuritis an inflammation of a nerve, cystitis an inflammation of the bladder, and so on. This word-ending is so well recognized that it has been used by nonmedical people, humorously if inaccurately, to

Any area of the body may become inflamed. The eyes are especially sensitive to the effects of hay fever, which may be caused by a variety of allergens, such as pollen.

The cardinal signs of inflammation

So far as is known, the cardinal signs of inflammation were first formally described about 2,000 years ago by Aurelius Cornelius Celsus in the fourth book of his great eight-book medical treatise *De Medicina*. Celsus, writing in Latin, described the four signs *rubor*, *calor*, *dolor*, and *tumor*—respectively redness, heat, pain, and swelling. Strictly speaking only three of these—redness, heat, and swelling—are signs. Pain, being purely subjective, is actually a symptom. Later another writer, believed to be the Roman physician Galen, added a final feature, *functio laesa*, meaning "loss of function"

invent words such as *examinitis* an *scribbleritis.* The term *dermatitis* is no as is commonly thought, the name of disease. Dermatitis is the most obviou physical sign of the very large number different diseases that can cause inflar mations of the skin (see Dermatitis).

So inflammation is not a disease in i own right but simply a defensi

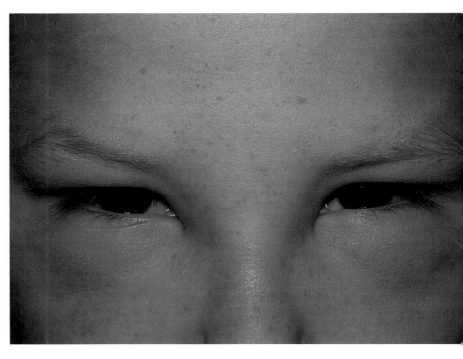

esponse of the body to various threats. It s, of course, a principal feature of thousands of diseases.

Causes of inflammation

The long list of causes of inflammation includes almost anything that can injure any part of the body. The principal causes are heat; cold; cutting; sustained friction; crushing; corrosive acids and alkalis; chemical poisons; certain body fluids, such as bile or urine, when displaced from their normal sites into the tissues; ultraviolet radiation (as in sunlight); ionizing radiation (as in X rays and gamma rays); loss of blood supply to living tissue; abnormal functioning of the immune system, with attack on tissues by immune system cells (autoimmunity); and other defects of the immune system, such as hypersensitivity reactions (allergy).

However, most common of all causes of inflammation are the toxic substances and immune system reactions produced by infecting or infesting organisms. These include viruses, bacteria, fungi, single-celled creatures (protozoa), and larger parasites, such as worms and various insect pests. All of these things can, and commonly do, induce inflammation, and although they are very different by nature, the response to all of them is remarkably similar.

The purpose of inflammation

Without the inflammatory response humans would not live very long, because they would quickly be overwhelmed by germs that produce toxins so virulent that their body cells would be killed. Some of the bacterial toxins are among the most poisonous substances known to science; a tiny dose, measured in millionths of a gram, may be sufficient to kill a human being.

So the first purpose of inflammation is to attack, inactivate, and destroy invading germs before they can become established and reproduce themselves in sufficient numbers to kill the body.

Inflammation involves local changes that result in enormous numbers of immune system cells being brought to the site of invasion. However, inflammation occurs under many circumstances other than as a result of the invasion by germs. Whenever there is tissue damage, inflammation results and the second purpose of inflammation is to enable the body to start to repair this damage.

Acute and chronic inflammation

Both of these purposes require a greatly increased blood supply to the affected area so that sufficient numbers of the different kinds of cells concerned with defense and repair become available.

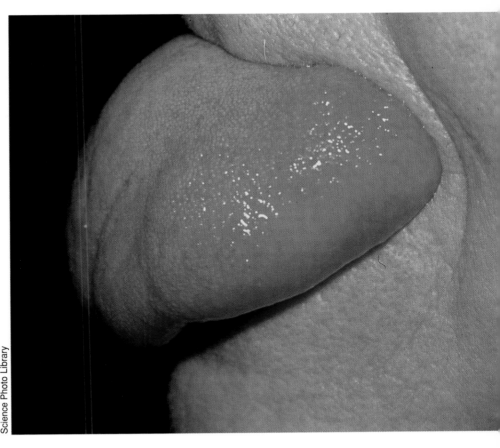

Science Photo Library

Inflammation is, in most cases, protective and leads to a return to normality and repair of damage. This applies to what is called acute inflammation, which is a short, sharp engagement that is soon successfully over.

However, inflammation does not always take this form. Sometimes the balance of the forces between the attack and the resistance of the immune system is more equal and the inflammation becomes more persistent; it may last for weeks and sometimes even months. This condition is called chronic inflammation, and it may lead to the formation of undesirable scar tissue, or it may have other unfortunate effects, such as abnormal adhesions between body surfaces.

The nature of inflammation

Inflammation essentially involves the small blood vessels, and therefore it is only possible for it to affect tissues that contain blood vessels. It cannot occur in tissues such as the corneas or crystalline lenses of the eyes, which are free from blood vessels.

However, these tissues are exceptions to the rule, and almost all other body tissues are copiously supplied with small vessels. The most profuse type of blood vessel in the body are the capillaries; these are tiny thin-walled networks of

In angioneurotic edema, inflammation of the tongue may result from an allergic reaction to foods, such as eggs. It may also cause breathing difficulties (see Allergies).

tubes that lie between the smallest arteries and the smallest veins.

Capillaries perform an important function in inflammation, therefore a brief description is necessary.

Function of capillaries

Capillaries are present in such enormous quantities almost everywhere in the body that if all other structures were removed, the human shape would still be recognizable. Their walls consist of a single layer of flattened cells joined edge-to-edge with tiny gaps at these junctions. The average diameter of the capillaries is about equal to or slightly greater than that of a red blood cell.

The pressure of the blood in the capillaries is very low, but it is highest at the point at which they branch off from the small arteries and lowest where they join the small veins. As a result there is a constant inflow of watery fluid from the blood through the capillary wall at the arterial end and an outflow of fluid at the venous end.

This fluid bathes all the cells of the body, and it is by way of this fluid that oxygen and dissolved nutrients are supplied to the cells and waste products, such as carbon dioxide and cell metabolic discharge, are removed.

Blood cell emigration

In healthy body tissue the red blood cells cannot pass through the walls of the capillaries, but there are other cells in the blood that can accomplish this task. Large protein molecules are also too big to get through the gaps in the capillary walls when the tissue is healthy.

However, when a tissue suffers from inflammation, its supplying blood vessels widen and the blood flow through it increases in a marked way. At the same time the cells in the walls of the capillaries separate sufficiently to allow protein molecules in the blood, including antibodies, to pass out.

This leads to a protein-rich discharge in the inflamed area. White blood cells also emigrate from the blood vessels by squeezing through these tiny openings, proceeding to investigate and to try to deal with the cause of the inflammation. The widening of the blood vessels and the increased fluid outflow from the capillaries account for the redness and heat, and the increased fluid in the tissues accounts for the swelling.

Prostaglandins

The pain of inflammation is caused by the release of powerful substances called prostaglandins from damaged cells. These stimulate pain nerve endings. Certain drugs, such as aspirin, prevent the release of prostaglandins (see Prostaglandins). This is how they relieve pain (see Pain).

White blood cells

The key operators in inflammation due to infection are the white blood cells. These are all cells of the immune system and are easily distinguished from the far more numerous red blood cells whose function is to carry oxygen from the lungs to the other tissues (see Blood).

The white blood cells come in various forms, including the small round B and T lymphocytes that produce antibodies and perform many other immune functions (see Immune System). However, the most obvious cells in inflammation are those known as phagocytes. The ending -cyte means "cell" and the root phagos means "eating." Therefore, phagocytes are "eating cells," and this is, literally, their function.

Phagocytes

Amoebic and gellike with an elastic outer membrane, phagocytes have no particular shape and move around by pushing out a kind of temporary limb (a pseudopodium—literally a "false foot") and then flowing into it. It is the ability to change shape and to send out protrusions that allows phagocytes to get through the tiny gaps in the walls of the capillaries.

Pseudopodia have another function, and it is this function that gives phagocytes their name. If a phagocyte encounters a foreign object, such as a bacterium or a piece of dead organic debris, it puts out a tubelike pseudopodium to surround the object. It then flows into the pseudopodium and around the object so that the latter is incorporated into the phagocyte's body.

The interior of the phagocyte is filled with fluid that contains a number of powerful chemical activators, called enzymes. These enzymes are capable of digesting and breaking up most kinds of organic material (see Enzymes).

Oxidants

In the presence of bacteria and other organisms, enzymes inside the white blood cells produce a powerful oxygen free radical known as superoxide. This immediately generates the strong oxidant hydrogen peroxide.

The red, inflamed, and scaly areas of this child's mouth are due to perioral dermatitis. Dermatitis refers to an inflammation of the skin due to an allergy or an unknown cause.

Hydrogen peroxide then acts on chloride in the phagocyte to form the chemical compound hypochlorous acid (this is also the basis of a widely used domestic disinfectant) that soon completely destroys the germs.

This disposal method by the phagocytes has negative repercussions if the inflammation persists for too long. In a condition where there is chronic (long-term) inflammation, successive waves of millions of phagocytes descend on the affected area of the body.

Unfortunately the free radicals do not stay in the phagocytes, and large quantities are released into the surrounding body tissues. Hydrogen peroxide and hypochlorous acid are seriously damaging to cells of all kinds, and this is the reason why chronic inflammation can be associated with tissue destruction.

Repair cells

Cells that work to repair damage, such as the little protein factories called fibroblasts, also accumulate at the sites of inflammation. As soon as the acute inflammatory stage is over and the cause has been dealt with, these repair cells proceed to do everything they can to correct the original damage. In addition they repair any damage that has been caused by the inflammatory process.

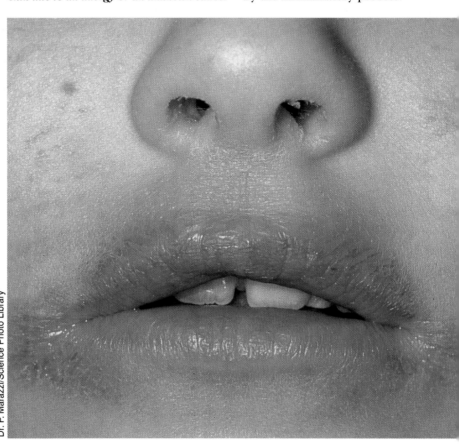

Dr. P. Marazzi/Science Photo Library

Influenza

Q The factory where I work offers free flu injections. Should I have one, and will it have any harmful side effects?

A An injection won't do you any harm at all, and the only side effects (which don't occur in all cases) are a sore arm and a raised temperature for 24 hours. The injection will offer you 60 percent protection against the flu in the winter of the year when you have it, and even if you do get the flu, it may be a much milder attack than you would otherwise have had.

Q My son, who is 12, has caught the flu at school. He shares a room with his younger brother. Should I move the younger boy to another room?

A People who are ill sleep badly, and your son may need attention during the night, so it would probably be better to move the younger boy. As for preventing him from catching the flu, it is probably too late to do that. The flu is infectious for one or two days before symptoms occur; it is almost impossible to stop it from spreading around a family.

Q Each time I catch the flu, I have different symptoms. Sometimes I just have a bad cold with a fever while other times I feel very tired and weak. Why should this be?

A There are three main strains of flu virus—types A, B, and C—and each one causes different symptoms. Type C is the mildest and causes similar symptoms to a cold. Type A is the most severe and causes the typical flu symptoms—fever, aching muscles, a sore throat, and a cough.

Q What is the difference between a mild flu and a bad cold?

A Colds and the flu are both caused by viruses. Colds usually cause little more than a runny nose whereas the flu tends to make people feverish. However, cold and flu symptoms often overlap, even though the viruses causing the illnesses are different.

Influenza is one of the most common illnesses and one of the most infectious. What can be done to guard against catching the flu and to keep attacks to a minimum?

Jonathan Watts/Science Photo Library

The influenza virus spreads in tiny droplets of water expelled from the nose when an infected person sneezes.

Influenza often occurs in epidemics when many people catch it at once. This usually happens in the winter, but people can get the flu at any time of the year.

Cause
The virus that causes influenza is special in that it is always changing its appearance to fool the body's defense mechanisms (see Immune system). It changes every year by a process called drift, and this results in outbreaks of the flu. Every 30–40 years a bigger change, known as shift, takes place, during which a different virus appears and causes a worldwide epidemic, or pandemic. Occasionally the flu virus changes to a form that resembles a previous virus, so that people who were infected by the first virus are immune to the second one.

Influenza is transmitted from person to person by coughing and sneezing. Drop-lets of secretions containing the virus from the infected person are breathed in by someone who is not infected, and this person starts to have the symptoms from one to three days later.

The part of animals in the spread of influenza is not well-known. Certainly domestic pets do not carry the disease. There is some evidence, however, that farm animals—for example, horses, hens, and pigs—do get a similar illness. The pig is thought to act as a potential carrier of swine influenza, which caused a pandemic in 1918–19.

Symptoms
Flu symptoms come on suddenly, with shivering and generalized aching in the

arms, legs, and back. The patient may have a headache, aching eyes, a sore or dry throat, and sometimes a cough and a runny nose. Occasionally there may also be the symptoms of a stomach upset, with vomiting and diarrhea. The body temperature at this point is above normal, usually between 101°F (38.4°C) and 102°F (39°C). The symptoms and fever continue for two to five days and leave the patient feeling tired and weak. He or she may also feel depressed and washed out. A sufferer should be reassured that this is quite normal after the flu and may last a few weeks. The cough may also persist for one to two weeks after the other symptoms have disappeared.

If a patient with the flu is examined by a doctor when he or she is ill, there is usually little sign of illness, except for a fever and an inflamed throat. These are the classic signs of the flu. If a patient has some immunity, he or she may often have a milder illness with fewer symptoms and only a small rise in temperature.

In case of the flu . . .

- Go to bed and keep warm
- Drink plenty of fluids; this is much more important than food. Drinks containing sugar provide some energy
- Take one or two acetaminophen pills every four hours to relieve aches and lower temperature
- Be careful to cough and sneeze into a handkerchief to limit the spread of infection
- When the temperature returns to normal, get up but take things easy for a few days
- If your fever lasts more than 3 to 4 days or is higher than 102°F (39°C), ask your doctor for advice

---

To aid a quick recovery after the first flu symptoms appear, go straight to bed and drink plenty of fluids.

The difference in immunity explains why some people get the disease worse than others, and why some people who have been in very close contact with an infected person may not feel ill at all. People become immune once they have had influenza because their body's defense mechanism recognizes the virus when it reappears and so prevents it from multiplying. This recognition does not happen if the flu virus has altered its appearance.

Complications and treatment

Influenza can strike all age groups, but the elderly are particularly prone to the complications of the flu.

The most common complication is a chest infection. This can vary from a mild cough to pneumonia. Sometimes the virus itself causes this, but more commonly another germ enters the body which has been weakened by the flu, and infects the chest. Older people and those who already have chest trouble are more likely to develop a chest infection after an attack of the flu.

If the flu patient has a severe cough, is producing green or yellow phlegm, has chest pains, or feels breathless, it is best to call the doctor. People who have other things wrong with them—for example, chest trouble, heart disease, or kidney problems—should let their doctor know if they catch the flu, because he or she may want to give them an antibiotic to prevent complications from developing.

If an attack of the flu seems prolonged and is not progressing normally, it is wise to contact the doctor.

In rare cases the flu virus can cause severe pneumonia, or pneumonia can be caused by another germ, which gets into the body when it is already undermined by the flu (see Pneumonia). In very severe cases of the flu virus itself, the heart or brain can be affected.

Prevention

There is at present no cure for the flu. The flu virus is always changing to fool the body's defenses, which is why vaccination does not always work.

In spite of this difficulty, vaccination is very useful, especially in communities such as schools, factories, and retirement or nursing homes. It is also useful in attempts to prevent the flu in people who are elderly or likely to develop more serious complications because of some other illness, such as chest trouble.

The flu injection (shot) is given in a single dose in the fall. It usually has no side effects, but occasionally it can make the arm sore or cause a slight rise in temperature that may last for up to 24 hours (see Vaccinations).

Ingrown toenail

Q If I let my toenails grow too long, will they begin to grow inward?

A No. Long toenails seem to grow straight. Cutting the nails too short encourages them to grow inward, and this should be avoided. Always cut cleanly and never pick at them; nails that are too short leave the fleshy side of the toe unprotected and open to the risk of infection (see Nails).

Q I have just had an operation for an ingrown toenail and the doctor told me not to cut it even if it sticks out over the end of the toe. Is this right?

A Yes. Never cut back an ingrown toenail. Keep the nail clean and remove any dirt or grime from under the nail. Bathe the toe regularly and dry it thoroughly, and, above all, wear loose-fitting shoes until the line of nail growth is well established. When the new nail has grown 0.125 in (3 mm) over the edge of the toe, then it is time to cut it firmly and neatly.

Q I have a chronically infected ingrown toenail and a growth has occurred on the edge. Is this serious?

A No. Where there is chronic inflammation, fibrous tissue full of tiny blood vessels often grows up from the site; this is called granulation tissue. It is best to ask your doctor to remove it: this is usually done by applying a stick of silver nitrate. When it subsides there is a good chance the nail will return to normal.

Q Are some people more prone to ingrown toenails than others? My family seem to suffer from this problem more than others I know.

A There is a great element of chance in who will get ingrown toenails, although it does seem that some people are more likely to develop them than others. However, ingrown toenails are not inherited. The only way to prevent them is to cut the toenails properly and wear good-fitting shoes.

This common condition is painful and ugly. Treatment is effective, but good foot care and wearing good-fitting shoes can prevent the problem of ingrown toenails from occurring in the first place.

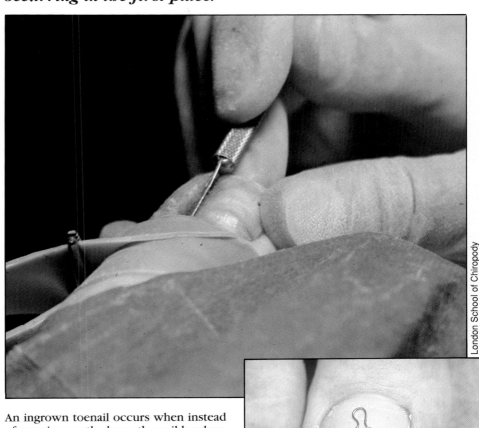

London School of Chiropody

An ingrown toenail occurs when instead of growing neatly down the nail borders, the nail edge pushes into the soft tissue alongside it and causes swelling and pain. It is the big toe that is nearly always affected, and trouble may arise when the soft tissue becomes infected.

Causes
The most common causes are the tearing of the nail so that the edge is unprotected, or nails that are cut incorrectly. Tight shoes pressing on the growing nail and hot sweaty feet are two other factors that can cause an ingrown toenail (see Feet).

Symptoms
An ingrown toenail is painful and looks deformed. The pain disappears when the foot is rested, but it resumes when the person walks and the shoe presses down on it. Initially the area around the nail becomes slightly red and swollen, but in time it may become infected. This leads to increased swelling and a possible discharge of pus, so that the area becomes painful and sticky.

In the large picture (above) a splinter of ingrowing nail is removed with a surgical knife. The inset shows a nail brace lifting a nail away from the soft side tissue so that the nail will grow correctly when the brace is removed.

Dangers
There is usually little danger from an ingrown toenail. The most common complication is an infection, which usually remains confined to the toe. In some rare cases the infection can spread or can be a sign of diabetes.

An untreated infection becomes chronic. In most cases the nail grows in a deformed fashion, or it may even come off due to the spread of infection.

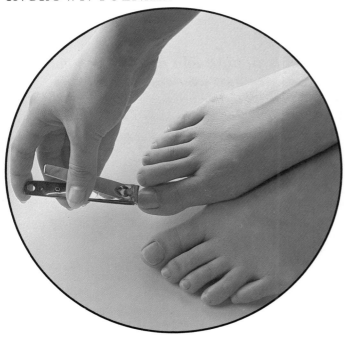

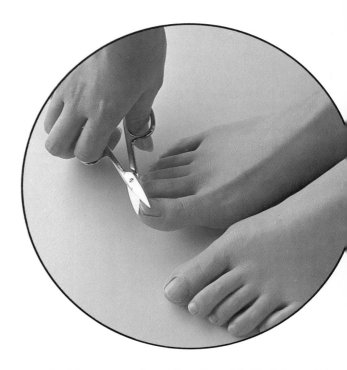

Treatment

The initial treatment involves resting the foot; relieving any pressure from footwear; regular bathing in hot salty water; and if there is an infection present, the use of an antibiotic. These measures cure a large proportion of cases, but in some people the condition is both chronic and recurrent; the tendency of the nail to grow inward never completely disappears, and the site continues to become infected from time to time.

Various surgical operations have been used to treat ingrown toenails. Their chief disadvantage is that they tend to immobilize the patient for two to three weeks. The first option is a nail wedge resection,

Everyone can have attractive feet, but nails have to be cut carefully and appropriate footwear must be worn.

Clippers (left) or nail scissors (right) may be used to cut toenails. Nails must be cut straight across and not too short, or they may become ingrown.

Prevention

- Cut nails straight across using sharp nail scissors or clippers
- Avoid cutting them too short
- Never pick at nails; cut them
- Regularly clean under the nails with an orange stick
- Wear properly fitting shoes and immediately change socks when they become hot and sweaty
- If you tend to have ingrown toenails, relieve the pressure and rest and bathe the toe when the area becomes red or painful

where the affected half of the nail is c‍ off under a local anesthetic; this simp‍ procedure provides a full cure for a gre‍ number of patients (see Anesthetic).

Another possibility is pulling off th‍ whole nail under a local anesthetic. Th‍ allows a new nail to grow again over‍ period of several months. In most cas‍ patients find that the condition does n‍ recur after this treatment.

In some cases a plastic gutter is place‍ along the side of the nail. This allow‍ growth to continue without the n‍ growing into and damaging side tissue.‍ local anesthetic will be used for this.

If everything else fails, in the very sm‍ minority of chronic cases, the nail a‍ the nail-forming tissue (nailbed) can ‍ removed. This surgical procedure is us‍ ally performed under a general anesthe‍ ic. When it heals the nail never regrov‍ and the area where the nail used to ‍ eventually becomes covered in a toug‍ protective skin.

Outlook

The outlook for this common conditic‍ depends on the individual patient. ‍ some cases rest and bathing produc‍ relief within two to three days. Whe‍ there is an infection, it may take sever‍ days to clear up.

It can take several months for the na‍ to grow back after surgery. Dressings (s‍ Dressings) and loose-fitting, open sho‍ must be worn for some time.

Occasionally the newly growing n‍ begins to grow inward, and then there‍ no solution other than to have the n‍ and nailbed removed. This provides‍ complete permanent cure.

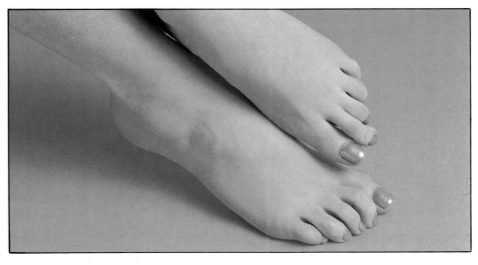

Inhalants

Q My four-year-old brother has asthma. Will he be able to use an aerosol inhaler?

A It depends on the child. Having an asthma attack with wheezing and difficulty in breathing can make young children panic. Using an aerosol inhaler requires a certain amount of concentration and good timing, particularly of the breathing. Some four-year-olds can manage this, others cannot. Those who have difficulties are prescribed an inhaler that gives a dose of powdered inhalant. Using this requires no skill at all—it is as simple as taking in a deep breath—and it is just as effective as an aerosol. However, the powder inhaler is not as convenient to carry as the aerosol, because you need a bottle of capsules too. A spacer tube that attaches to the inhaler can be very helpful.

Q My grandmother thinks that asthma inhalers do more harm than good and that a few lungfuls of fresh air would be just as effective against an attack of asthma. Is this right?

A Unfortunately for asthmatics this is completely untrue. Fresh air does not stop asthma. Your grandmother is probably influenced by stories about asthma inhalers that went around some years back. They had a bad reputation because the drug they contained, though effective in stopping asthma attacks, was capable of overstimulating the heart if taken in excessive doses. Nowadays the drugs used in aerosol inhalers have practically no effect on the heart, and the inhalers are easily carried in a pocket and superbly effective.

Q I use an inhaler containing a steroid drug for my asthma. The other day I heard that steroids have side effects. Will they affect me?

A No. The dose of steroid you take in your aerosol is very small, between 10 and 100 times less than that which you would have to take by mouth. You would have to grossly overuse your steroid inhalant to be in danger.

Drugs for treating asthma and emphysema, and the inhalers used to take them, have greatly improved in recent years so that they are both effective and safe in the prevention and treatment of asthma attacks.

Easy to use and convenient to carry around, this type of aerosol inhaler stops all but the worst asthma attacks.

Inhalants are medicines that are breathed in, and undoubtedly their most significant use these days is to prevent or cure the wheezing, tightness in the chest, and severe breathing difficulties that are experienced by people suffering from distressing asthma attacks (see Asthma) or emphysema (see Emphysema). Although they are very different diseases, they are treated the same way.

An inhaler is the device used to deliver the inhalant. The aerosol inhaler turns the medicine into a fine spray by means of a harmless gas called freon. Both the drugs and the gas are kept under pressure in canisters. When the valve of the canister is opened, the gas escapes, taking with it a fine spray just like an aerosol.

Three main types of medicine are given by inhaler: bronchodilators (medicines that widen the bronchial tubes and give immediate symptomatic relief), steroid medicines (long term treatment that prevents and controls asthma); and anti-allergy medicines (which block the body's reaction to the allergens; see Allergies).

Why inhaled medicine is used

Asthma is an inflammatory disease of the bronchioles that makes them prone to irritation from pollutants and allergens. The inflammation causes the muscles to contract and spasm, narrowing the airways and causing the patient to wheeze to force air into the oxygen-deprived lungs.

It therefore makes sense to give the patient a medicine that acts only upon the lungs, sparing all other parts of the body. Inhaled medicines do just this. Furthermore only a fraction of the dose normally required by mouth need be given, and because only a small proportion of that small dose is absorbed, there are very few side effects.

This combination of specific action without side effects is ideal, and is the main reason why the emphasis in treatment of asthma has changed over recent decades from pills taken by mouth to inhalants.

Bronchodilator aerosols

These are taken to stop an asthma attack after it has started. They work by relaxing the smooth muscle that surrounds the bronchial tubes. They act rapidly and give complete relief within minutes. However, they treat only the symptoms and not the cause. The effect wears off fairly quickly, too, but having stopped wheezing, the patient usually stabilizes for several, typically four, hours, after which there may be another attack. For this reason the inhaler is needed frequently and people with asthma tend to carry their inhalers around with them constantly.

The dose needed depends on the type of bronchodilator used, but generally one puff (occasionally two) is enough to stop an asthma attack in its early stages.

The aerosol method of delivery represents a great step forward in asthma treatment. Before this method was introduced, the inhalant was given by a cumbersome contraption with a rubber bulb and a glass

The nasal inhaler (below) is a special type used to treat irritations, like hay fever, in the passages of the nose (see Hay fever).

or plastic siphon in a container that had to be topped off with the inhalant. This apparatus was inconvenient to carry around and likely to become blocked.

The aerosol is about half the size of a pack of cigarettes and practically never causes problems. Exactly the right amount of inhalant is ejected each time; this is described as a metered dose.

Steroid aerosols

Steroid drugs act by controlling the bronchial smooth muscle so that it is less likely to contract and cause asthma. They do not stop an attack, as a bronchodilator does. They are purely preventive and tend to be most effective after a course of doses has been built up over several days.

For this reason the steroid is inhaled at regular intervals, perhaps every six hours. It is more effective on some patients than others, but used in conjunction with the bronchodilator it can at least control all but the most severe asthma, which in any case needs hospital treatment. Such a medicine is prophylactic—one taken for prevention, not relief.

Aerosol inhaler technique

Using an aerosol inhaler properly requires a very small amount of skill. The can is shaken and held upside down, insuring that it is vertical. The patient breathes out completely and then, with the nozzle of

the aerosol between the lips, begins t breathe in slowly and deeply.

Shortly after starting to breathe in, th spray is released simply by pressing o the canister in its holder. The patient con tinues to breathe in until the lungs ar full. The breath is held for five second Another puff may be taken if it is needec

The mistake most commonly made is t deliver the spray before starting t breathe in. If that is done most of the dru is either dispersed around the mouth c inadvertently swallowed.

To make the timing less critical, specia devices called spacers have been intre duced. These separate the aerosol fro the mouth by a long tube of plastic. Th aerosol gathers in the tube, and fro there it can be inhaled with the nex intake of breath as it happens.

Using an aerosol inhaler is easy. A do tor will demonstrate the technique whe he or she first prescribes it. Howeve those with young asthmatic childre know that sometimes the breathing diff culty that is experienced in an asthm attack can make it difficult to concentra on the most simple procedure.

Powder inhalants

Bronchodilators and steroids can be give as powder inhalants. They are prescribe by doctors if a patient has difficulty usir an aerosol. This type of inhalant is gainir in popularity in the US with the ban c chlorofluorocarbons (CFCs; see Pollution

A capsule containing a powder loaded into a cylindrical plastic devic and cut in half by a built-in blade. Th patient then breathes in through th device, which spills the contents of th capsule into the inhaled airstream.

A slightly different form of powder deli ery has been designed for a different dru The drug sodium cromoglycate contro allergic reactions, which are a major cau of asthma. A capsule containing the drug loaded into a plastic device, which spir rather than spills, its powdered conten into an inhaled airstream. Like the steroid sodium cromoglycate is prophylactic.

Dangers

No serious side effects have been repo ed with inhaled steroids. In the past, ho ever, bronchodilators did have a bad rep tation. It was suspected that the bro chodilating drug that was then in wic use was capable of overstimulating th heart if it was used excessively.

Today bronchodilators are used f emergencies only while steroids are use daily to control symptoms. People wi asthma should keep to the recommende dosage of bronchodilators, although the is a large safety margin should they take puff too many during an attack.

Inhibitions

Q My sister seems unable to stand up for herself in any argument with her husband. Is there anything that can be done about this inhibition?

A Yes. First of all, however, you must be sure that she really wants to change and that it is not just you who is getting upset about it. If she really does want to lose this inhibition, she should ask her doctor to arrange for her to attend a class in assertion training. This will help her express her own point of view more strongly.

Q My husband gets very loud and exuberant at parties, and it embarrasses me. What can I do?

A Try to focus not on your husband, but on the reactions of those around him. Concentrate on one person at a time and judge to what extent they accept or even encourage his behavior. If everything seems fine and other people seem perfectly comfortable, then don't worry about it. If you are sure that they are only putting up with him out of politeness, however, tell your husband firmly that he is only being tolerated, not admired. Do not tell him this at the time, nor just after the event. Save it until you are getting ready for the next party. This timing is very important.

Q My mother is very inhibited about being seen in her underwear in the changing rooms of swimming pools. Is this the result of her being an only child and being used to privacy from an early age?

A Being an only child can have this kind of effect, but such an inhibition can have a number of other causes, such as parental prudery, cultural or religious beliefs, or being convinced that one's body is unattractive. Alternatively your mother may simply be unused to this relatively new kind of changing room. It might help if you go to the swimming pool together and she sees you dressing and undressing in such surroundings. She may also prefer to change in one of the bathroom stalls.

Most of us have minor inhibitions, but inhibitions that cause serious problems, such as avoidance of social or sexual situations, can make life a misery. Skilled help, however, can ease these problems.

Bubbles/David Lane

A modest level of inhibition in the human makeup is useful, because it helps to balance at least some of the wilder excesses of which one could be capable. Too much, however, can make life miserable.

Inhibition and guilt are actually two sides of the same coin; both reflect a difference between our desires and our beliefs. While guilt is caused by doing what we know (or think) we should not do, inhibition prevents us from doing what we know (or think) we should be able to do.

Research shows that most people have inhibitions of some kind. However, we seldom notice other people's inhibitions because it is difficult to notice something that a person does not do. As a result we tend to conclude that inhibitions in others are rare.

Because inhibition derives partly from moral conflicts, certain groups of people tend to be more prone to it than others. Older people may be more inhibited than young adults due to the climate of moral strictness in which they grew up.

An inhibited person tends to stay in the background and may not even like facing him- or herself in the mirror.

Adolescents, on the other hand, may have more inhibitions simply because they have not yet learned to strike a balance between their desire to free themselves from parental restrictions, their wish to retain some values that will stabilize their lives, and being accepted by their peers. Letters to newspaper advice columns from young people concerned about their reluctance to do what everyone else does are common, and there is evidence that a shift in personality toward greater reserve and shyness does, in fact, take place during the adolescent years.

Causes

Since inhibition involves both a reluctance to engage in outgoing behavior and a fear of not doing so, it can be seen that two components, shyness toward other people and anxiety, are involved in its development. Although changes in these character

traits can occur due to upbringing and experience, an individual's general level of shyness and proneness to anxiety are to some extent set from birth, and they may even be partly genetically determined.

The extent to which a person feels inhibited may nevertheless differ considerably from situation to situation. For example, there is the type of man who is completely uninhibited at a bar, at a football game, and in his work at the factory, yet who is totally ill at ease in the company of women unless he can regard them as platonic friends rather than as potential girlfriends or wives.

Signs
Inhibition can occur in many contexts but the most common are in social and sexual situations. The physical symptoms are those of straightforward anxiety—quickening heartbeat and pulse, hollow feeling in the pit of the stomach, dryness in the mouth, slight perspiration, and trembling in the limbs.

In social situations the person will tend to stay in the background, saying little when spoken to and finding great difficulty in maintaining any flow of conversation. His or her body will be tense, and he or she may sit too upright in a chair, sometimes twining their legs around each other or around a chair leg and clasping a drink too tightly. There may also be difficulty in meeting other people's eyes.

Sexual inhibition can happen even in those whose social competence is fine. They may be good at flirtation and able to make their partner emotionally happy, yet be physically reticent when it comes to sex itself. This can be frightening to those who are still developing their sexual identities, because they are often totally unaware of their inhibitions until sexual situations occur.

Problems and their treatment
By and large people's inhibitions do not need treatment, because they act as a natural defense against excesses of behavior that might be regretted in retrospect. Inhibitive tendencies, however, might be harmful when they have an adverse effect on a person's lifestyle. A person who is sexually inhibited, for example, puts a strain on his or her relationship with a partner from which it may not recover. Similarly a person crippled by social inhibition can become prey to loneliness and depression if they do not make an effort to combat these conditions.

Extreme social or sexual inhibitions can, however, now be treated with some degree of success. A professional therapist will treat social inhibition by building up a person's social skills, literally teaching him or her the techniques of conversation and interaction and rewarding the patient with praise and encouragement for every positive move that he or she

Being with self-assured people in a lively social situation can sometimes make inhibited people feel isolated. It is important to make them feel part of the group without putting too much pressure on them to join in.

makes. The process sounds basic, but can be very effective.

Sexual inhibition can generally be treated using the sensate focus technique devised by American sex therapists Masters and Johnson. This focuses attention on the pleasure-giving and pleasure-accepting aspects of sexual activity without reference to intercourse itself. Because the focus is on what one feels rather than on what one has to do, inhibition can be bypassed and can begin to die away.

Outlook
Treatments generally last for only a few months, although results will probably be obtained long before that, and the outcome is usually good. Nevertheless it must be emphasized that although change is easy, the integration of change into a person's lifestyle is more difficult and depends to a great extent on whether the person really desires it. For some people inhibitions are a defense and a refuge from certain aspects of their lives, and the rewards that they experience from throwing away those defenses must be seen to be worthwhile if the inhibitions are to disappear forever.

Injections

Q My son is only three and dreads having the routine injections needed for immunization. He really is scared; what should I do?

A Don't tell him that an injection won't hurt at all. He will soon learn that it does and then trust you less. For now just divert his attention and then, when the time comes, explain how important the injection is for his health. Try and arrange for the injection to be done quickly and efficiently with as little waiting as possible. Some doctors offer children medications mixed in a sweet drink.

Q Why do some injections hurt more than others?

A How much an injection hurts depends on the site of the injection, the size of the needle, and the amount of fluid to be introduced. The bigger the needle and the larger the amount of fluid, the greater the pain, because the tissues are forced to expand more. Some tissues, such as skin, are taut and therefore more painful when they expand. Subcutaneous (beneath the skin) fatty tissue is less so; muscle is midway between the two, unless the patient tenses up. Thus a relaxed patient having an injection into a muscle will feel little pain, whereas a tense person has an increased sensitivity to pain.

Q When I had a typhoid injection some time ago, I couldn't use my arm the day after. Why did this happen?

A There was a reaction from the tissues of the body as the injected substance was absorbed. This occurs because most vaccines consist of foreign proteins. The body mounts a defense in response, producing antibodies that can eliminate the disease and give you immunity. This defensive response may involve swelling and inflammation, which is felt as pain and stiffness. However, the response varies from person to person. A painful, swollen, useless arm is rare these days, because modern vaccines tend to produce less of a reaction.

Injections are an extremely effective way of giving drugs to treat illness and to immunize against disease. They are rarely painful and are certainly not to be feared.

Anthea Sievking/Vision International

Babies' injections are done so quickly that they are hardly aware of them. A quick cuddle will soothe away tears.

There are three main ways of taking medical drugs. The easiest method is to give them by mouth, or if rapid absorption is required, they can be inserted into the rectum as a suppository.

However, there are many drugs that cannot be given in either fashion, usually because the acid that occurs naturally in the stomach as an essential aid to digestion would destroy or change the substance. Injections get around this problem by introducing a drug or vaccine directly into tissue or the bloodstream.

The usual method of giving injections is through a hypodermic needle. These are usually very thin needles with a pointed end and are used to administer medicine beneath the skin.

The basic procedure for all injections is to clean the skin, then push the needle through the skin to the depth required. Pressure on the plunger then forces liquid out through the hole in the end of the needle into the tissue, which is consequently forced to expand. It is this expansion that causes the characteristic aching pain of an injection. The narrower the needle and the smaller the amount of fluid injected, the less painful the injection will be.

Methods of injection

Almost all injections are into skin, tissue beneath the skin (e.g. blood), or muscle.

In a subcutaneous injection fluid is injected into the soft fatty tissue under the skin. The drug disperses into the surrounding cells and is carried away relatively slowly by the bloodstream. This tissue expands fairly easily and the injection is consequently not particularly painful. This method is ideal for giving vaccines or drugs.

Less common is an injection into the dermis, or lower layer of the skin. This is called an intradermal injection, and because the skin has a relatively poor blood supply, it is useful for some types of immunization or allergy testing. Since skin is a relatively taut tissue, the pain of expansion tends to be felt more here.

Muscle has a plentiful blood supply and so a drug deposited there is carried away into the bloodstream quickly, usually in a matter of minutes, and its effect is soon established. Muscle is also capable of absorbing a relatively large quantity of fluid and this may be useful if a large dose is needed. In terms of pain an intramuscular injection is midway between a subcutaneous and an intradermal injection.

Intravenous injection

This means injecting into a vein, in other words directly into the bloodstream. The procedure requires skill; a suitable vein has to be found and pierced with the needle, which then has to be held correctly so that it does not slip. A doctor usually gives the injection.

Some drugs can only be given intravenously, but the most common reason for using this method is the need for speedy distribution of the drug. Veins carry deoxygenated blood back from the tissues to the heart and lungs for reoxygenation, from where it is pumped all over the body. Arteries only carry blood outward from the heart to a specific site.

Other techniques

It is possible to inject substances almost anywhere in the body, and of course medicine frequently presents cases that require other techniques of injection.

For intravenous injections the site may be difficult to locate because veins do not always run near the surface and because they do not necessarily stand out.

A cuff is placed around the limb to be injected. This cuts off the blood flow in the vein, which starts to swell. When the vein is clearly seen, the needle is inserted into it under the skin. The plunger is withdrawn a fraction to check that blood flows into the needle; when the doctor is sure the needle is in a vein, he or she releases the cuff and presses the plunger.

Occasionally arteries are injected if the drug that is being used needs to travel to a specific site. Equally a joint may be injected for a particular purpose, such as a treatment for arthritis (see Arthritis).

Dangers

The chief danger of injections is infection. The needle and syringe have to be completely sterile to prevent bacteria being injected into the tissue along with the drug, so the skin is wiped with rubbing alcohol to prevent infection (see Infection and Infectious disease).

Another danger is that the tip of the needle might accidentally penetrate an artery. If this happens a drug could reach a small area in a dangerously large quantity. To prevent this, nurses are usually trained to draw back on the plunger of the syringe before injecting to check that there is no blood.

Most vaccinations are given in this manner. The vaccine flows down the hollow needle into the fatty tissue below the skin.

How and why injections are given

Type of injection	How and where applied	Typical reasons for giving the injection
Subcutaneous	A small needle, usually inserted under the skin of upper arm; left arm if patient is right-handed and vice versa	Immunizations; daily insulin for diabetics; monthly injections of vitamin B_{12} for pernicious anemia sufferers
Intramuscular	A longer needle is used than for subcutaneous injections because it must reach a deeper level. Usually given in buttock muscle, carefully avoiding sciatic nerve	Some drugs can be given in this way if needed quickly, including antibiotics for severe infection; iron for severe anemia; and painkillers for severe pain
Intravenous	Given by a doctor into a vein, commonly in the crease of the elbow, but also elsewhere	Emergency route for quick administration of lifesaving drugs; also anesthetics
In a closed space of the body	May be the peritoneum (abdominal lining); spinal canal; or a joint	Specific treatment of a part of the body; site varies according to complaint

Accidentally injecting into a nerve can also sometimes cause damage, but doctors and nurses are careful when they give injections, so this rarely happens. Injections are slightly painful, but many people make them more so by worrying about the pain. This makes the muscle tense and consequently worsens the aching caused by expansion. Relaxing will certainly reduce any pain.

Subcutaneous injection

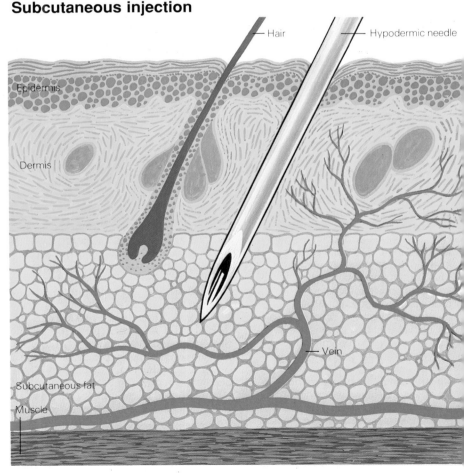

Hair

Hypodermic needle

Epidermis

Dermis

Vein

Subcutaneous fat

Muscle

Insecurity

Q My three-year-old sister takes an old piece of blanket to bed and she won't be parted from it. Is she insecure?

A Many children have comfort objects that give them a sense of security at bedtime. However, they usually outgrow the need for the comfort object by the time they go to school, so don't worry.

Q I come from an uneducated family. I have been to college and have a very good job, but I feel inferior whenever I meet new people. How can I overcome this feeling?

A People who have achieved far more than they or their families ever expected often feel they cannot live up to their achievements. Your difficulty with new people is symptomatic of this. However, anxieties can also cloud one's perceptions of reality. When meeting new people, focus not on yourself but on them. Relegate time to judge yourself when surrounded by friends and family.

Q My 13-year-old son is handsome and intelligent but he has no self-confidence. What can be done?

A Teenage years are a difficult time. Apart from having to cope with body changes, there are all the other adolescent problems to deal with as well. The only way you can help is to stand by your son, and offer reassurance, support, and advice (when asked). If he appears troubled, seek outside advice.

Q I have a caring husband, two lovely children, and a really interesting part-time job. However, I am very insecure when my mother-in-law stays over because she is so critical. What can I do about it?

A Mothers-in-law can be critical, though often we imagine that they are worse than they are. If you and your family are happy with your standard of housekeeping and lifestyle, that's all that matters. Take her criticisms with a pinch of salt, and steer clear of arguments.

Insecurity can begin in childhood, so it is important to encourage self-confidence in children. However, everyone can feel insecure at times. Understanding such feelings and thinking positively can help overcome them.

Sally and Richard Greenhill

Insecurity happens to all of us. Starting a new job, moving to a different town, taking examinations, speaking in front of a group of people, and a host of other life situations are bound to bring up feelings of uncertainty about ourselves. Our worries may be exaggerated, but usually we can summon up the courage to handle the situation, so long as there are other areas of our life in which we feel secure.

However, there are some people who are so wracked with anxiety that they are unable to stand back and see things in perspective. Their worries are not simply responses to isolated events: they are far more deep-rooted and have become almost a permanent state of mind (see Anxiety). They feel inadequate not just in certain situations but in coping with life in general. Many have lost contact with reality and are unable to build up confidence through experience the way that a more balanced person can.

Insecurity, regardless of whether it is a transitory phenomenon or a more deep-rooted problem, can be controlled, provided the person can come to terms with

Feelings of security—and a fostering of love, confidence, and independence—should be established early in a child's life.

the situations that give rise to it and with the disabling feeling itself.

Causes

Feelings of insecurity often arise from childhood experiences. Individual personality probably plays a large part as well. Yet why one person should be more secure than another is not fully understood; perhaps it is nature (see Genetics), perhaps it is nurture (see Environment), or perhaps it is how the person interprets their experiences.

From early in a person's life, attitudes and behavior patterns are established and, if nothing is done to change them, they will continue into adulthood.

Security, or insecurity, is established through the way parents treat a baby. Since their treatment of the child is the child's only guide to his or her own image, that is the self-image that will become established.

confidence to handle this, he or she will not even try, rather than risk failure and possible disappointment.

Without a happy balance between emotional security and independence, a child will grow up feeling anxious. Made to feel like an outsider (and an unlovable one at that), fearful of new situations, confused about talents and capabilities (particularly if the parents are overcritical and at the same time have overly high expectations), the child will develop into an insecure teenager and then into an insecure adult.

If the insecurities are few and defined, it may be that other aspects of personality or character will be able to provide some compensation. Also although the person may remain insecure in those areas, the general trend of his or her life will be largely unaffected.

However, insecurity becomes a major problem when it begins to dominate a person's existence (becoming the immediate response to relationships, opportunities, changes in circumstance, and so on). Then chances of having a full life are limited and neuroses will develop.

Childhood insecurity that begins at home, will often spill over into school, where peer pressure from other children and the fear of failure itself can have long-lasting effects.

Tom Belshaw

Children are often insecure when they encounter new situations, so affection and understanding should be shown (above).

If parents are distant, unaffectionate, and unresponsive to demands for attention, the child will feel unwanted, and think that he or she is not worth caring about. Because no warm and close relationship is formed, a child will be unable to see him- or herself as lovable. Having had no experience of loving, he or she will either not be capable of giving love or will lack the confidence to offer love. All future relationships may well be jeopardized by this lack of emotional security.

Of equal importance to providing a secure emotional base is the need to foster enough confidence in the child to handle new situations. Such independence cannot be gained if parents shield the child from experience, arouse fears about performing tasks, or are overly critical. Responses like these will only serve to dampen the child's own initiative and create an even greater dependence on the parents (see Inhibitions).

Such a child may grow up with a timid nature, afraid to do things alone, and uncertain about his or her own abilities. Additionally, he or she may develop a fear of being criticized, or rebuffed, and because the child does not have enough

Zefa

Events that change a person's life—marrying, having children, starting a new job—can cause anxiety. However, if you feel secure the adjustments are easier.

Insecurity in children

Making a small child feel secure requires a great deal of effort on the part of the parents. However, such selflessness should not be at the complete expense of the parents' own lives.

Babies and small children recognize caring from the age of three months. The more they are smiled at and cuddled, played with, and talked to, the more their feelings of security will increase. In the first year they may become panicky if a parent leaves them for more than a moment; at this point the parent should stay nearby as much as possible, but the child also needs to get used to being with other people.

When the small child is learning to walk and talk, the parents should be patient, supportive, and very encouraging whatever his or her rate of progress may be.

Children are prone to a host of fears, such as being alone in a room at bedtime, seeing strange animals at a zoo, and starting a new school. Their fears should never be laughed at; indeed parents should try to explain the situation to the child in simple language, and support him or her without being overprotective. He or she

Tom Belshaw

will soon gain confidence so long as the parents are there as a safe base.

As children grow older they will confront an increasing number of new life situations, many of which may arouse insecure feelings. Parents must stress these feelings are totally natural, and that the child or adolescent is not alone in having them. One of the most worrying things for young people is the fear of failure, of disappointing themselves, their parents, or perhaps their friends and teachers. The emphasis here should be on doing your best, and as long as you try, your best is enough.

At the same time it is important to insure that children know that not everyone excels at every skill and talent and that other people's skillfulness in a certain area may be balanced by a lack in other areas. In this way some measure of self-esteem can be established, in addition to confidence. If children and adolescents have a sense of identity and a feeling of worth, they will be able to accept and use all sides of their personality positively.

Coping with the different situations they will meet in life therefore becomes easier.

Insecurity in adults

It is rare that people reach adulthood overflowing with confidence. Certainly they will have a fair idea of their strengths and weaknesses, although they have probably exaggerated the weaknesses and underestimated the strengths. In doing so, they have simply reinforced their insecurity.

Because of this, when new situations present themselves, a person's first response is fear, which can sometimes be carried to paranoid lengths. What the insecure person should realize is that other people probably feel the same way and that such insecurity is not abnormal.

If necessary insecure people should think about all their achievements rather than their failures: focusing and doing positively constructive things during the day, and accentuating these positive accomplishments at night; from this, true confidence will develop.

Insomnia

Q The more I worry, the more difficult it is to drop off to sleep. What should I do?

A You are probably feeling very anxious, and a hypnotic (sleep-inducing) drug or a mild tranquilizer may help you. Once you get used to sleeping, stop taking the drug.

Q We seem to be a family of insomniacs. Can insomnia run in families?

A There is no research to prove this. However, family lifestyles, such as going to bed late or having a cup of tea or coffee just before bedtime, can certainly contribute to disturbed sleep patterns.

Q I have been given sleeping pills. If I take them, will I become addicted?

A Tranquilizers can easily become habit-forming and are best used on a short-term basis. Don't hesitate to discuss this with your doctor (see Hypnotic drugs).

Q After the death of my father, I have been having difficulty getting to sleep, and when I do I often wake during the night. Is this the result of depression?

A This is very likely. Sleeplessness is a true sign of depression, and typically so if you can get to sleep sometimes and then wake in the early hours. Your doctor will probably recommend not a sleeping pill, but an antidepressant drug. Once this begins to work, you should sleep soundly.

Q I have no trouble sleeping during the day but find that I cannot sleep at night. What should I do?

A You have probably managed to reverse your sleeping rhythm. It is important for you to see your doctor for a checkup, then try cutting out your daytime naps and you should find it easier to sleep at night. You may need a mild tranquilizer for the first few nights, but you will soon settle back into your normal sleeping habits.

Being unable to sleep is something that most of us experience from time to time, and it is usually only a short-term inconvenience. Long-term insomnia may indicate an underlying problem requiring medical help.

The exact biological functions of sleep remain unknown. It is common experience, however, that lack of sleep leads to deterioration in both mental and physical performance, so it is clear that sleep is essential for good health. Recent research has added support to the theory that during the periods of rapid eye movement (REM) sleep, consolidation and reinforcement of memory occurs. Dreaming is also believed to have physiological functions; in addition to structuring and interpretation memory data, it is thought to help in the activation of the neural networks of the brain and the disposal of redundant and useless information (see Dreaming).

Insomnia is most common in middle-aged and elderly people. This is mainly because as we age, our bodies require less sleep. When insomnia occurs in a younger person, it is more likely to be a sign of some other disorder, such as anxiety or depression (see Depression).

People sometimes mistakenly believe they are suffering from insomnia because of a misconception about the amount of sleep they need. Sleep needs vary greatly, with some people requiring less than four hours every night and others needing more than 10. Others who think they have insomnia are simply out of phase, lying awake for hours after going to bed but sleeping normally if allowed to sleep late in the morning.

Patterns of insomnia

People suffering from insomnia may show a variety of patterns. They may have difficulty in getting to sleep, difficulty in maintaining sleep, repeated brief periods of wakefulness, or early morning waken

Those who suffer from insomnia should get as much fresh air and exercise as possible. This can be very relaxing, and it may also help to induce sleep later on.

BSIP Zarand/Science Photo Library

840

ng. The particular pattern may indicate he cause of the trouble to a sleep disorder specialist. If there is no obvious ause, insomnia is said to be primary. Secondary insomnia has numerous causes, both psychological and physical.

A person with insomnia may suffer rom a wide variety of symptoms. The most common of these are daytime atigue, irritability, anxiety, depression, ack of concentration, and aches and pains in the muscles.

Diagnosis

The diagnosis of the cause of insomnia may be obvious, but in some cases it will equire special investigations. The most sophisticated of these investigations is nown as all-night polysomnographic (PSG) study. PSG involves the simultaneous recording of a number of physiological variables, which include respiratory ffort, the action of the heart (see lectrocardiogram), brain wave patterns see Electroencephalogram), muscle ctivity (electromyogram), mouth and ose airflow measurement, and blood xygen saturation levels to monitor the ffectiveness of breathing.

Overnight polysomnography is the est way to confirm that the insomnia is aused by excessive daytime napping, or the result of interference with breathing by the tongue or other causes of airway obstruction (the obstructive sleep pnea syndrome).

Causes

There are many causes of sleeplessness, ut only a few of them appear to have ny direct medical causes (see Sleep and eep disorders).

When a person is ill, constant waking r fitful sleeping is a common occurrence. In acute illness, pain or fever may revent sleep, and excessive sweating or ckness may make the patient wake frequently. In cases of chronic illness (such heart or lung disease) shortness of reath, or pain caused by leg cramps or odominal spasms can cause wakefulness. Patients with heart disease or rostate enlargement may need to pass ater several times at night, resulting in sturbed sleep.

Mild anxiety and depression are both ommon causes of insomnia. Although red and well aware that sleep is the swer, the sufferer is unable to drop off. he harder he or she thinks and worries bout the inability to sleep, the less likely eep becomes.

In cases of severe depression, the person may fall asleep quickly but wake after nly two or three hours and then be able to get any further sleep, leaving m or her feeling constantly tired.

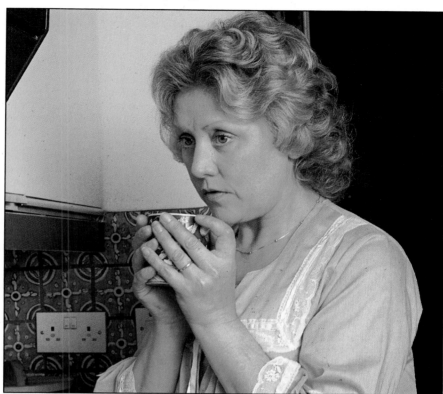

Coping with insomnia

Do
- Get plenty of exercise and fresh air; this stimulates sleep later
- Have a hot milky drink last thing at night; this helps sound sleep
- Learn relaxation techniques; counting sheep helps some people, but others need different methods
- Avoid overeating and drinking too late at night
- Insure that you sleep in a well-ventilated bedroom
- Seek outside help for worries that keep you awake
- Go to bed when you are tired; simply staying up for as long as you can may make you overtired
- Insure that you are warm and comfortable in bed

Don't
- Take stimulants such as tea or coffee just before going to bed; they will keep you awake
- Keep sleeping pills by the bed; you may wake and take more, forgetting when you took the last dose
- Take other people's sleeping pills; individuals get used to their own tablets and the dose required by one person may be quite different from that required by another
- Give old people sleeping pills without first checking with the doctor; the tablets can make them confused and can even cause incontinence
- Sleep in nightwear that restricts you in any way; it is best to sleep naked or in a very loose garment

Eating a large meal immediately before going to bed, drinking too much alcohol, or sleeping in a badly ventilated room can also have an adverse effect on sound sleep. Even if people sleep throughout the night in these circumstances, they often feel that they have not slept at all the next morning.

There are many other causes of insomnia. These include worm infestation, drug

and alcohol abuse, hydrocarbon poisoning, mercury poisoning, organophosphate poisoning, manganese poisoning, high altitude sickness, jet lag, liver failure, periodic cessation of breathing (obstructive sleep apnea syndrome), bacterial meningitis, thyroid gland overactivity, stress reaction, bereavement, Zidovudine treatment for AIDS (see AIDS), discontinuation of antipsychotic drugs, benzodiazepine withdrawal, opiate withdrawal (See Drug abuse), restless legs syndrome, periodic limb movements, circadian rhythm disorders, and terminal illness.

Jet lag

This is an important cause of insomnia that occurs in people flying from east to west, or vice versa, across several different time zones. In addition to insomnia there may be loss of the ability to concentrate, tiredness, loss of appetite, and irritability.

Jet lag may be a danger when air crews are affected and is an important consideration for businesspeople who are traveling to take part in serious negotiations. It is essential for them to schedule meetings so that there has been time for at least some degree of recovery from jetlag insomnia.

Travel from east to west results in delayed sleep. It is usually easy for someone who has traveled in this direction to get to sleep, because he or she is settling down so late. But sleep is then disturbed when the normal waking time of the home time zone is reached. Adaptation is fairly rapid. If business is urgent, meetings should be scheduled for a time at which the person would normally be fully alert in their home time zone. Traveling east causes more of a disturbance, because time zone changes effectively shorten the traveler's day.

Getting to sleep may be difficult, because the traveler is having to settle down in the afternoon of their home time zone. He or she may wish to see a doctor, who can prescribe a fast-acting sleeping pill (see Hypnotic drugs).

Treatment

Home treatment for insomnia is very effective, providing there is no underlying medical or emotional cause. Avoiding daytime naps, getting plenty of fresh air and exercise, and having a hot milky drink before going to bed have been shown to induce sleep in most people suffering from insomnia.

Where the insomnia is the result of a medical illness, such as heart disease, then sleeplessness will only improve on treatment of the heart condition. When a person is suffering from acute depression, antidepressive drugs are the best answer, because they can return the sufferer's sleep pattern to normal, long before his or her mood improves.

People whose insomnia is the result of acute anxiety usually require sleeping pills. These are hypnotic drugs and, although they are ideal for dealing with short-term insomnia, they can be both habit-forming and addictive.

In the past many sleeping pills contained barbiturate drugs that produced

People with insomnia sleep more than they think they do, but they wake more often than normal sleepers. It is the quality, not the quantity, of sleep that is the problem.

serious side effects, such as dramatic mood changes. Because the drugs were not excreted from the body for several hours, they caused a serious hangover in the morning. The more modern sleeping drugs, however, claim to have a shorter action period and they cause less hangover effect.

Most doctors generally prescribe sleeping pills on a short-term basis, and it is only in fairly exceptional cases that they are prescribed over a longer period. A regular supply of sleeping pills may be useful for an elderly patient, but for a younger person, a healthier lifestyle or attention to the cause of the insomnia is of greater help.

In cases where acute anxiety is the cause of insomnia, once the problem is solved the outlook is good. Early-morning waking due to depression is likely to worsen unless antidepressant treatment is given; if sleeping pills are also prescribed a normal sleep pattern can usually be achieved within a week. After that time the patient is, if at all possible, advised to slowly withdraw the use of the sleeping tablets and rely on more natural methods of inducing sleep.

Although insomnia is totally different from being deprived of sleep, the end results can be similar. When people are deprived of sleep they become irritable with changing moods, and mental as well as physical illness can result.

Permanent insomnia produces mood changes and irritability, and chronic insomnia makes a person tense and edgy, which in turn can affect performance at work. If home treatment does not help, a visit to the doctor is usually worthwhile.

People suffering from terminal illness often sleep badly because of unrelieved physical or mental distress. They may be affected by pain or discomfort, cramps, sweats, fear of incontinence, or many other physical disorders for which relief is available.

More commonly with the terminally ill insomnia is the result of fear of dying in the night, or of simple anxiety or depression. It is reasonable to expect medical staff to investigate these possibilities (see Hospices), because they can be greatly helped by sensitive and informed counseling, and, when appropriate, by suitable medication.

Many terminally ill patients wish to be given a strong hypnotic drug so that they can sleep, particularly if they are in pain. Those drugs that are most appropriate include benzodiazepines, such as temazepam or diazepam. For the short term management of severe anxiety in such circumstances, a sedative tricyclic antidepressant drug, such as amitriptyline, is usually given.

Oscar Burriel/Science Photo Library

Insulin

Q Two years ago I was diagnosed as a diabetic, and I have been taking insulin since then. Will I have to take it for the rest of my life?

A It is likely that you will. However, insulin is sometimes only required to tide diabetics over a difficult period, after which they may manage with just a special diet. Some diabetic women only require insulin while they are pregnant. In some cases pregnancy actually brings out a tendency to diabetes, and the woman is treated with insulin until after the birth, when she can return to normal and insulin is no longer needed.

Q Can you have too much insulin in your body as well as too little?

A Yes. This can happen as a result of excessive insulin production. Perhaps the most striking example is a rare condition called insulinoma, where too much insulin is secreted by an insulin-producing tumor of the pancreas. Symptoms may include loss of consciousness and seizures, but the condition may go undetected for years. The treatment includes surgery and drugs, depending on the type of tumor and the gravity of the condition.

Q My son is diabetic; should I encourage him to give himself his own insulin injections or should I continue to do them for him?

A This depends on his age. Obviously very young children need to have the injections given to them by an adult, but many specialists believe that children do better if they are encouraged to take control of the condition and give their own injections right from the start or as soon as possible. Even children as young as seven or eight may manage their own injections with the help and encouragement of their parents. Learning to do it properly at an early age will also help your son to be independent and can even give him some pride in the achievement of managing to do this important thing for himself.

Insulin was one of the major discoveries of the early part of the 20th century. It is now the main treatment for diabetes, offering hope for sufferers.

How insulin is made by the body

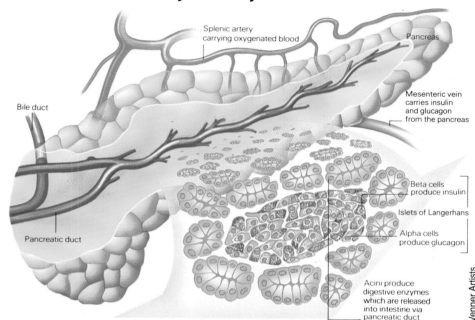

Splenic artery carrying oxygenated blood

Pancreas

Mesenteric vein carries insulin and glucagon from the pancreas

Bile duct

Pancreatic duct

Beta cells produce insulin

Islets of Langerhans

Alpha cells produce glucagon

Acini produce digestive enzymes which are released into intestine via pancreatic duct

Venner Artists

Insulin is a hormone made by the islets of Langerhans, a cluster of hormone-producing cells in the pancreas (see Pancreas). The role of insulin is to keep levels of sugar in the blood within normal levels. A lack of insulin causes diabetes mellitus (see Diabetes), a condition that can be treated with insulin injections.

How it works

If the level of sugar in the blood begins to rise above a certain level, the islets of Langerhans release insulin into the bloodstream. The insulin acts to oppose the effects of hormones, such as cortisone and adrenaline, which raise the level of sugar in the blood (see Hormones).

Insulin allows sugar to pass from the bloodstream into the body's cells where it can be used as fuel. If the body produces only a very small amount of insulin or no insulin at all, there is no mechanism for controlling the blood sugar level, because the sugar in the blood cannot be converted into fuel for the cells, and therefore diabetes results.

Treatment

The treatment for diabetes is to replace the insufficiently produced or absent hormone with either insulin from animals or synthetic insulin.

The hormones insulin and glucagon are produced in the islets of Langerhans. They enter the bloodstream via the mesenteric vein and balance the body's sugar level. An insulin deficiency causes diabetes; treatment replaces the insulin.

Unfortunately insulin is destroyed by gastric juices if taken by mouth and so it is given by self-injection. In general diabetics have two injections of insulin a day, one before breakfast and one before their evening meal.

Insulin shock

People with diabetes who accidentally take too much insulin may develop insulin shock because the quantity of sugar in the blood is drastically reduced. Immediate action is necessary to prevent possibly fatal consequences.

The symptoms of insulin shock include agitation, trembling, sweating, pallor, speech difficulty, and unconsciousness. Someone suffering from the preliminary symptoms is given sugar in the form of candy or fruit. An unconscious patient is given an injection of adrenaline into a muscle or glucose solution into a vein.

Insulin has saved the lives of countless diabetics, and its effectiveness is constantly improving as research continues.

Intercourse

Q I am two months' pregnant. Is it safe for me to continue to have intercourse?

A Quite safe, unless you have a history of miscarriage or premature delivery. If this is the case your doctor will warn you of any risks. In late pregnancy intercourse may be uncomfortable, but it will not damage you or your baby. You could try different positions or other ways of lovemaking apart from intercourse.

Q I've heard that there are various pills that make men more virile. Do they work?

A No. These are nothing more than extremely expensive caffeine or vitamin pills; they will not affect sexual potency. Any effect will be psychological; men who believe that such pills will make intercourse last longer will feel more confident about lovemaking.

Q My husband and I enjoy intercourse, but we have never experienced simultaneous orgasm. Is this normal?

A Yes, absolutely. Few couples experience simultaneous orgasm, so there is no need to worry. Simultaneous orgasm can be very exciting, but it should not be the ultimate goal. If you both find lovemaking pleasurable and satisfying, there is nothing to be concerned about.

Q Since I started taking the Pill, I have no interest in sex. What should I do?

A Try taking a different pill, such as a low dose progesterone-only mini-pill, or one with a greater proportion of estrogen. If this doesn't help, consider using another contraceptive method such as a condom.

Q My girlfriend and I only have intercourse twice a week. Is this normal?

A Frequency is only a problem if one or both partners perceive it as such. If you are both content, there is nothing to worry about.

Sexual intercourse, although essential for human reproduction, is also an expression of love, affection, and attraction between two people. It involves a complex relationship between body and mind.

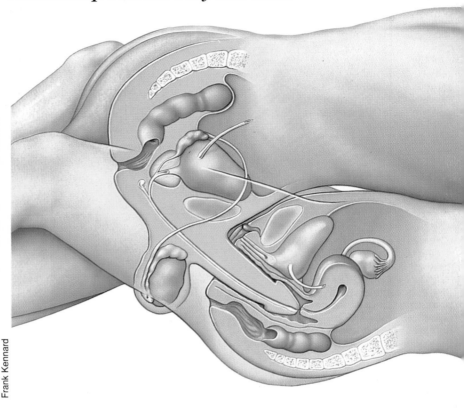

Frank Kennard

The term *intercourse* is really an abbreviation of the phrase "sexual intercourse." The word literally means "a running between" and implies any sort of mutual association between two or more people. Unfortunately it is frequently but wrongly used only as a synonym for coitus or copulation.

When first introduced, the phrase "sexual intercourse" was intended as a polite (or euphemistic) way of referring to an activity then seldom explicitly described outside medical circles. Appreciation of this point of popular usage is important, because sexual intercourse involves far more than copulation. Sexual relations between couples should extend well beyond the entering into and movement of the penis in the vagina to produce mutually pleasurable sensations that result in orgasm (sexual climax).

Sexual intercourse also encompasses a wide spectrum of expressions of mutual appreciation, respect, affection, support, and love. It includes all activities carried out between a couple mutually interested in any form of expression of physical love, whether extending to full coitus or not. It would, for instance, include mutual masturbation.

This emphasis on mutuality, and on the mental or even spiritual aspects of the matter, implies that many sexual acts—such as one-night stands, casual promiscuity, sex with prostitutes, rape, or sex with an unwilling partner—cannot properly be described as sexual intercourse. They are certainly sexual, but they are not intercourse, which implies a fully voluntary two-way process.

Conception may result if sexual intercourse takes place when the woman is ovulating. However, most couples are not trying to achieve a pregnancy every time sexual intercourse takes place, and thus the act becomes part of an expression of love and sexuality.

Intercourse involves more than a purely physical response; thoughts and emotions play a large part in the process. This interrelation results in the bodies of both the man and the woman going through complicated series of stages before, during, and after climax, regardless of the technique used. The famous sex therapists Masters and Johnson describe four stages that the body goes through during the orgasmic cycle.

The excitement phase

Arousal usually begins with the emotional wish for sex, triggered by feelings of being attracted to the partner. Complex hormonal scents (pheromones) may play a part in this attraction. The body quickly responds to the mind. The sexual organs of both men and women become engorged with blood. In a man this will result in the erection of the penis, which swells and becomes darker in color.

Penile erection depends on the structure of the penis. It contains three longitudinal columns of spongy material. Two of these lie side by side and are called the corpora cavernosa. The third, through which the urine tube (the urethra) passes, lies centrally under the two others and is known as the corpus spongiosum. These three columns are supplied with blood by two arteries. The diameter of the arteries is under the control of smooth muscle, whose state of tension depends largely on psychic stimuli.

During sexual interest the arteries widen so that blood under high pressure is pumped into the three spongy columns. The result is that they fill with blood and the penis becomes erect. This process is called tumescence and its reversal, detumescence.

When fully erect the penis points at an upward angle appropriate to the axis of the vagina. The veins that drain the penis are soft and thin-walled, and are easily compressed and closed by the expansion of the corpora. This helps to maintain an erection. There are no muscles in the penis (see Erection and ejaculation).

The internal sexual organs of the woman also become filled with blood. So does the vulva (the external sexual organs; see Vulva). The vagina expands in both length and width, and its walls begin to produce a lubricant that eases the entrance of the penis. Another important source of lubrication is the pair of Bartholin's glands that open just behind the vaginal orifice. These glands secrete a clear mucus that becomes smeared on the glans (the head of the penis) and is therefore carried into the vagina. The clitoris, the most sensitive part of the female genitals, often, but by no means always, becomes erect.

The skin of both the man and the woman becomes more sensitive, particularly around the erogenous zones—the lips, nipples, buttocks, and genitals. This in turn heightens arousal if those parts of

Tom Belshaw

the body receive stimulation during foreplay. Breathing becomes deeper and faster, and the pupils of the eyes may dilate. Both the man and the woman may develop a fine flush on both the chest and neck. This flush is more commonly seen in women than in men and is often of a strikingly mottled character. Intercourse may begin at this stage. The flush (if present) will often persist throughout the remainder of the act and will usually fade slowly afterward as sexual excitement declines.

The plateau phase

Excitement continues to increase for both partners. The vagina becomes about 2 in (5 cm) longer than normal, and the entrance to the vagina narrows to grip the penis. The clitoris draws back into its hood. The penis will have expanded to its maximum size, and the testicles become larger and rise up toward the body. Small drops of lubricant mucus identical to the mucus produced by the Bartholin's glands appear at the urethral opening of the penis. This is sometimes confused with seminal fluid, which contains sperm and has a somewhat milky appearance. It is important to recognize, however, that at this stage, and at any time prior to orgasm, small quantities of seminal fluid may escape spontaneously. For this reason barrier methods of contraception, such as a condom, may fail unless they are adopted before penetration.

The penis and the vagina move together rhythmically to produce the maximum pleasure and sensation for both partners.

Kissing and caressing play an important role in the excitement phase.

This movement causes friction on the penis, as well as on the clitoris and inside the vagina, depending on the position. Both the man and the woman will feel highly aroused, and their bodies will tense a little.

Orgasm

For the female, orgasm starts with a rush of sensation that begins in the clitoris, then spreads to the vagina and throughout the rest of the body. The muscles around the vagina, vulva, and anus go into a series of contractions that last for a number of seconds. This is an intense physical experience and is the climax of pleasure in lovemaking (see Orgasm).

The man experiences a buildup of feeling in his genitals. Sperm will have been pushed up the two vasa deferentia from the testicles and will meet the seminal fluid produced from the seminal vesicles. Sperm do not swim up each vas deferens as is commonly stated; they are forced up by pressure from the production of new sperm in the seminiferous tubules of the testicles. The sperm and seminal fluid are then forced to the internal entrance of the urethra leading to the penis by the action of the prostate gland.

The muscles that surround the root of the penis produce a series of contractions, and ejaculation begins. The amount of sperm and seminal fluid will be between 0.07–0.20 fl oz (2–6 ml). The internal contractions, as well as the buildup that immediately precedes them, are intensely pleasurable.

The resolution phase

This phase begins immediately after orgasm. The body relaxes and breathing becomes more gentle. The clitoris immediately returns to its nonaroused state, and the blood that has been engorging the internal organs slowly reduces in quantity. In women this takes about 30 minutes. The man's penis loses its erection and goes back to its nonaroused state. The testicles also get smaller.

During the resolution phase both the man and the woman feel a sensation of release and calm. They may wish to rest or fall asleep for a short time. The orgasmic cycle may begin again, but men take longer than women to get into the physical state where this is possible.

The role of the mind

Thoughts and feelings can have a great effect on the experience of sexual intercourse. If either partner is tired, under stress, depressed, inhibited, or preoccupied, the body will not begin to respond sexually or go into the first phase of the orgasmic cycle. Anxieties about work, tensions in the relationship, lack of privacy, financial worries, fears about performance, illness, or too much food or drink can also inhibit sexual response.

Finally attitudes to sex and intercourse learned from family, friends, and religion can have a powerful effect on the body's responses. Many men believe that they should always take the sexual initiative, and this can place a man under great stress. Further, many men and women have been brought up with the belief that sex is dirty and often regard their genitals as unpleasant or unattractive. Enjoyable and fulfilling sexual intercourse may not be possible until each partner has accepted his or her own body, and learned to enjoy the pleasurable sensations it can give them.

Problems

Most problems that people experience in sexual intercourse stem from the mind rather than the body. However, physical causes should always be ruled out before anyone with a sexual problem seeks help through psychosexual therapy.

Male problems usually take the form of impotence, ejaculatory failure, or premature ejaculation. There is rarely anything physically wrong, and the problem is often made worse by worry (see Impotence).

Women are sometimes worried that sexual intercourse will cause pain, or they associate it with a painful experience in the past. Women who have recently given birth or who have gynecological problems may feel protective about their bodies and resist sexual intercourse. This fear of pain can cause vaginismus, an involuntary contraction of the muscles around the vagina and those of the floor of the pelvis, which makes it impossible for the penis to enter.

Emotional factors and attitudes to sexual intercourse and lovemaking may result in dyspareunia, or painful intercourse. If the woman's mind is unresponsive, then her body will not respond and the Bartholin's glands will not secrete mucus. Also, the fluid that passes through the vaginal walls to the interior of the vagina will be inadequate, and dryness will impede introduction of the penis.

Lastly, many women are unable to achieve orgasm during sexual intercourse, although they may have no problems with the first two phases of arousal. Women who do not climax through sexual intercourse alone may need additional stimulation of the clitoris before they climax with their partner. This is not a problem and does not indicate any sexual dysfunction or abnormality.

Many women, even those who have a good sexual relationship and enjoy sex, never have an orgasm, unlike most men, who have no trouble achieving orgasm. The unwarranted emphasis that is commonly placed on the female orgasm has led many women to experience unjustified feelings of guilt, and it is not at all unusual for women to simulate orgasm so as not to disappoint their partners.

Couples who have problems that they cannot sort out themselves would be well advised to seek professional help.

A couple who are happy and relaxed together are most likely to find intercourse a pleasurable and fulfilling experience.

Zefa

Internal examination

Q My doctor insisted that I have an internal examination before going on the Pill. Why was this necessary?

A Your doctor was simply insuring that you were well and healthy before prescribing this form of contraceptive. You probably had your blood pressure, weight, and family medical history checked too. This is all part of a good preventive medicine routine.

Q I've never had an internal examination before and I'm terrified of having one. My doctor says I need to have a Pap smear. Is there anything I can do to avoid having this test?

A No, not unless you want to risk leaving a condition that might need attention untreated. An internal examination only takes a few minutes and will not damage you in any way. Discuss your fear with your doctor, who will do his or her best to help you relax. Your doctor is likely to have met many women who feel as you do and will understand your feelings. If your doctor is a man and you feel shy about being examined by him, ask to see a female doctor.

Q I am due to visit my doctor for an internal examination when I have my period. Is the examination possible during menstruation?

A Menstruation makes many of the tests difficult to perform, so you should try to make another appointment. Say why you want to change the date so that they will fit you in as soon as possible.

Q I've recently had an unusual discharge and think I should go to the doctor. Would an internal examination really be possible since I am a virgin?

A Yes, it would. In the same way as it is possible for virgins to use internal sanitary tampons, it is possible for an internal examination to be carried out. There is no need to worry and you should visit your doctor as soon as possible.

An internal examination is an essential part of preventive medicine. Because every woman is likely to have one at some time in her life, it can be reassuring to know how and why this examination is done.

An internal examination is a way of assessing the health of the external and internal sexual organs—the vagina, the uterus, the cervix (neck of the uterus; see Cervix and cervical smears), the ovaries (see Ovaries), and the fallopian tubes (the tubes that lead from the ovaries to the uterus). It also provides the opportunity for an important part of preventive medicine, the Pap smear, to be performed. The examination will be done at regular intervals and as part of the checkup a woman has when she is prescribed birth control, treated for any sexually transmitted disease, or when she is pregnant.

If a woman does not fall into any of these categories, then her doctor should give her an internal examination regularly and a Pap smear usually every year or two to insure that all is well.

Why it is necessary

The purpose of an internal examination is to diagnose any gynecological problems that a woman has or is likely to have in the future. Since it is often possible to foresee problems before they become serious, an internal examination is therefore an essential part of female preventive medicine; a precaution to maintain her health. Before checking the internal organs, the doctor will first look at the vulva to insure that it is healthy and that there are no signs of inflammation (see Inflammation). The doctor will also notice the size of the clitoris and labia minora (inner lips of the vulva) and whether or not there is any unusual discharge that may indicate the presence of infection (see Vaginal discharge).

The muscular tone of the sexual organs will also be assessed, particularly after childbirth. The woman may be asked to cough to check that the muscle that closes the urethra (the tube that leads out from the bladder) is working properly. The Bartholin's glands at the entrance to the vagina will also be checked for any inflammation or infection.

The doctor will then check the internal organs for any signs of a gynecological problem. If a woman is pregnant, the duration and health of the pregnancy can be checked. At each stage of the examination, the doctor will be checking for different conditions.

How the examination is done

The doctor will begin the internal examination by inserting a finger into the vagina (see Vagina). Thin plastic gloves are worn for this, and the doctor will use some lubricating jelly to make the internal examination easier.

How a Pap smear is done

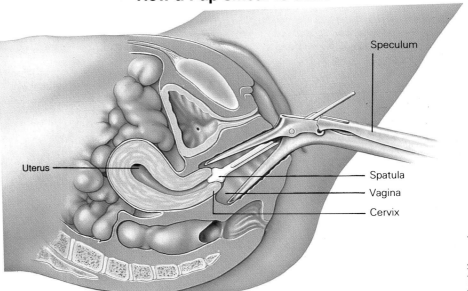

Speculum

Uterus

Spatula

Vagina

Cervix

Frank Kennard

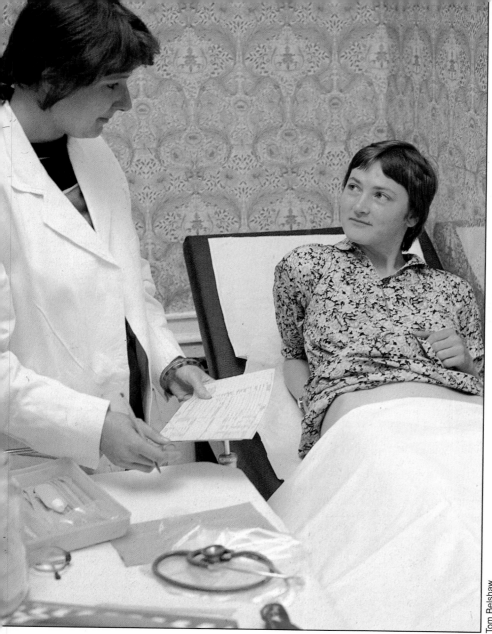
Tom Belshaw

checking for other kinds of infections or diseases, a smear of discharge will be taken for testing. The speculum will then be closed gently and removed.

A bimanual examination
Bimanual literally means "with two hands." The doctor will insert two fingers of one hand into the vagina and press the outside of the abdominal wall with the other. This enables the doctor to feel the shape, size, and position of the internal sexual organs. The causes of any inflammation or infection can be diagnosed. The bimanual examination is especially useful during pregnancy because the uterus and cervix change shape and feel different to the touch. The cervix and the uterus become softer, and the size of the uterus is an indication of the duration of the pregnancy.

The doctor will make sure that the ovaries are in place and that they are healthy. Some women find it a little uncomfortable when the doctor checks their ovaries, but this is the only way the doctor can tell that they are in the correct place.

After the examination
Your doctor should inform you of any problems that have been found during the examination, because they may need to be treated. Results of any tests will take a day or so to obtain, but these should also be given to you. Often doctors feel that there is no need to tell a woman the results of any test unless there is something wrong, but fortunately some doctors are aware that women are eager to know the results of tests, particularly if they are given a clean bill of health.

Worries
It is clear that the internal examination is a vital part of health care. It carries with it no physical dangers, and there is no risk in having the examination during pregnancy. Even so, many women are worried by the idea of an internal examination, either because of embarrassment or fear that it will hurt.

This is perfectly natural. Many women feel nervous and vulnerable because intimate parts of the body are being touched and examined by a relative stranger. However, doctors are aware that women can feel tense about an internal examination and will do their best to create a relaxed atmosphere.

Women themselves can find that they feel more relaxed if they try consciously to relax the neck, back, jaw, and hands, as well as breathing through the mouth during the examination. This will make the examination easier for the doctor and more comfortable for the woman.

An internal examination is quick and simple to perform and should be done at least once a year as part of a good preventive medicine routine.

By feeling the vaginal walls, the doctor can check that the vagina is healthy and that there are no unusual inflammations or swellings.

The doctor will then insert a speculum, that makes it possible for the vaginal walls and the cervix to be seen and examined. The speculum is a small instrument, shaped somewhat like a duck's bill, that can be gently opened to make the vaginal walls and the cervix clearly visible. If the speculum is made of metal, the doctor should warm it to make the examination more comfortable.

At this point a Pap smear may be done. The doctor inserts a small spatula into the vagina and scrapes away a tiny amount of the cervix, which will then be analyzed by a pathology laboratory for any signs of disease or abnormality.

Frequency of testing
The frequency of the Pap smear will depend on the woman's age, how many children she has, and whether she is sexually active. However, medical opinion varies as to how often this should be done. Many birth control clinics like to take a Pap smear once a year, others once every three to five years. Any woman who has never had a Pap smear should ask her doctor to do one at the earliest opportunity, since it makes it possible to diagnose conditions that could lead to cancer. Early treatment of these conditions can prevent cancer from developing.

A Pap smear will not hurt but may feel a little uncomfortable for the second or two it takes to do it. If the doctor is

Intoxication

Q Does alcoholic intoxication have any lasting effects?

A That depends on whether the intoxication is an occasional affair or a regular habit. Repeated abuse of alcohol can cause liver damage, bleeding in the stomach, irritability, violence, impotence, lack of concentration and drive, and insomnia. Moderate drinking is generally safe, although tolerance varies by individual, and everyone should know their own limit. Alcohol is a potent enough poison to be dangerous if taken in excess, even in just one session. For example, if you were able to drink heavily all day without stopping you might kill yourself. However, for most people this is impossible because they would be unconscious long before then.

Q When a substance is labeled nontoxic, does it mean that it cannot make people become drunk?

A No. It means that the substance is not poisonous. In other words the substance will not do you any harm if it is taken accidentally. It doesn't mean that the substance will not catch fire, cause intoxication, or irritate some skins.

Q My grandfather is 70 years old and not very strong. He drinks a lot of whiskey, often a half a bottle each day. Most of the time it doesn't seem to affect him. Could he have built up a resistance?

A Yes. If someone drinks excessively as a matter of routine he or she will build up a resistance to the amount of alcohol they can consume. This means that the liver, which is responsible for breaking down alcohol, gets more efficient with practice. However, that does not mean that your grandfather is damaging his health any the less. It also suggests that if he is not already a dependent drinker, he may develop into one. The more alcohol a person can drink with no apparent physical or mental effects, the more he or she will drink.

In the short term intoxication means, at the very least, an increased menace on the roads. In the long run it causes irreparable, even fatal, damage to the health.

The Breathalyzer tests a driver's level of intoxication. If the yellow crystals turn green, the driver is over the safety limit.

Strictly speaking the word *intoxication* refers to poisoning of any kind, but alcoholic intoxication is the most common, followed by the poisoning of alcohol combined with certain medications. Alcohol can accentuate the effects of some medications, sometimes with very dangerous results, so patients should never disregard their doctor's warnings.

Absorption

The alcohol in beer, wines, and liquors is called ethyl alcohol (or ethanol). In its pure form ethanol is a colorless and almost tasteless liquid.

Alcohol is absorbed primarily in the stomach, by diffusion rather than digestion. The absorbed alcohol then spreads rapidly throughout the body in the bloodstream. When large quantities of food are in the stomach, however, alcohol is absorbed more slowly. This is why it is good to eat when drinking alcohol.

The threshold of intoxication

The body can deal with modest amounts of alcohol without significant effects. As you drink the body breaks down the alcohol, mainly in the liver. It is broken down at a steady rate of about 0.0007 oz of alcohol per 3.4 fl oz (20 mg per 100 ml) of body fluid per hour.

It takes about 12 hours to break down the alcohol consumed in half a bottle of whiskey, so in theory you could go to bed and wake up still intoxicated. Similarly, by drinking moderate amounts of alcohol steadily around the clock, you could maintain a permanent state of intoxication.

Short-term effects

The short-term physical effects of alcohol and intoxication include satisfying thirst, relieving tension, and anesthetizing the senses. Alcohol also causes slurring of speech, irritation of the stomach lining, vomiting, impotence in men, and it can sometimes cause depression.

Long-term effects

Drinking too much alcohol often leads to alcohol dependence. The dividing line between moderate drinking and dependence is almost nonexistent. Some people can become dependent if they hav~~e~~ more than 5 pt (2.76 l) of beer a day.

Chronic or long-term alcohol intoxic~~a~~tion can lead to: cirrhosis of the live~~r~~ which is fatal if it is not caught early (se~~e~~ Liver and liver diseases); and vitamin deficiency, which may damage the hear~~t~~ brain, and kidneys (see Vitamin B).

Dependent drinkers suffer from th~~e~~ DTs, or delirium tremens, when th~~e~~ intoxication wears off. There is shakin~~g~~ anxiety, hallucinations, depression, an~~d~~ insomnia, which disappear when the~~y~~ have another alcoholic drink. Alcoh~~ol~~ withdrawal can be fatal.

Dependent drinkers need profession~~al~~ help. Health services provide this, as d~~o~~ groups like Alcoholics Anonymous. Man~~y~~ treatments are offered, which involv~~e~~ either gradual or abrupt withdrawal, a~~s~~ well as counseling. Sometimes a drug i~~s~~ given that makes the patient feel ill (vom~~-~~ iting, headache, flushing) if they drin~~k~~ alcohol, and this acts as aversion therap~~y~~.

Outlook

Serious alcoholism is recognized as a per~~-~~ sonality disorder, and such cases onl~~y~~ wish to be permanently intoxicate~~d~~. Continued psychiatric help is one way t~~o~~ beat this type of drinking problem.

Where the will to be cured is strong~~,~~ the chances of a return to normal life ar~~e~~ good, but this means giving up drinking~~.~~

Observing the effects of alcohol intoxicatio~~n~~ in a parent can be a frightening experience for children.

Stages of intoxication

Level of alcohol in blood (figures for a man of average height and weight)	Stage
From 0 to 0.0028 oz (0 to 80 mg) per 3.4 fl oz (100 ml) of blood. To achieve this, about 3 fl oz of straight whiskey or 2 pt (0.9 l) of beer must be drunk	The legal limit for drivers in the US is 0.0035 oz (100 mg). Most regular drinkers behave soberly with this amount inside them. Even so it can be shown that their reactions are slower than usual and their ability to judge distances is impaired
From 0.0028 to 0.00525 oz (80 to 150 mg)	You are the heart and soul of the party, but if someone crosses you, you may become aggressive
From 0.00525 to 0.0105 oz (150 to 300 mg)	You are beginning to show the outward signs of intoxication; unsteadiness on the feet and a tendency to knock things over or be violent. You may have difficulty inserting a door key
From 0.0105 to 0.01225 oz (300 to 350 mg)	You have difficulty in standing, are unable to speak distinctly, and may be vomiting
More than 0.01225 oz (350 mg)	You are flat on your back in a drunken stupor and at risk of inhaling your own vomit (which can cause suffocation). Your breathing may be impaired, and dangerously low body temperature could set in if you are outside in the cold. A lethal dose of alcohol is not much more than what is already in your body

Intravenous infusion

Q What happens if an intravenous infusion feeds too quickly or slowly?

A There is little danger if this occurs for a short period, although neither situation is desirable. A counter or container that allows fluid through in measured amounts is used where the control of fluid amount is critical or where excess fluid would be dangerous.

Q Is an intravenous infusion used only in emergencies?

A No. An IV is often used to prevent complications from developing. When a patient has had abdominal surgery, it may not be possible for him or her to eat or drink. An IV can prevent dehydration and assist in recovery.

Q Are intravenous infusions always inserted into arms?

A If a vein is not available in the arm, a leg vein can be used. An arm vein is preferable since a leg vein is more likely to become inflamed and blocked. Veins in the forearm are preferable to those in the elbow or wrist since a cannula (the tube through which fluid passes into the patient) may bend or be knocked out when a person bends their arm. Scalp veins or leg veins are often used in infants.

Q I am due to have a major operation and will probably be put on an IV. Is this going to be very painful?

A Once the cannula is inserted it is completely painless, although it is inconvenient since you can't move the arm. The area may become slightly inflamed, but this soon disappears when the IV is removed.

Q How does a doctor decide how much fluid to give?

A Clinical assessments of the patient and blood tests indicate the amount of fluids and salts missing in the body. When close control of the blood volume is needed, a central venous pressure line may be inserted near the heart.

If a patient urgently needs fluids because of disease, surgery, or an accident, they can be directly introduced into the bloodstream via an intravenous infusion.

An intravenous infusion, which is commonly called an IV, is used to feed fluids directly into the bloodstream. Its purpose is usually to correct a serious lack of the nutrients or fluids on which the body's cells depend.

Such a deficiency may be caused by a number of factors. For instance, prolonged vomiting or diarrhea causes a great loss of fluid and essential nutrients, while major surgery or certain conditions may affect a patient's ability to take fluids or drugs by mouth.

Blood transfusions

An IV is required to introduce a blood transfusion into the body. This is necessary after massive blood loss or to compensate for a lack of red blood cells in the blood of anemic patients. The object of a blood transfusion is to increase the amount of hemoglobin, the substance that carries oxygen around the bloodstream, in the body (see Blood).

How it works

The fluid passes from a bag or bottle suspended on a stand into a chamber known as an infusion-set. In it, the fluid is visible and the rate of flow can be checked. From here the liquid passes down a length of flexible tubing at a rate controlled by a screw clip on the cannula, a flexible tube.

A suitable vein is found, most commonly in the forearm, and the area around it is cleaned thoroughly. A doctor or nurse inserts a needle surrounded by a plastic sheath into the vein. When the needle is removed, the sheath is held firmly in position with adhesive tape and a splint. This prevents the sheath from pulling out of the patient's vein if he or she makes a sudden movement or has a spasm.

The patient may feel a slight pain as the needle is inserted, but otherwise there is no discomfort. The arm has to be kept still; if the cannula pulls out, the infusion will slow down or stop. Any inflammation and swelling caused by particularly long use of an IV disappears shortly after it has been removed from the patient.

Being on an intravenous infusion is inconvenient but painless. To insure that the needle does not move, the area around where it is inserted is usually wrapped in cotton padding and a splint is bandaged on.

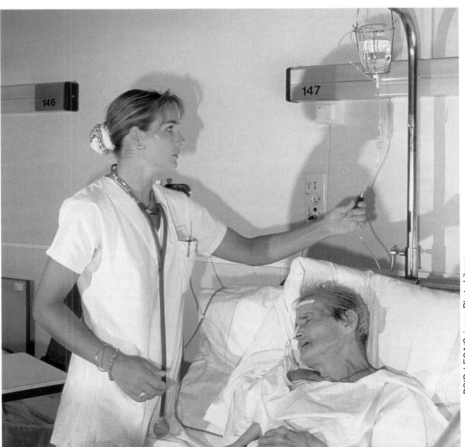

Iridology

Q What do orthodox doctors think about iridology?

A Few of them accept that there are detailed links between parts of the body and areas of the iris in the way that iridologists do. Many conventional doctors consider iridology to be unscientific and therefore useless. They also feel that there is a danger that an iridologist may fail to diagnose a condition that needs urgent surgery or control by a drug.

Q I wear contact lenses. Will this make any difference?

A You will be asked to remove contact lenses or glasses before the iridologist examines your eyes.

Q Will the iridologist ask me lots of questions?

A Yes, he or she will ask questions after the examination and may also ask you to fill out a questionnaire about your personal and family medical history. The consultation may include simple tests for blood pressure or tests to assess the condition of the heart and blood sugar levels.

Q My little brother is very hyperactive. Could iridology help him, or would he find the examination too stressful?

A The iris is not fully formed until a child is about six years old, so this is the earliest age iridology can be useful. Iridology is often used in cases of hyperactivity in children. To keep stress levels down, the young child should sit on a parent's knee opposite a bright natural light source (like a window), instead of the practitioner shining a penlight into the eyes.

Q How long does an iridology consultation last, and is it expensive?

A Iridologists work in different ways, and a consultation may last from 30 minutes to two hours. Prices vary too, so check this when you make an appointment.

The markings in the eyes are as individual as fingerprints. So is it true that iridologists can tell you a great deal about your health just by gazing into your eyes?

According to iridologists, the iris (the colored portion of the eye) reflects the state of a person's physical health. From its coloring, condition, and markings, they claim to be able not only to diagnose present and past conditions, but also to give advance warning of possible future ill health. Iridology is only used for diagnosis, it is not a type of healing or therapy.

The iris is said to represent a body map, divided into sections corresponding to different parts and systems. The kidneys, for example, are represented in a segment at the bottom; the lymphatic and circulatory systems lie in an outer ring. The left eye, say iridologists, corresponds to the left-hand side of the body and the right eye to the right-hand side. White marks on the iris show signs of stress and inflammation in the relevant organ, dark marks indicate a malfunction. The dark rim around the iris of many smokers is said to show the accumulation of toxins in the body.

Origins

As long ago as the time of the ancient Greeks, the iris was considered to be a barometer of a person's health. It was noted that the colored part of the eye was full of colors and different markings, and it was named accordingly after Iris, the goddess of the rainbow. The Greek doctor Hippocrates, the founder of medicine, wrote that it was important to examine the eyes carefully when assessing the state of a patient's health.

Modern iridology, which is also called ophthalmic somatology, began in the mid-19th century with a Hungarian doctor, Ignatz von Peczely. During his childhood he nursed an owl with a broken leg and noticed a black mark in the bird's eye that disappeared as its leg healed.

After he qualified as a doctor and took up an appointment in a hospital in Budapest, Peczely began to carry out his own research by studying the irises of his patients before and after treatment. He drew up charts of their irises and discovered that the same condition in different patients seemed to cause a mark to appear in the same part of the iris.

From this research he was able to draw charts showing the various sectors of the iris and their relationship with the body's various parts and systems; these charts form the basis of iridology today.

After Peczely published his research some doctors in Europe began to use iridology as a diagnostic tool, and early in the 20th century a Swedish homeopath introduced it to the United States (see Homeopathy). Fifty years later an American naturopath, Bernard Jensen, refined and developed the original iridology charts, and these are the charts used by many contemporary iridologists (see Naturopathy). Others tend to use charts that combine the research of various other practitioners. However, the basic principle of iris analysis remains the same as it was a century and a half ago, when first practiced by Peczely.

How it works

People are born with strengths and weaknesses, and iridologists claim that these are reflected in the iris of the eye (see Eyes and Eyesight). According to this theory the iris functions like a pre-recorded tape, showing all that has happened to the body since birth. Taking into account genetic factors, underlying trends can be identified and future problems predicted from the iris color and markings.

Iridology classifies people into three broad categories according to their basic eye color. It is claimed that each of these categories has a tendency toward certain conditions and diseases.

Lymphatic constitution

People with blue/gray eyes have a lymphatic constitution, which is said to give

What does iridology offer?

Iridology practitioners say that health problems show up on the iris map before their symptoms become apparent in the body. So iridology offers a kind of early warning system of things that may be about to go wrong. Steps can then be taken to put things right.

What iridology cannot reveal
- Viral infections, such as measles or a cold
- Pregnancy
- Mental illness, such as schizophrenia
- The likelihood of developing cancer

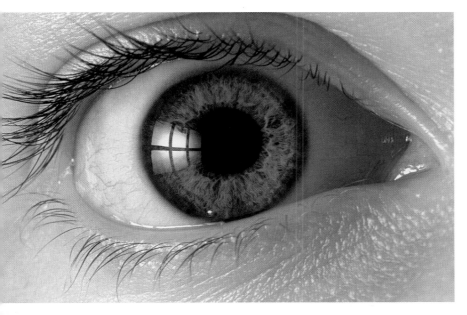

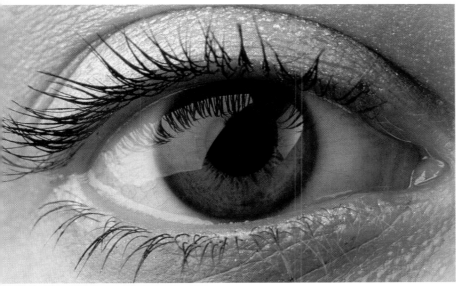

Dark flecks in the blue iris (top) indicate a lack of energy in the body organ to which they relate. People with brown eyes (above) may be prone to digestive problems.

iridologist will construct a detailed map of the individual eye markings to make a more accurate diagnosis.

Eyelines

There are about 500 recognized iris markings that can be identified by the iridologist. These consist of lines, flecks, wedges, wisps, clouds, cobwebs, rings, arcs, and patterns, many of which have pretty names like tulips and honeycombs. They are not considered random but are all related to the organs in the body, according to their position.

The shape and size of each mark has its own particular significance in iridology. In general white markings are indicators of overactivity and irritation, and dark markings indicate underactivity and weakness. The practitioner will also ask questions in an attempt to reveal whether a condition is active or dormant.

The consultation

A consultation lasts between 30 minutes and two hours. The iris is examined with a light and a magnifying glass or iris microscope, and a drawing is made. The light causes the pupil to contract, so that the greatest area of the iris can be seen. It also shows the structure of the iris so that the individual pattern is apparent. Some iridologists take close-up photographs of each iris, enlarging them to about 20 times normal size. These are used only for reference; a diagnosis would never be based on photographs, because printing variations can produce misleading results.

The patient will be told what the diagnosis reveals, including the causes of any current diseases and conditions. He or she will also be informed about the body's strengths and weaknesses and any underlying tendencies toward disease, and will be advised on changes to diet and lifestyle. If a serious condition is identified, the iridologist will suggest that the patient consult their regular doctor. A follow-up visit may be required, especially if any photographs have been taken.

Many iridologists are also trained in another therapy, such as naturopathy or herbalism, and use iridology as an extra diagnostic tool. If nonserious conditions are identified during the consultation, the therapist may offer to treat the patient using his or her own brand of therapy.

Preventive medicine

Many people use iridology as a form of preventive medicine. They have a consultation with an iridologist even when they are feeling well, to get a snapshot of their current state of health and to be alerted to any problems that may result in illness. They are then able to take steps to correct the problems.

an individual a tendency toward allergies, arthritis and rheumatism, fluid retention, respiratory infections (like bronchitis), swollen glands, and flabbiness.

People with green eyes also have the lymphatic constitution. This is because green eyes are thought to be the result of yellow coloring over a blue iris, giving the same tendencies as for the blue/gray eye category.

In addition, green-eyed people may have a sluggish liver, evening nausea, and early gallstones. They may also suffer from skin problems and swollen glands and they may be prone to allergies.

Hematogenous constitution

Brown-eyed people can expect to be told they have a hematogenous constitution. This indicates a tendency toward circulatory problems, mineral deficiencies (like anemia), glandular disorders, digestive and gastric problems (like constipation), skin problems, and diabetes.

Biliary/mixed constitution

Anyone with hazel eyes can expect to have a biliary/mixed constitution. A mixture of the two basic eye colors gives people with hazel eyes a mix of the two main categories. They may also have liver and gallbladder problems.

However, all these constitutional indications are only guidelines; not everyone with brown eyes will suffer excessively from constipation. At a consultation the

Iron

Q Do you lose iron if you give blood regularly?

A Yes. If you give blood once every three months, then you lose about twice as much iron as normal. However, a good mixed diet is more than adequate to replace this loss.

Q Is it true that spinach contains a lot of iron?

A In fact, it contains a moderate amount. Green vegetables are not the best source of iron. Dried peas and beans, and unrefined flour, contain more than most green vegetables. Spinach contains about 4 mg of iron per 3.5 oz (100 g) of spinach, which is a moderate amount. However, iron from vegetables is not so easily absorbed by the intestine as iron from meat.

Q I was given iron pills by my doctor and my feces turned a funny black color. Is this normal?

A Yes. Black feces are a common side effect of taking iron supplements. Iron may also produce either diarrhea or constipation, but generally any side effects are minimal.

Q Should I take iron pills while I am having a period?

A No. A mixed diet should provide adequate iron, even for women having periods or who are pregnant, except occasionally during the last four months of pregnancy. However, vegetarian women may find it necessary to take iron supplements during their reproductive years.

Q I have heard that iron pills are dangerous for children. Is this true?

A It is unusual for children to suffer from anemia due to iron deficiency, but when they do they can be given iron under medical supervision. However, iron pills can poison children if an overdose is taken, and for this reason they should be kept well out of children's reach.

Just as iron plays a vital role in industry, its presence in the body is essential for health. When a deficiency occurs, problems can arise, but the right diet and iron supplements can restore the balance.

Jerry Harpur/John Lewis

A diet containing plenty of iron-rich foods is especially important during pregnancy, when the developing fetus absorbs much of the woman's iron stores.

Anemia is a blood disorder involving the red blood cells that carry oxygen to all parts of the body (see Anemia). Anemia caused by iron deficiency is one of the most common deficiency disorders in women. It rarely occurs in healthy men. This is because women lose iron regularly in the blood shed during menstruation, and tend not to take enough iron in their diet to replace it (see Menstruation). Iron deficiency anemia in children, men, or postmenopausal women, however, suggests that there is a problem elsewhere. There may be a slow bleeding duodenal ulcer (see Ulcers) or, particularly in children, some disease causing abnormal iron absorption from food in the intestine.

Iron is a chemical element found in the body's red blood cells. It cannot be produced in the body so, to maintain good health, it is essential to eat some foods that contain iron (see Blood).

The role of iron

The red blood cells contain hemoglobin, which is responsible for the vital activity of carrying oxygen from the lungs to the tissues. It also gives blood its red coloring. Iron is an essential ingredient of hemoglobin, and a lack of iron is by far the most common cause of anemia.

Anemia may result in tiredness, breathlessness, and a general feeling of ill health (see Fatigue). Iron deficiency can also cause ridges and brittleness in the nails which may become spoon shaped in severe cases), while the corners of the mouth may become sore, and there may be thinning of the lining of the esophagus and stomach, causing indigestion.

The body contains about 0.1 oz (3–4 g) of iron. Seventy percent of this is present in the red blood cells that circulate in the bloodstream, with a further small amount in the bone marrow. About 20 percent of the iron is stored in the liver and the spleen, much of it in the form of ferritin –an iron-containing protein. A small amount of the body's iron is not concerned with the manufacture of hemoglobin but is involved in other important cellular functions. Many of the enzymes that regulate a normal cell's activity depend upon iron (see Enzymes).

Iron loss

The main cause of iron loss is through bleeding. However, since iron is widely distributed in the tissues, the loss of cells from surfaces like the skin and the lining of the intestine also leads to iron loss.

The total amount lost in this way each day is about 1 mg. In women, although menstrual bleeding occurs only once a month, the average loss due to this amounts to a further 1 mg per day. Thus women normally lose about twice as much iron as men.

Female iron loss is also increased during pregnancy, when the fetus and the placenta absorb much of the woman's iron stores. The total daily iron requirement during pregnancy is almost double that of a nonpregnant woman during her reproductive years. During the last four months of pregnancy, a great deal of iron goes into building the blood volume of the baby ready for birth. During these four months up to 7.5 mg of iron is required per day. For this reason iron supplements are frequently prescribed, but usually not until after the 14th week of pregnancy. This is because iron pills can cause disturbance of the intestine and lead either to constipation or diarrhea, occasionally to nausea, and in some cases even to actual vomiting.

Since the normal iron stores are quite large, it would take a normal man about three years to develop iron deficiency anemia. However, iron deficiency comes on much quicker if there is blood loss, such as might occur if someone suffers

The iron used in industry is the same basic chemical element as the iron found in the body. When metals are combined with other chemicals they produce salts, and this is the form that iron takes in the body. This iron is known biologically as ferrous salts. The best source of iron in the food that we eat is red meat, particularly liver.

Foods containing iron

The recommended iron intake is 10 mg per day for children and adults; iron supplements may be prescribed by a doctor during pregnancy and for iron deficiency anemia. Iron levels are given in milligrams per 3.5 oz (100 g) of food, but these levels are subject to variation, particularly in the vegetables, due to the variable amount of iron in the soil.

Food	Iron level
Liver	6.0–14.10
Beef	2.0–4.5
Milk	0.1–4.5
Eggs	2.0–3.0
Lentils	1.9–14.0
Unrefined wheat flour	3.0
Refined wheat flour	0.7–1.5
Potatoes and root vegetables	0.3–2.0
Spinach	4.0 approx
Other green vegetables	very variable
Parsley	8.0
Lettuce	0.8

from slow bleeding from, for example, ulcers or hemorrhoids.

Severe anemia is immediately obvious because the sufferer will become very pale. Less severe degrees can be detected by blood tests. If there is a low hemoglobin level in the blood, whether it is due to lack of iron is confirmed by looking at the red blood cells under a microscope. When iron deficiency anemia is present, the red blood cells become smaller, whereas in other causes of anemia they tend to enlarge or remain of normal size. To avoid confusion, the level of iron in the blood is measured. Treatment is with iron pills, which are taken until the level of hemoglobin is back to normal. This will be confirmed by a blood test.

Iron absorption

Iron is absorbed from the small intestine (see Alimentary canal). The normal absorption is only in the region of 1 mg per day, and this only balances the normal losses. The fact that iron loss and iron absorption are set in this critical balance explains why it is relatively easy for a person to have an iron deficiency, and therefore, why it is quite a common complaint.

In fact, only about 10 percent of the iron we actually eat ever gets absorbed by the body, although this proportion may be higher when there is iron deficiency. Since the normal loss is about 1 mg, people should therefore eat about 10 mg of iron per day, though menstruating women obviously need more and should try to eat more of the foods that are rich in iron, such as liver.

Iron is mainly found in red meat, particularly liver. There is also a considerable amount in lentils and in unrefined wheat flour. Purified white flour contains less iron, although iron is artificially added to flour and to many breakfast cereals.

Excess iron

Iron overload in the system can occur for a number of reasons, including excessive iron absorption from the intestine, or unnecessarily large doses taken over a long period. Excess iron may affect the liver, causing cirrhosis, and may accumulate in the pancreas, giving rise to diabetes (see Diabetes), or in the testes, which may then cease to produce male hormones (see Testes).

The treatment for iron overload is repeated removal of blood at intervals. This lowers the level of iron in the body. Once cirrhosis is established repeated removal of iron will not make it disappear, but may help to slow down the progress of the disease (see Cirrhosis).

Tony Stone Associates

Irritable bowel syndrome

Q My sister always has diarrhea and stomach pains before her exams. Does she have irritable bowel syndrome?

A No. Many people have this kind of reaction near important exams. The whole nervous system is affected, and this causes the intestine to become overactive. With an irritable intestine there is a similar kind of spasm, but it lasts much longer and may arise without obvious stress.

Q My doctor thinks I have irritable bowel syndrome, and wants me to go to the hospital for further tests. Why?

A Because there are no positive features that identify irritable bowel syndrome, diagnosis has to be made by excluding other possible causes, and these need hospital tests. Your doctor may not expect to find anything serious, so the tests are for reassurance only.

Q My doctor has suggested that I have a high-fiber diet for my irritable colon, but I hate the taste of bran. Are there any alternatives?

A Most fiber in the average diet comes from vegetables and fruits, and eating plenty of these will help. Whole meal bread is also a good source, and some breakfast cereals contain bran or other fiber in a more palatable form. If necessary your doctor may advise fiber in the form of special tablet-shaped fiber preparations that are taken several times a day with meals.

Q I have irritable bowel syndrome, and now my son has similar symptoms. Should I give him the same treatment?

A No, you must take him to the doctor. Irritable bowel syndrome does not run in families, and just because you suffer from it doesn't mean that your son is likely to have it. Also similar symptoms may indicate another more serious condition, and every case merits individual consideration from a doctor to exclude these.

This condition, which commonly afflicts young adults, is also known as spastic colon, mucous colitis, or nervous diarrhea. It responds quite well to treatment.

Most cases of irritable bowel syndrome arise spontaneously. Psychological factors are thought to play a part; those affected are often anxious and tense. However, since all anxious people do not manifest symptoms, and some who are not obviously anxious have them, there is thought to be an underlying disorder, consisting of more frequent than normal pressure waves that force the food through the intestines. Another factor may be the taking of too many laxatives by those obsessed with intestinal function.

Symptoms vary from mild discomfort to excruciating pain, which can be continuous or comes in spasms; it may affect the whole abdomen or only one region. It is often aggravated by food and relieved by urinating, defecating, or passing gas.

Patients may feel bloated, and hear stomach rumbles and sense turbulence in the gastrointestinal tract (see Alimentary canal). When there is constipation, the feces are often hard and ribbonlike, pellety, or covered in mucus.

Irritable bowel syndrome may be confused with various forms of colitis (chronic diarrhea), intestinal polyps (benign growths), ulcers, diverticulosis (bulges in the intestine due to inflammation), and intestinal cancer, but medical examinations usually rule these out.

Treatment and outlook

Part of treatment is ruling out more serious diseases, such as dysentery, lactose intolerance, or inflammatory bowel disease (see Diverticulosis). A high-fiber diet adds bulk to the intestinal contents, making food pass easier and quicker. When constipation or diarrhea persist, antispasmodic drugs may give relief.

Counseling (especially on avoiding stressful situations) may also be needed.

When frequent pressure waves reach a spastic segment of the intestine, the buildup of food or gas causes a full feeling (left).

How irritable colon arises

Frank Kennard

Colon

Ileum

Spastic (contracted) segment

Rectum

Roger Payling

Roger Payling

Working off stress by engaging in sports activities (above) can be a remedy for irritable bowel syndrome. A stressful job involving constant challenge and problem solving (left) may contribute to developing the disease.

Irritants

Q My son recently swallowed some kerosene. I was going to make him vomit by giving him salty water to drink, but a neighbor told me not to and to take him straight to the hospital. Was she right?

A Some irritants cause intense burning in the mucous membranes of the mouth and throat and do less harm in the stomach. Vomiting will only cause more damage. A drink of milk is the best emergency treatment for all gastric irritants. The patient should then go to the hospital, where a stomach pump can be used to empty the stomach safely.

Q When I splashed some car battery acid up into my face, I instantly put my head under the water tap. Was this the best thing to do?

A Yes. First aid for all acid or alkali burns involves doing just that. Dilute the acid, remove all contaminated clothing, and get medical help. Even if the eyes are affected, speedy and plentiful dilution of the corrosive agent can prevent further damage.

Q How can I tell if the household cleaning compounds I use are irritants?

A Bottles containing chemicals for cleaning or bleaching state clearly on the label "Poison: do not swallow." They should always be kept in a locked cupboard and away from children.

Q My son made some horrible gas with his chemistry set and coughed for ages. Could he have done any lasting damage?

A Only a few gaseous irritants cause damage long after they are absorbed into the system. In most cases the initial exposure is so unpleasant that the person inhaling the gas moves away before any lasting damage is done. Chemistry sets used without supervision can be dangerous. Even the gas producing stink bomb, hydrogen sulfide, is a strong respiratory irritant.

There are many different irritants that can affect the human body, and they can produce symptoms ranging from mild discomfort to severe pain. Fortunately prompt medical treatment is usually successful.

Irritants are any substances—animal, vegetable, mineral, or chemical—that cause inflammation and irritation when they come into contact with the human body. They can be specific to the individual, taking the form of an allergy, or they can be poisonous or corrosive substances that are toxic to everyone.

How the body is affected

Irritants usually affect several areas of the body at once, with symptoms starting at the point of entry.

The skin: Some chemicals spilled onto the skin react with it to produce a mild burn. Acids and alkalis may produce no reaction at first, then cause a sensation of heat followed by itching and redness or, in more severe cases, blistering and pain.

The eyes: The eyes absorb chemicals quickly. They react by watering profusely, and the eyelids go into spasm as they try to shut out the irritant. In severe cases the mucous membrane covering the eye becomes inflamed and, unless the irritant is removed, ulceration will lead to scarring and possible blindness.

The nose and lungs: Gaseous irritants can be inhaled into the lungs through the nose or mouth. In the nose they cause a profuse nasal discharge and a burning sensation. In the lungs they cause coughing spasms and sensations of choking, followed by asthma and wheezing as the fluid from the blood pours into the lungs.

The mouth and gut: Irritants that are swallowed cause pain and burning in the mouth, followed by abdominal pain. There may be burns on the skin around the mouth, vomiting of blood, and shreds of stomach mucosa. Medical help is needed.

Treatment

Treatment consists of first identifying the irritant and then removing it, either by dilution or by using an antidote that renders it chemically ineffective. Any damage sustained by the body is then treated with drugs.

Dealing with irritants

FIRST AID

If a corrosive irritant is swallowed, never induce vomiting. Irritants burn the mouth and throat but are less harmful when mixed with the acid of the stomach. Give the patient milk since this neutralizes both acids and alkalis. Get medical help immediately.

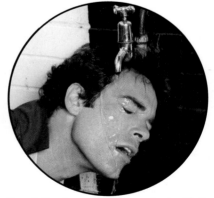

If an irritant comes into contact with the skin, wash the area with cold water, then bland soap and water. Cover broken skin with a clean dressing and get medical aid. If the eyes are affected, wash the irritant out with plenty of cold water and then go to the hospital.

Isolation

Q **I am worried that my son may give my husband mumps if he catches it at school. Should I isolate him?**

A A man with mumps is likely to be more seriously ill than a child who has contracted it. Inflammation of the testes can occur, and this is unpleasant and painful. However, your son would be infectious before he shows any symptoms, so isolating him when he becomes ill may be too late. Remember that in this condition the virus passes from one person to another in the saliva and in airborne droplets from coughing and sneezing. Your husband may have had mumps as a child. If this is the case, he would be very unlikely to get it again.

Q **My one-year-old daughter has been put into isolation because she has pneumonia. Will she suffer from the lack of personal contact?**

A Always communicate your worries to the nursing staff. They will tell you what you can do for your child in the way of feeding, playing, reading from a picture book, and so on. If your daughter is very ill, just try to be with her as much as possible. However, remember to always keep to the strict rules of the ward.

Q **Should a person with sickness and diarrhea be isolated?**

A Not necessarily. Most cases clear up quickly in a few hours or days. If the trouble continues see your doctor. Exceptions to this are those in contact with children, hospital workers, and workers in the food and catering industries, who should stay off work until pronounced better by their doctor.

Q **Would I be put into isolation if I contracted tuberculosis?**

A Indeed you would. Tuberculosis is a highly infectious disease and used to be a killer. However, modern drug treatment is almost always successful (see Tuberculosis).

Isolating the patient was once the only method of containing infectious diseases. Since the introduction of immunization and antibiotics, however, it is now only used in very special circumstances.

Isolation is the medical term for separating a patient from the community to prevent the spread of infection. Usually the patient has an illness that may endanger others; however, isolation is also used to protect the patient from any infection that others may pass on to him or her. A person with a faulty immune system (see Immune systems) can die from common, normally mild illnesses, such as influenza or chicken pox.

The isolation room may be in a general hospital next to a general ward, or in an infectious diseases unit, or in a separate infectious diseases hospital.

Diminishing need

Nowadays, as a result of immunization programs, antibiotics, and higher standards of hygiene, comparatively few people with an infectious disease ever require admission to the hospital, let alone being placed in isolation. However, in the past many patients were admitted suffering from infectious diseases or their complications, and they either frequently died or were permanently disabled.

Keeping children amused and occupied plays an important part when nursing them in isolation at home.

Although premature babies are kept in isolation, their mothers are encouraged to help with their care as soon as possible.

In those days isolating the patient was the only means of limiting the spread of infectious diseases such as diphtheria, leprosy, poliomyelitis, and tuberculosis.

Normally patients are now only put into isolation in the hospital when it is suspected that they have one of the more serious infectious diseases, such as typhoid or dysentery. However, patients with blood disorders (such as leukemia) or lymph gland disorders, and patients receiving certain anticancer drugs, are frequently kept in isolation because they tend to be very susceptible to infections, as are patients with severe burns.

Premature babies are also looked after in isolation, in incubators housed in special units run by highly skilled staff, to reduce the risk of infection. As soon as they are strong enough to be handled, however, their mothers are encouraged to cuddle and feed them.

Barrier nursing

To prevent direct infection from patients in isolation with suspected or proven diseases, the technique known as barrier nursing is used. Gowns are provided for all medical and nursing staff attending the patient, and for any visitors. These are worn on top of ordinary clothes, to insure that any infection from the patient is contained, and is not transferred onto skin or clothing. Hands must be carefully washed on entering the room, before taking off the gown, and again after leaving the room. For diseases spread by droplet infection sneezed out in the patient's saliva (such as whooping cough or pneumonia), a mask is also worn by nursing staff and visitors.

Flatware and linens are kept separate, because everything that has been near the patient is considered to be a possible source of infection. All dressings, needles, syringes, etc., must be incinerated. Obviously, too, the patient's urine and feces must be very carefully disposed of, particularly if there is any possibility that these contain infection, as in cases of typhoid or dysentery.

Reverse barrier nursing

Patients who are especially susceptible to infection have to be treated in isolation by so-called reverse barrier nursing to prevent them from catching anything. Here meticulous care must be taken to insure that no one with any infection, however minor, is allowed near the patient. Hands must be washed before going into the room. Masks are worn and disposable gowns put on. In some cases it may be necessary to kill all germs in the patient's food by treating it with radioactivity. The air supply is filtered and made to flow in one direction only.

These types of precautions are taken particularly where patients with bone marrow disease are concerned. They are also used for patients who are taking drugs to reduce the possibility of rejection following transplantation of organs (see Transplants).

Minor infections

There are many minor infectious diseases, normally thought of as childhood infections—such as chicken pox or measles—where the patient should be kept at home, though not in strict isolation, to protect others. This is especially important in the case of rubella (German measles), where contact with a woman in the early stages of pregnancy who has not had this illness may seriously damage the unborn baby (see Rubella).

However, many parents believe that children should be encouraged to catch certain minor infectious diseases at a fairly early age and get them over with, as they tend to have less serious effects on children than when the same infection is contracted in adulthood.

Isometrics

Q My boyfriend would like to have bulging biceps, and I gather that isometric exercises could achieve this—but how long would it take before there was a noticeable improvement?

A If your boyfriend did isometric exercises properly, he would probably be able to measure, and to feel, a change in all the muscles involved after four weeks. However, to achieve the figure of a bodybuilder takes many months of intensive work at isometric exercises, combined with weight-lifting and other fitness routines.

Q I am a dedicated football player. Would it help me to do some isometrics as well as jogging as part of my training?

A Yes. Isometrics will help you to develop specific sets of muscles that need to be extra strong for your sport. However, to get the results you want, you need to know exactly how to put isometrics to work for you. Ask a trainer for advice.

Q What is the hard evidence that isometrics gives good results? It's fine looking at photographs in old magazine ads of Charles Atlas and other musclemen, but is it really possible to build up a body like that just with isometrics?

A Charles Atlas's body does seem incredible, but he did indeed claim that it was achieved through pure isometrics. Other bodybuilders have achieved similar results with a combination of isometrics and additional routines such as weight lifting.

Q I would like to get more exercise, but I do not have the time or the money to play sports or to go to the gym. Are isometrics the answer?

A No. Isometrics are only for building up the muscles. They do not improve suppleness and, more important, they will not improve the condition of your heart, which is one of the main objects of most forms of exercise.

Isometric exercises can build up muscles at a remarkable speed, but they should be combined with an overall physical fitness routine in order to benefit general health.

Isometric exercises are a quick and easy way of increasing muscular strength and improving posture. Quite simply, they build muscles by the action of pushing or pulling against a stationary object.

The alternative, and generally more familiar, form of muscle building is isotonic exercise. This involves movable objects just as weight lifting does.

The need for exercise

Exhausted though a person may feel at the end of the day, those who do not exercise regularly use only about 20 percent of their potential muscle power in a normal day's activity.

This drastic underuse of the muscles means that many people have few reserves of strength at their command. This could mean straining muscles and ligaments when sudden extra exertion is required, such as running to catch a train. Even occasional isometric exercises will help strengthen flabby muscles. Always stretch out first, and don't push too hard or strain yourself at first.

One man who proved the power of isometrics in no uncertain terms was the legendary Charles Atlas. In 1921 he won the title of "the most perfectly developed man in the world" using pure isometric exercises. Photographs of him posing with one hand pressed against the opposite forearm showed a typical exercise that made the technique popular.

Muscle tone and strength

The main advantage of the isometric method is that strength and muscle tone are increased very quickly. As little as a minute and a half's workout a day will give surprisingly positive results.

Because isometrics concentrate heavily on one muscle or set of muscles, all e

One example of an isometric exercise (below) is to lie on your back with knees bent and feet firmly on the floor. Pushing the feet against the floor, raise your trunk, bringing your arms to knee level, and then beyond as shown. Count to six; relax; and then repeat the exercise 10 times.

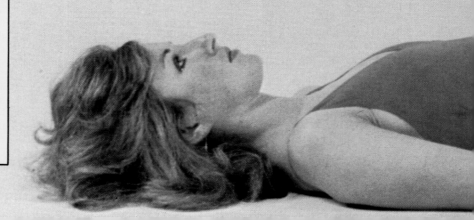

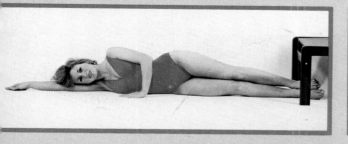

Below: Stand with your feet apart, holding a towel in one hand at knee level as shown. Wrap the towel under one heel and pull, counting to six. Relax; then repeat the exercise four times on each side.

Above: Lie on your side, one arm stretched under your head and feet under a table. Keeping legs rigid, raise them to touch the underside of the table; push upward. Count to six; relax; repeat five times on each side.

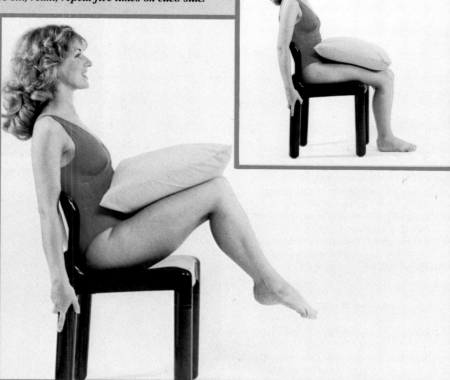

Above: Sit on a straight-backed chair. Place a cushion on your lap; grip the sides of the chair as shown. Raise your thighs, trying to squeeze the cushion against your stomach. Count to six; then relax. Repeat the exercise three times.

ISOMETRICS

John Walmsley

Isometric exercises are designed to strengthen the muscles by the action of pushing against an immovable object, such as a desk (above). This means that even the deskbound, who normally find it difficult to take time to exercise, can exercise for a few seconds every day to strengthen their muscles (above right, and right).

those muscle fibers are put to use. Exercises that involve movement of the body concentrate less on a particular set of muscles, so only some of the fibers are used. Depending on how strong and developed a person wants to become, he or she can vary the number and frequency of the exercises performed.

Although an excellent way to develop muscle, isometric exercises are certainly not the answer for general fitness. Strength and fitness should not be confused with each other; isometrics can make the body strong, but not fit. Because sweating does not occur during the exercises and because the joints are not involved, isometrics are not helpful for general suppleness or for dieting. Ideally they should be combined with another type of exercise—such as bending and stretching, cycling, or running—which involves the whole body, gets the blood flowing, and makes the heart work harder (see Exercise).

Though isometrics are perfectly safe for most people, they should still be approached with care. When muscles are severely tightened for a time, veins and arteries are compressed and blood pressure rises. Isometrics are not recommended for those with heart trouble.

When and how to do them

Isometric exercises can be done anywhere—in an automobile, at a desk—in fact, wherever a person happens to be. They are simple to do; they do not cause much fatigue; and each one lasts only a few seconds. Unlike other types of exercise, no expensive equipment is required; a stationary object such as a steering wheel, a desk, or a clenched fist is all that is necessary.

For example, while waiting in an automobile in a traffic jam, it is easy to strengthen arm and chest muscles by

putting the hands on either side of the steering wheel and pressing inward hard. In the office, upper back muscles can be developed by sitting about 1 ft (30 cm) away from a desk, then placing the palms of the hands on it, and pressing downward hard.

For a more thorough series of exercises, attach a long piece of rope or cord to either end of a pole (a broom handle is ideal); then stand on the rope and use the pole for a series of pushing and pulling exercises that strengthen the arm, shoulder, leg, back, and chest muscles.

For all of these exercises and for all isometric exercises, each exertion should last a minimum of six seconds. About different exercises per day are sufficient to condition the whole body.

For the person who wants to take isometrics seriously and also to have some fun, a record of progress can be kept by measuring the muscles as they develop and recording the scores. This can be done by measuring the diameter of each area of concentration—upper arm, chest, neck, hips, thighs, or calves—every four weeks. The progress will be dramatic at first, but later it will even out. The chart will remain useful, however, for monitoring the progress of each set of muscles—and if one falls behind, it can be given special attention to bring it back into line.

There are isometric exercises to suit every person, whatever age, shape, and fitness level. For those who are interested in isometrics, manuals and videos are widely available, which show the safe and effective performance of the exercises.

Itches

Q My mother always says that you should not scratch if you itch. Why is this; what harm could it do?

A There is no harm occasionally scratching an area that itches. This is quite normal and is very relieving. When, however, there is a particular cause for the itching, such as inflammation or a skin disease, then rubbing or scratching the area will only make the condition worse. Scratching may also break the skin and cause infection.

Q Should all itchy rashes be seen by a doctor, and is it safe to put calamine lotion on them first?

A Unless you know the exact cause of the rash, you should see your doctor; the rash could be a sign of a more serious condition. Meanwhile apply calamine lotion if you wish. It is bland and harmless, provided the skin is not broken, and as it cools the skin it seems to have a direct action in reducing any itching.

Q I have varicose eczema on both legs, and it always seems worse in the morning. The doctor says that I am scratching it, but I am not. What could be making it worse?

A You may be scratching yourself in your sleep. This is very common, especially for people with varicose veins and eczema, because the irritation is so intense. Try wearing stockings at night, and ask your doctor to prescribe antihistamines, which will help to reduce the itching.

Q I am a diabetic and I have always suffered from itches. Can you explain why?

A The high blood sugar levels in diabetes often produce skin itching. Because of their raised blood sugar levels, diabetics are prone to fungal infections, such as thrush, and these can be very irritating. Your doctor can prescribe treatment to relieve these conditions.

Itches are essential to the well-being and safety of the body. They tell us when something is wrong and warn us of illnesses and skin diseases that may require treatment.

An itch is a feeling of irritation that is almost always accompanied by a desire to scratch or rub the affected area in order to relieve it. An itch may occur on any part of the body surface, in particular, the skin around the eyes and ears or the area around the genitals.

Itching sensations vary greatly, depending on their cause. They can be mild tingling feelings, easily relieved by a quick scratch, or they can be so severe that the sufferer is driven into a complete frenzy by the feeling that ants are crawling all over the skin.

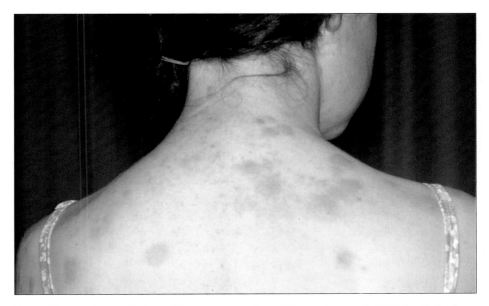

Insect bites can be particularly itchy; none more so than bites left by the mosquito (above).

One of the symptoms of chilblains (below) is an itchy, tingly feeling, but the urge to scratch should be resisted.

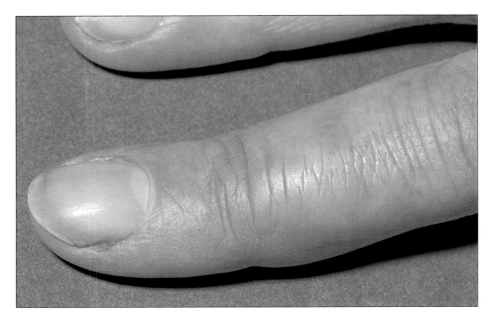

Causes

Itching is caused by the stimulation of the tiny nerve endings that lie just under the skin. This stimulation can be direct, for instance, when an insect crawls over the skin, or when someone wears something rough against the skin. It can also be brought about indirectly by the release of histamine, a chemical substance present in the body that causes an inflammation of the nerve endings—this happens when a person is bitten or stung by an insect, or is stung by a plant, or has an allergic reaction to a particular substance (see Allergies).

Medical conditions that affect the nerve endings can also produce itching. This can be seen in diabetes; in some cases of anemia and overactive thyroid (thyrotoxicosis); and in the malignant, but treatable, condition of the lymph glands, Hodgkin's disease (see Hodgkin's disease). In severe cases of jaundice, it is the presence of the bile salts deposited in the skin itself that produces a very intense irritation (see Jaundice).

Skin diseases and conditions are probably the most common causes of itching. In seborrheic dermatitis, for instance, it is the excessive grease production that causes itches (see Dermatitis). In eczema (see Eczema) and psoriasis (see Psoriasis) there is also severe itching in the affected areas. Chilblains and fungal infections, such as athlete's foot, cause localized itching for as long as the conditions remain present and active (see Athlete's foot).

Other factors

Itching can be totally psychological in origin, resulting from tension and anxiety, or just from thinking about fleas, lice, or itching itself.

For a variety of reasons, such as dry skin and stretching (which makes the nerve ends more sensitive), itching occurs in some pregnant women and is known as pruritus of pregnancy. Itching also occurs in the very old, due to lack of skin moisture, or else because of a shortage of iron stores in the bloodstream. Some individuals feel itching in their legs following a hot bath.

Early warning system

An itch is a warning that something is wrong. Sometimes it indicates an insect's presence, sometimes a rash that is a sign of illness.

If the eyes itch this may be an early sign of conjunctivitis or hay fever. Ears itch occasionally when a piece of wax is loose and about to fall out (see Wax in ear). However, if itching persists or becomes intense, it could also be a sign that there is inflammation of the outer ear, known as otitis externa. This condition can be

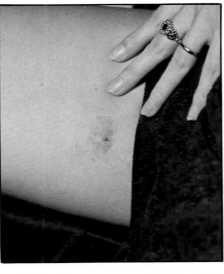

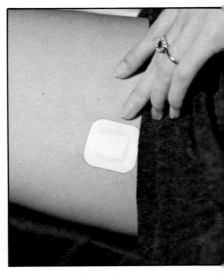

painful and causes extreme irritation if left untreated; fortunately it can also be cured quite easily and quickly with antibiotics (see Otitis).

Itches around the genitals can be a sign of a urinary tract infection or of a yeast infection (see Yeast). In children the most common cause of this type of itch is the presence of threadworms living in the rectum (see Worms).

A small wound, still stitched, can cause severe itching; it is a positive part of the healing process. Covering the wound with an adhesive bandage will prevent scratching and the risk of infection.

It is not unusual to feel slight itching after a bath. This can be caused by bathwater that is too hot, or the drying effect of some soaps. Some bath oil in the water will help.

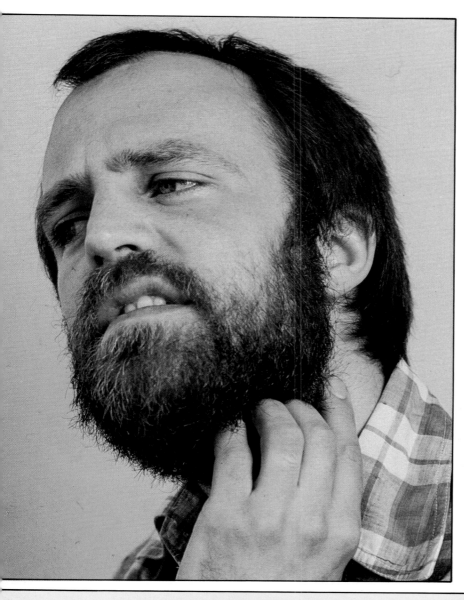

Itching can have totally psychological causes, such as tension and worry; but itchy beards are usually the result of poor hygiene or skin complaints.

Dangers

Like most symptoms itching can occasionally be a sign of a dangerous condition, particularly in the case of a severe allergic reaction, or where undiagnosed skin itching may be caused by thyroid disease or diabetes.

In conditions such as severe eczema or psoriasis, itching can lead to damaging scratching, and this can very easily cause the spread of inflammation, and make the condition worse by breaking the skin and leaving it open to infection.

Because of dangers such as these it is always important to discover the cause of a persistent itch, even if it is not particularly severe, and to insure that it is treated as soon as possible.

Treatment and outlook

The treatment of itches depends very much on the cause, although anti-inflammatory and antihistamine drugs nearly always help.

Itching quickly subsides when the cause is removed or is successfully treated. However, in cases of allergy to common substances, such as pollen or dog or cat hair, itching will inevitably recur every time the individual comes into contact with the allergen.

In skin diseases itching is only a symptom of the condition taking place in the skin, and it will remain for as long as the condition is present. However, the irritation can usually be eased considerably by the use of anti-inflammatory drugs or steroid creams (e.g., hydrocortisone). The doctor will prescribe these.

Causes and treatment of common itches

Condition	Causes of irritation	Treatment and advice
Seborrheic dermatitis	Excessive grease production has an irritant effect	Control of grease production sometimes helped with animal-fat-free diet, open air, and exercise
Psoriasis and eczema	Hereditary and recurrent skin conditions where inflammation in the skin causes severe irritation	Irritation controlled by steroid creams and coal tar creams; scratching very harmful as it introduces infection
Fungal infections (athlete's foot and yeast infection)	Irritation due to presence of fungi living in the skin	Antifungal treatment clears fungus; scratching causes infection to spread
Chilblains	Exposure to cold and damp, combined with poor circulation, causes inflammation	Keep hands and feet warm and dry; scratching will cause pain
Insect bites	Bites cause an irritant chemical to be released in the body, which causes a local allergy	Antihistamine drugs and cold packs; scratching spreads irritant and makes condition worse
Food allergy	Allergy to certain foods, like strawberries, causes itchy skin rash	Antihistamine drugs; cool baths; scratching not usually harmful; avoid allergen

Jaundice

Q My baby developed jaundice a few days after he was born, and he was given treatment under a powerful light. Why was this?

A It has been found that ultraviolet light increases the breakdown of bilirubin, the substance released by used red blood cells when they are removed from the bloodstream. Bilirubin produces the yellow color in the skin. Jaundice is very common in young babies before the liver is functioning properly because bilirubin is eliminated from the system via the liver. High levels of bilirubin can be dangerous. Treatment with ultraviolet light tides the baby over until its liver is mature enough to excrete bilirubin.

Q My skin looks sallow and yellow when I am tired. Is this mild jaundice?

A It is possible that you have a slightly higher level of bilirubin in your blood than is normal. There is a congenital disorder called Gilbert's syndrome where people suffer from a long-term, low-grade jaundice. The condition is very common. It may be worsened by fasting or infection, but does not usually cause any trouble.

Q I have just recovered from hepatitis and have been told not to drink any alcohol for several months. Why is this?

A Alcohol is poisonous to liver cells, particularly if they have been affected by the hepatitis virus. If you were to drink straight after an attack of hepatitis, the liver would be further compromised and the jaundice would come back and could cause permanent damage.

Q Why do doctors in blood transfusion units always ask people who want to donate blood if they have had jaundice?

A Hepatitis can be transmitted by transfusion. For this reason blood transfusion units do not take blood from people who have had jaundice in the past, just in case they are carrying the hepatitis virus in their blood.

A person who looks yellow is described as being jaundiced. However, jaundice is not a disease in itself, but a sign of disorder in the liver or elsewhere. Treatment depends on the disorder, which needs prompt diagnosis.

In a jaundiced person the skin and the whites of the eyes take on a yellow tinge. This comes about because a natural coloring substance called bilirubin is released from the red blood cells.

Red blood cells have an average life of 120 days. At the end of that time they deteriorate and cannot function properly any longer. They are constantly being broken down by the spleen and replaced so that they can carry out their vital functions in the body efficiently (see Spleen).

The main component of the red blood cell is the protein and iron compound hemoglobin. This is the substance that links with oxygen in the lungs and carries it to the tissues of the body. Hemoglobin contains a portion called heme. When this is broken down chemically, a substance called bilirubin i

Different types of jaundice

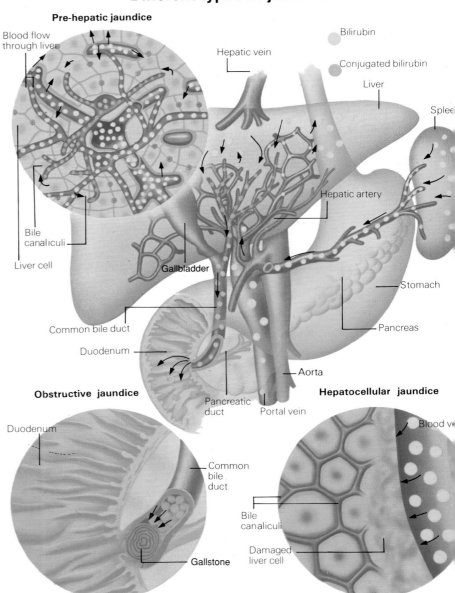

Pre-hepatic jaundice
Blood flow through liver
Hepatic vein
Bilirubin
Conjugated bilirubin
Liver
Splee
Hepatic artery
Bile canaliculi
Liver cell
Gallbladder
Stomach
Pancreas
Common bile duct
Duodenum
Aorta
Obstructive jaundice
Pancreatic duct
Portal vein
Hepatocellular jaundice
Duodenum
Blood v
Common bile duct
Bile canaliculi
Gallstone
Damaged liver cell

eleased. In a healthy person this is carried to the liver to be disposed of. The liver subjects it to a process called conjugation. This makes the bilirubin dissolve so that it can be excreted in the bile that is produced by the liver.

Disposing of bilirubin

Bilirubin is the principal coloring material of the bile (see Bile). Liver cells remove it from the blood and secrete it as bile, which is stored and concentrated in the gallbladder, which is situated immediately under the liver.

From the gallbladder bile passes down the bile duct to the small intestine, where the bile salts it contains emulsify dietary fat and allow the absorption of fatty food (see Digestion). Much of the bile is reabsorbed from the intestine into the blood.

Bile contains considerable quantities of cholesterol, most of which is reabsorbed into the blood. However, it is possible to have too much cholesterol in the body, which may lead to atherosclerosis. The liver can only compensate for this to a certain extent, so it is a good idea to reduce dietary fat intake (see Fats).

Color of feces

It is the bilirubin that is responsible for the dark brown color of feces, because it is broken down by intestinal bacteria into brownish yellow pigments. Some of the bile pigments reabsorbed into the blood are excreted in the urine and cause its yellow color.

If the liver becomes diseased, or if the bilirubin cannot escape because the bile ducts are blocked, the person may become jaundiced (see Liver and liver diseases). The raised level of bilirubin in the blood, resulting from one or more of these problems in the stages of its release and elimination, will impart the yellow color of jaundice to the skin and the whites of the eyes of the patient.

Different causes of jaundice

There are several different types of jaundice, and each one has a different cause.

In the first type the amount of bilirubin is just too great for the liver to process. This happens because an excessive number of blood cells are being broken down, and the

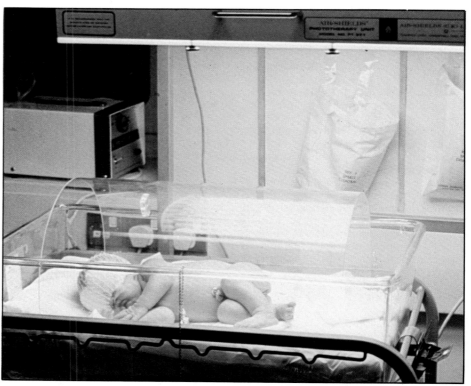

St. Mary's Hospital, London

liver cannot cope with them. Therefore the person may become jaundiced, even though there is no actual problem with the liver. This is called prehepatic jaundice.

Any condition that upsets the well-being of the liver cells may cause jaundice by interfering with the conjugation process. This type of jaundice is known as hepatocellular (liver cell) jaundice.

After conjugation the bilirubin has to be excreted through the biliary system—the bile ducts within the liver, the gallbladder, and the common bile duct that leads down into the intestine at the duodenum. Any obstruction in this system will lead to jaundice, and this is known as obstructive jaundice.

Types of jaundice

Prehepatic jaundice: This type is rather uncommon, but there are certain congenital (present from birth) disorders of blood cell function that lead to increased breakdown of abnormal red blood cells. There are other circumstances, such as hemolytic anemia, in which too many red blood cells are broken down.

Hepatocellular jaundice: Hepatitis (virus infection of the liver) is very common and causes jaundice because it inflames the liver cells (see Hepatitis).

Drugs, such as the contraceptive Pill, antidiabetic drugs, and some antibiotics, may also cause inflammation of the liver cells or small bile ducts. Such inflammation will produce jaundice, but these are very rare cases.

A jaundiced newborn baby may be treated with a powerful light. This is called phototherapy and is painless. It helps to break down the bilirubin that is causing the condition. Bandages protect the eyes.

Alcohol is a frequent cause of jaundice. It may bring on a single attack after a prolonged drinking session, or the jaundice may result from alcoholic cirrhosis (a liver disease that causes progressive liver destruction).

Obstructive jaundice: Anything that interferes with the formation of bile or its free flow out of the liver, down the bile duct, or into the intestine, will lead to a damming-back of bilirubin and a rise in its levels in the blood. This is because red cell breakdown will continue whether or not the bile can achieve its normal circulation and disposal.

Effect on feces

Failure of bile to get into the intestine means that the feces will be deprived of much of their normal coloring matter and will appear pale and claylike. Also, because of the absence of emulsifying bile salts, fat in the diet will not be properly absorbed and will remain in the feces. This will make them less dense so that they will float and be difficult to flush away (see Feces).

The rising levels of conjugated bilirubin in the blood cause an increased quantity to be excreted in the urine, which becomes very dark. These two signs—

Bilirubin is a product of the breakdown of used red blood cells in the spleen. Prehepatic jaundice occurs if the spleen breaks down too many blood cells and produces too much bilirubin for the liver to cope with. Some of the bilirubin travels through the liver and comes back into the blood system in the hepatic vein. Hepatocellular jaundice occurs if the liver cells are damaged. Obstructive jaundice is caused by a blockage.

light feces and dark urine—are classic indications of obstructive jaundice.

Gallstones

Obstructive jaundice may be caused by various disorders, the most common of which are gallstones. These are formed in the gallbladder and may consist of cholesterol or bile pigments.

Gallstones are very common and only a small proportion of people who have them suffer any harm. A stone that blocks the duct from the gallbladder to the main bile duct will not cause obstructive jaundice, but there will be severe inflammation of the gallbladder. A large stone in the main bile duct may, however, lead to a complete blockage and severe jaundice (see Gallbladder and stones). Incomplete blockage may cause variable jaundice, which fluctuates in severity.

Importance of investigation

Jaundice must always be investigated and the cause found; it must never be assumed to be due to gallstones.

Another important and serious cause of obstructive jaundice is cancer of the head of the pancreas. The pancreas secretes digestive enzymes and its duct enters the intestine at the same point as the bile duct. A tumor in the part of the pancreas nearest to the intestine can readily block off the opening of the bile duct into the bowel. This sort of tumor is the fifth most common cause of cancer death, and unfortunately the outlook for the patient is very gloomy (see Pancreas).

Other causes of obstructive jaundice include: liver cirrhosis from alcohol or drugs, cirrhosis present at birth (primary biliary cirrhosis), various forms of hepatitis, Hodgkin's lymphoma, severe bacterial infections, pregnancy, cystic fibrosis, worm parasites, cancer of the bile duct, benign tumors of the bile duct, cancer in local lymph nodes, and biliary cirrhosis from pancreatitis.

Biliary obstruction

In addition to the jaundice and the feces and urine signs, biliary obstruction may cause fever, shivering, pain, and liver abscesses (a cavity containing pus surrounded by inflamed tissues; see Abscess). The malabsorption of food resulting from the loss of bile salts may lead to weight loss, a tendency to bleed from failure of vitamin K absorption, and bone changes from failure of vitamin D absorption. These two vitamins are fat-soluble and are present in fatty food.

Symptoms

Yellowness is usually the first symptom of jaundice, showing first in the whites of the eyes and then in the skin. There may also be some pain as a result of the underlying disease.

Patients often have pale stools and dark urine because bilirubin is not reaching the intestines. Conjugated bilirubin is leaking from the liver cells back into the blood; because it is soluble, it can pass through the kidneys and come out in the urine, making it darker.

Diagnosis

It is particularly important to diagnose the exact cause of an attack of jaundice.

The hepatocellular sort, for example, may not always require specific treatment. In contrast, however, a gallstone blocking the common bile duct needs to be removed by surgery so that it does not cause an infection in the bile duct behind the obstruction.

Blood tests may be used in the diagnosis, and if necessary an ultrasound scan or computed tomography (CT) scan will show the bile ducts in the liver (see Scans). If the ducts are dilated, then the cause is likely to be an obstruction, whereas if they are normal a hepatocellular cause is more likely to be found.

Suspected obstruction

When an obstruction is suspected it may be diagnosed in one of two ways. The first is to insert a fine needle into the liver through the right side. This will enter one of the many small bile ducts and dye can then be injected to outline the obstruction. This is called percutaneous transhepatic cholangiography.

Alternatively a flexible gastroscope may be passed down to the bile duct, a tiny tube inserted, and X-ray dye injected to show the site of any obstruction (see Endoscope). Both these diagnostic techniques are carried out in the hospital.

Treatment and outlook

Treatment of prehepatic jaundice will depend on what is causing the problem. Most of the hepatocellular forms clear up without specific treatment. Jaundice more serious if it results from cirrhosis however; there is no specific treatment other than preventive measures, such as avoiding alcohol (see Alcoholism).

Jaundice in newborn babies

Jaundice in newborn babies is very common, resulting from the liver being not quite mature enough to cope with the normal breakdown of red blood cells.

Because the liver is immature, the bilirubin in a baby's bloodstream tends to be unconjugated. High levels of unconjugated bilirubin in the blood may lead to being deposited in various parts of the brain, causing permanent damage. This means that severe jaundice in babies within the first few days of life has to be treated promptly. Treatment under a powerful light increases the breakdown of bilirubin in the skin, but a complete change of blood, called an exchange transfusion, may be necessary in the first few days of life. After this the liver starts to conjugate the bilirubin.

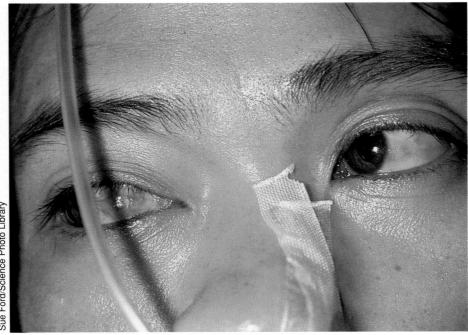

Sue Ford/Science Photo Library

Yellowing of the whites of the eyes is usually the first symptom of jaundice and indicates that there is a disorder elsewhere in the body.

Jogging

Q Everyone I know seems to have taken up jogging. Why is it considered such a great fitness activity?

A It might seem difficult to understand why so many people jog as though their lives depended on it. However, in many senses, your life *might* depend on jogging, or at any rate on participating in vigorous exercise that will involve your heart and lungs. Stress, high-fat diets, and lack of exercise all contribute to heart disease, which is one of the most common causes of death. Jogging can be an enjoyable way of keeping healthy.

Q I am 52 and would like to go jogging. Am I too old?

A In theory, no. People in their 80s go jogging, and their good health and general fitness owes much to the fact that they are so active. If they pace themselves carefully, they will experience no ill effects whatsoever. For anyone over 45, it is a good idea to have a medical checkup beforehand.

Q I want a release from my business worries. Would jogging be of any use?

A It might be, but it is not as suitable for your needs as a sport that is mentally demanding, such as fencing, which would occupy your mind more, and thereby distract you from your worries. Some people find that the gentle rhythm of jogging does clear their mind, once they have set up a routine, but if you are an incurable worrier, you would probably do well to find another form of exercise.

Q People seem to go to great lengths to look fashionable when they are jogging. Is it necessary to spend so much money on tracksuits?

A No. People probably feel less self-conscious about jogging if they feel they look fashionable. In fact, any comfortable clothing will do, such as shorts and T-shirt or tracksuit, and properly-fitted rubber-soled running shoes.

Jogging is a very popular form of exercise. Many people wonder whether it would be right for them to take it up and exactly what the benefits would be.

Jogging first became a craze in the 1970s, and it is easy to see why it became popular and why its popularity has lasted. Since people became aware that lack of exercise contributed to heart disease, and health experts began to advocate the usefulness of a gentle run, jogging has been a natural choice for anyone who wishes to improve his or her health.

Aerobics

Jogging is a prime example of aerobic exercise. Aerobic exercises are those that cause a marked temporary increase in the rate of breathing and heartbeat. These two activities govern the amount of oxygen the body can process (see Exercise).

Oxygen, the colorless, odorless gas that makes up about 20 percent of the air we breathe, is vital to the body. Without it our cells are unable to burn nutrients to provide energy. If the body is deprived of oxygen for more than a few minutes, the organs and tissues become damaged (in the case of the brain, irreparably so) and eventually die.

The muscles, in particular, use oxygen when they are exercised. They are supplied with it through the bloodstream, which has a chemical makeup that lets it carry oxygen to all the different parts of the body.

Oxygen enters the bloodstream via the lungs; each time we breathe in, the tiny blood vessels (capillaries; see Lung and lung diseases) woven into their spongy fabric receive a supply of oxygen. This oxygenated blood then returns to the heart, to be pumped around the body. So in terms of oxygen processing, the heart and lungs act as a team.

The benefits of exercise

Work your muscles hard, for example, by running a mile and a half at a steady pace, and they will make heavy inroads on their supply of oxygen. To replace it, oxygen processing by the heart and lungs has to be stepped up. The body does this by increasing the rate of the breathing and heartbeat. It also sends more than the usual volume of blood to the heart, which

Be comfortable when you jog: wear loose-fitting, lightweight clothing and properly-fitted, rubber-soled running shoes with a good arch support. They should be broken in before using them regularly.

Tom Belshaw/Man's tracksuit: The Gymnasium

has to work harder to pump it around the body. The person pants to take in more air, and their heart beats very fast, all in order to step up the oxygen supply.

Uncomfortable as it is, being puffed is the whole aim of exercises such as jogging. For the heart is designed for far more strenuous activity than we normally give it, and if it is never put through its paces, it will get flabby, weak, and prone to disease.

The only way to exercise the heart is by getting breathless, and involving the heart as energetically as you possibly can in the oxygen-processing activity.

Stress

There are other ways of raising the heartbeat without taking aerobic exercise. The most obvious one is by becoming excited or by experiencing one of the many situations that doctors usually group together as causing stress.

The number of heartbeats per minute can rise steeply when you receive a nasty shock, but this is no substitute for aerobic exercise, because the heart is simply beating faster without having extra blood to pump. Indeed, the heart may be damaging itself when it races as a result of stress, for without the extra volume of blood on which to push, it can strain itself. This situation is similar to an engine that is racing out of gear.

This is why stress is a well-known factor in heart disease. The heart is built to withstand astonishing amounts of stress, both physical and emotional, but if the pressure of worries goes on too long, and if you sit all day without exercising, and also eat unhealthy foods, you may be asking too much of your heart. To make up for these unfair pressures, you should go to some lengths to give the heart what it needs in the way of aerobic exercise to keep it healthy.

Jogging guidelines

The golden rule of jogging is not to overdo it. If you go at a speed at which it would be uncomfortable to talk with a friend, you are going too fast. You should move at a slow pace, with the whole body, but especially the shoulders, relaxed. Remember that sprinting is not an aerobic exercise. It simply makes dramatic inroads on the body's supply of oxygen, without making the heart work for a prolonged period at the increased rate needed to replace the oxygen.

A sensible way to start jogging is by combining walking with jogging in 15-minute periods. Over a few days slowly cut down the walking periods until you are jogging for the whole time. Then go out for half an hour, using the walking-and-jogging combination again, and once

How to jog correctly . . . at any age

Buildup schedule A

For fairly fit under-35-year-olds
Week 1: Do at least half-an-hour's brisk walking a day. Walk at every opportunity. Use the stairs rather than the elevator. Get off the bus a stop or two earlier than you would normally. Walk to the store. It is important to spend the whole of your jogging sessions walking at a brisk pace
Week 2: Start by walking for five minutes. Then jog for 30 seconds, walk for 30 seconds, repeat ten times. Then jog for 45 seconds, walk for 45 seconds, repeat three times. Finally walk for five minutes
Week 3: First do a warm-up walk for five minutes. Jog one minute, walk

one minute, then repeat five times. Walk five minutes
Week 4: Again begin with a warm-up walk for two minutes. Then jog two minutes, walk one minute, then repeat the whole thing five times. Walk two minutes
Week 5 and thereafter: Warm-up walk one minute. Jog for three minutes, walk one minute, then repeat five times. Over the next few weeks, increase the time actually spent jogging, and cut down the number of walking breaks you have been taking, until you are eventually jogging the whole 20 minutes (this should happen at the end of the sixth week)

Pictor International

more cutting down on the walking periods until you are jogging for the whole 20 minutes of the program.

Targets

Obviously the amount of jogging a person needs to do to reach the peak of aerobic fitness (and stay there) is different for each one of us, according to how fit, how old, and how healthy we are.

A typical program (with medical approval) for people between 40 and 49 (assuming that they are fit enough to start without any warming-up period) might start with jogging 1 mile (1.61 km) in 18 minutes five times a week. Over the next 10 weeks, the jogger would aim for a series of targets. First 1 mile (1.61 km) in nine minutes; then 1 1/2 miles (2.42 km) in 14 minutes; and finally 2 miles (3.23 km) in 20 minutes.

After keeping this up for several more weeks, the exact number will vary from person to person, the individual will be what the experts call truly fit: capable of 1 1/2 miles (2.42 km) in 12 minutes. Done four times a week, this simple program will keep you in peak physical condition.

Dangers

Much has been made of the fact that some unlucky people have collapsed from heart failure on their first jogging sortie. It is true that jogging is not to be approached lightly, but equally certain is that many of the collapses have occurred because of the great numbers of people who go out jogging, rather than because the activity itself is dangerous.

Most people need no medical examination before starting to jog, and there is no risk attached to the exercise as long as it begins gently and increases gradually in vigor. However, people above the age of 45, those who have been previously inactive, and, above all, those with a history of heart problems should consult their doctor before starting.

Those who find that they have unexpected symptoms during the exercise, such as becoming quickly and hopelessly out of breath (so that they have to stop altogether) or experiencing heart palpitations and giddiness, should stop jogging and consult their doctor.

In general the long-term dangers of not exercising are greater than the short-term ones of unaccustomed exercise.

Perspective

While jogging is an excellent, indeed vital, exercise for the heart, it does not do as much as other forms of exercise for muscular strength (except in the leg muscles) and overall suppleness. To improve these you should do gymnastic and isometric exercises (see Isometrics).

Text reproduced by permission of The Health Education Council, London

Buildup schedule B

For not-so-fit over-35-year-olds
Week 1: Spend a determined week walking as much as possible as described in schedule A; work up to 30 minutes of brisk walking a day
Week 2: Start by walking for five minutes. Jog 15 seconds, walk 15 seconds, then repeat five times. Walk five minutes. Jog 15 seconds, walk 15 seconds, then repeat five times. Walk five minutes
Week 3: Warm-up walk five minutes. Jog 30 seconds, walk 30 seconds, repeat three times. Walk four minutes. Then jog 30 seconds, walk 30 seconds, then repeat three times. Walk five minutes

Week 4: Warm-up walk five minutes. Jog one minute, walk one minute, then repeat twice. Walk two minutes. Jog one minute, walk one minute, then repeat twice. Walk five minutes
Week 5: Warm-up walk five minutes. Jog one minute, walk one minute, repeat five times. Walk five minutes
Week 6: Warm-up walk two minutes. Jog two minutes, walk one minute, repeat five times. Walk two minutes
Week 7: Gradually increase the time spent jogging, and cut down the number of walking breaks, until by the end of the eighth week you are jogging for 10–12 minutes at a stretch, depending on your level of comfort

Joint replacement

Q When a joint is replaced, is the new joint taken from a human donor?

A No. Replacement joints are always artificial.

Q My grandmother fell and broke her thighbone. Now the surgeon wants to do a complete hip joint replacement. Is this a good idea?

A Many cases of fracture of the neck of the thighbone are best treated by a total hip joint replacement. This is because this kind of fracture often cuts off the blood supply to the head (ball) of the femur. The result is the death of the bone (ischemic necrosis) and crumbling, so that the joint is severely affected. In this case the only effective solution is to replace the joint.

Q Which joints can be successfully replaced?

A By far the greatest majority of joint replacement operations involve the hip and the knee. However, prosthetic joints have been designed for the finger and toe joints, the elbow, shoulder, ankle, and for the articulation of the jaw (the temporomandibular joint situated just in front of each ear).

Q Do these artificial joints last for a lifetime?

A That depends on the age of the recipient. In many cases a new hip joint provides excellent performance for the rest of a person's life, but it is true that in some cases problems, such as loosening of the joint's attachment to the bones, may arise. These may call for a further operation.

Q What does a joint revision operation involve?

A Joint revision surgery involves opening up the whole hip joint site, removing the loose or damaged artificial part with all the old cement, and replacing it with a new part. With the hip joint it may be necessary to revise only one of the two parts of the artificial joint.

One of the great advances of modern surgery is the ability to remove damaged joints and replace them with artificial ones. Through developments in bioengineering, millions of people have been relieved of joint pain and disability.

Joint replacement surgery was unheard-of until the early 1960s when the British orthopedic surgeon John Charnley began to develop the artificial hip joint and the necessary surgical techniques. The principles established by Charnley remain valid today, but advances in joint design, materials, and surgical technique have turned what was initially an experimental form of treatment into an everyday routine.

Many trials were necessary to determine the most suitable mechanical details, metals, plastics, adhesives, and combinations of materials. Often years had to pass before the results of these tests were known, so progress was slow. However, both hip and knee joint replacements are now spectacularly successful.

However, the frequency with which this kind of surgery is performed and the high success rate do not imply that joint replacement surgery is easy or trivial. Joint replacement surgery is always major surgery and inevitably involves some risk to the patient. These operations commonly take several hours.

Indications for joint replacement

The principal indication is a joint disorder that causes pain on movement and cannot be adequately controlled by

This plastic knee joint replacement, which has been fitted to a human bone sample, consists of new contact surfaces, artificial cartilage, and artificial tendons.

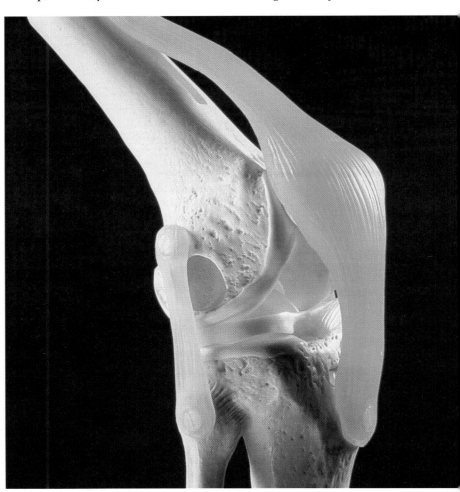

onsurgical means. Most patients who come to joint replacement surgery have had a fair trial of conservative treatment, such as weight reduction, modification of activity, the use of a cane, and painkilling and anti-inflammatory drugs. Surgery should not be undertaken unless the person concerned has been fully informed both of the expected benefits and the inevitable risks of such major surgery.

Hip joint replacement

The hip replacement was the first joint replacement to be carried out. It is still the most successful, and by far the most frequently performed operation. This is partly because of the relative simplicity of the hip joint, which is of the ball-and-socket type (see Hip).

Before the operation, a full medical review and overall examination are necessary. Different patients have different requirements, and much preliminary consideration by the surgeon is required as to the best choice and the correct size of prosthesis (artificial joint), the possible need for bone grafting, measures to ensure equal leg length, the need for blood transfusion, and so on.

There is now a huge choice of hip joint prostheses. The surgeon uses templates to determine the best type and size. Joints may be made-to-order or obtained as factory-made items. Preoperative planning will also involve a check of all X rays and scans (see X rays).

Technology

The artificial hip joint is in two parts. One is a metal part that fits into the sawed-off top of the thighbone (femur). This part has a long, pointed spike that is pushed down the hollow shaft of the bone and a spherical head offset to one side. Once properly fitted and aligned, this part has, traditionally, been cemented into the hollow of the bone using acrylic cement.

The other part is a cup into which the prosthetic head fits. This cup is also made of metal but has a high-density polyethylene liner. The cup has to be fitted to the bony socket in the side of the pelvis. Some of the earlier designs had cups that were all plastic, but these were found to deform under the pressure of the head and to wear rapidly. The metal cup supports the lining and provides a nondeforming surface that can more effectively be cemented to the bone of the pelvis.

One of the most common later complications is the loosening of the cup, the femoral component, or both. This is because it is inherently difficult to achieve long-term adhesion between a living bone and an inert material. The problem has recently led to much interest in the use of porous metallic surfaces with numerous small openings into which bone can grow to create a more secure long-term bond.

With this method cement cannot be used, so it is necessary for a high degree of precision in reaming out bone for the cup and the femoral component to secure the prosthesis. Sometimes small pegs are used to improve the initial stability of the cup and to prevent rotation that would break off the spicules (small protrusions) of invading bone. Some ingrowth of fibrous tissue also occurs. It is common for the upper part of the femoral component to be made with a porous surface. The early results of these porous prostheses are very encouraging.

Knee joint replacement

The knee proved to be a much more difficult joint to design and replace than the hip joint. Among other reasons this was because of the difficulty of reproducing the complex functions that occur at the knee joint during movement. The knee joint is not a simple hinge but also involves a degree of sliding (see Knee).

One orthopedic team tried nine different prosthetic knee joint designs over a period of 13 years. Each type had desirable features, but no one design appeared to have outstanding advantages over the others. This series, reported in 1985, involved 673 knee joint replacement operations. With gradual improvements in design, however, the results of knee joint replacement became acceptable.

A critical factor in the success of knee joint replacement is the precise alignment of the leg bones. This is difficult to achieve. The weight axis must pass through the center of the knee and the lower leg must be set at an outward angle of between five and nine degrees. To achieve these requirements the lower end of the femur and the upper surface of the lower leg bone (tibia) must be precisely cut so that their respective prosthetic components fit at the correct angle. These components carry sturdy pegs, and holes are accurately drilled in the two raw surfaces so that the artificial parts can be snugly and tightly fitted.

It is also very important to maintain the strength of the muscles and the integrity of the ligaments over the entire postoperative period. The main muscles on the front of the thigh (the quadriceps) will quickly lose power unless they are exercised regularly.

Problems may occur with an artificial kneecap (patella) after joint replacement. There may be undue wear on the plastic back surface or a fracture on the plastic. Patellar complications are the most frequent cause of trouble with knee joint replacements. Occasionally the major patellar tendon that connects the quadriceps muscle to the front of the tibia may even rupture.

At present most prosthetic knee joints are fixed with cement, but the best fixing methods have not yet been fully established. The long-term results of uncemented knee joints are not yet known. In general, however, satisfactory results are achieved at 10-year follow-ups in 90 percent of all knee joint replacements performed by experienced surgeons.

The ball and socket forms the main part of this prosthetic hip joint. The spherical part is made from zirconium to withstand wear and tear.

Joints

Q Is it really true that the muscles can restrict a joint's movement against a person's will?

A Yes. Limitation of joint movement usually results from spasm of the muscles surrounding the joint, and they go into spasm because of pain. In other words this is a type of protective mechanism to stop the joint from becoming dislocated and to minimize the effects of any injury.

Q Is it true that some joints don't move at all?

A Yes. The plates that make up the human skull are joined by suture joints called synarthroses. These joints are moveable at birth but quickly knit together to become totally immovable.

Q My son can crack his finger joints like gunfire. I keep telling him that it is bad for his fingers. Am I right in thinking that he could damage them?

A No damage occurs as a result of cracking your finger joints. The crack is caused by a slipping of the lateral tendons that hold the joints in place around the bone ends. A little time is required for the tendon to slip back into its original position, which is why you can only crack your fingers once and then have to wait a little while before you can do it again. Your son probably does it because he knows very well that it annoys you.

Q I have been a football player all my life and now have severe osteoarthritis of the hip. I am 45. Can I have the joint replaced so that I can continue to lead an active life?

A Although the replacement material used nowadays is excellent, many orthopedic surgeons are reluctant to replace the hip joint in patients under the age of 50 because of the possibility of the need for a further operation later on. However, with improved techniques and materials, this situation is likely to change within the next few years.

Joints give us our full range of body movements, but individual joints vary in the amount of flexibility they allow and in their vulnerability to injury.

There are two main types of joints—synovial joints and fibrous joints. Synovial joints are designed to allow a large range of movements, and they are lined with a slippery coating called synovium. Fibrous joints have no synovium; the bones are joined by tough fibrous tissue, permitting very little movement.

Synovial joints

The synovial joints can be subdivided depending on the range of movement of which they are capable. Hinge joints, such as the ones at the elbow and knee, allow bending and straightening movements. Gliding joints allow sliding movements in all directions because the opposing bone surfaces are flattened or slightly curved. Examples of these joints are found in the spinal bones, the wrist, and the tarsal bones of the feet. Pivot joints in the neck at the base of the skull and at the elbow are special types of hinge joints that rotate around the pivot. The pivot joint in the neck allows the head to turn and the one in the elbow allows twisting of the lower arm to enable movements such as turning a doorknob. Joints that can be moved in any direction, such as the hip and shoulder, are called ball-and-socket joints.

The joints in the fingers are typical examples of hinged synovial joints. The bone ends are covered in a tough elastic material called articulating cartilage (see Cartilage). The entire joint is enclosed in a very strong coating of tough gristle called the joint capsule. This holds the joint in place and thereby prevents any abnormal movement.

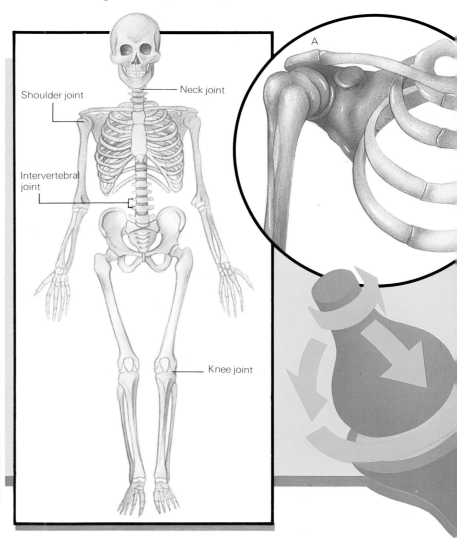

Shoulder joint

Neck joint

Intervertebral joint

Knee joint

A

Sue Dandre and John Hutchinson

874

Lining the inside of the joint, but not running over the articulating cartilage, is the synovium. This layer of tissue is often only one cell thick and provides fluid that oils the joint and prevents it from drying up. It is not absolutely essential for the normal functioning of the joint, and in certain conditions where the synovium becomes diseased, such as rheumatoid arthritis, it may be removed without damaging the joint in the short term (see arthritis). However, a healthy synovial membrane is thought to be essential to help prevent wear and tear of the joint.

Knee joint

The knee joint is a much more complicated structure than it would first appear, and it is commonly injured by athletes (see Knee). When you extend your knee beyond the straight position, it locks. This locking is brought about by a very slight but important twisting movement of the large bone in the lower part of the leg (the tibia). Then there are two pieces of cristle that act as padding between the cartilage linings of the thighbone (the

femur), the largest bone of the body. One piece of cartilage wedges the outside of the joint and the other the inside. These are called semilunar cartilages, since they are shaped like a crescent moon, with the points toward the inside of the joints.

The outside edge of each semilunar cartilage is attached to two very strong ligaments (elastic tissue that connects muscles; see Ligaments), one running down the outside of the leg and one down the inside. These form the lateral and medial colateral ligaments of the knee, with the cartilage forming a sandwich between them. Since the cartilages are attached at their points and their edges, a twisting movement of the knee that pulls the ligaments can tear the cartilages. A torn cartilage—common among football players—causes severe pain and sometimes an inability to bend the joint. If this persists the only treatment is to remove it. It may grow back, but in any event the muscles strengthen to compensate for the missing cartilage.

Both the knee and the hip joint have ligaments in the center of the joint for

Most common types of synovial joints

The human skeleton consists of 206 bones. We can bend and move because the bones have joints at each end. The synovial joints are the ones that allow the greatest range of movements, and there are several types.
A: Ball-and-socket joints, like the ones in the shoulder, allow movement in any direction.
B: Hinge joints, like the ones in the knee and elbow, only allow bending and straightening movements.
C: Pivot joints are special kinds of hinge joints that rotate around a central pivot. This kind of joint allows movements such as turning your head from side to side or twisting a screwdriver.
D: Gliding joints, which are found in the spine, wrists, and feet, allow a sliding movement, as happens when you twist your body from side to side.

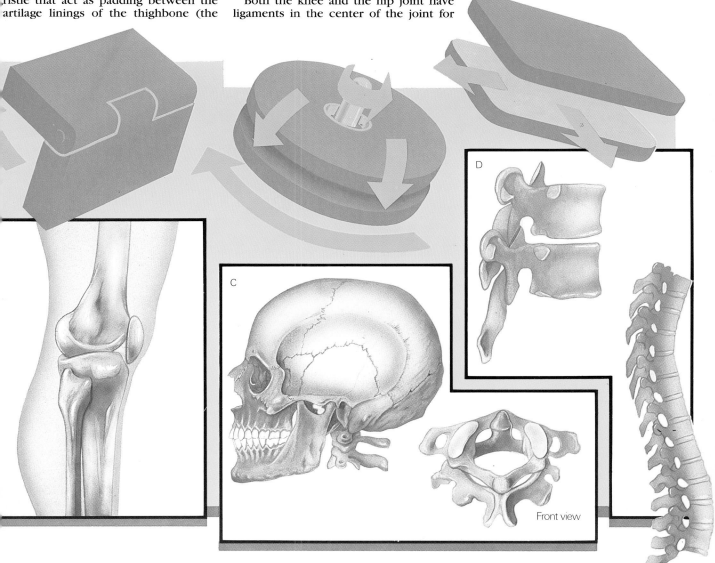

Front view

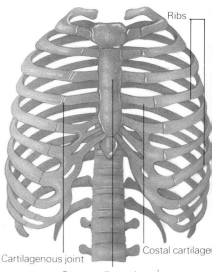

Q Is it possible to get osteoarthritis of the jaw?

A Yes, and this can be a very troublesome condition. It occurs more commonly in people who have lost their teeth. It may also give rise to pain elsewhere, for example a headache or earache. The most effective treatment is with an anti-inflammatory painkiller, such as aspirin.

Q My uncle has suffered from back pain for years. The doctors now tell him he needs an operation to set his back solid. What does this mean and how will it help relieve my uncle's pain?

A Pain in an arthritic back is caused by joint movement. If the joints can be prevented from moving, then the pain is relieved. An operation called a spinal fusion can be performed to fuse the bones together, usually just at the lower part of the back.

Q My mother has bad arthritis. She has read that aspirin is bad for her stomach. Is there an alternative medicine she can take instead of aspirin?

A All anti-inflammatory drugs cause a certain degree of irritation of the stomach. Aspirin is particularly bad in this respect, but it happens to be one of the most effective drugs. It is always better to use a soluble type of aspirin than one that doesn't dissolve in water and better still to have food in the stomach at the time the aspirin is taken.

Q My sister can make amazing movements with her thumb. Could she be double-jointed or is there a problem with her joints?

A There are no truly double-jointed people, although some people can move all their joints through a very large range of movements; this is usually because they have trained themselves to do so. However, it is common for an ordinary person to develop great mobility of just one or two joints and the thumb joint is a case in point.

added stability. In the case of the knee, there are two of them that cross, one from front to back and the other back to front (for this reason they are called anterior and posterior cruciate ligaments). These too can be torn, particularly when the knee is dislocated.

The synovial membrane lining the inside of the knee is very extensive and runs under the kneecap (patella) for about 1 in (2.5 cm) down the front of the shin. There are several bursae, small enclosed cavities, at the knee that are lined with synovial membrane and filled with synovial fluid. Constant kneeling or a bang on the knee can result in inflammation of the synovium, causing painful swelling due to increased production of fluid by the synovium. This is called bursitis (see Bursitis).

One of the most common diseases of the joints is rheumatoid arthritis (see Rheumatoid arthritis). Its cause is unknown, but it is characterized by an inflammation of the synovium, and, as a result, accumulation of fluid in the joints. This condition is quite distinct from wear and tear arthritis (see Osteoarthritis).

Synovial joints

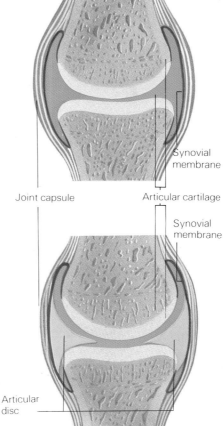

Joint capsule

Synovial membrane

Articular cartilage

Synovial membrane

Articular disc

Cartilaginous joints

Ribs

Cartilagenous joint

Costal cartilage

Sternum (breastbone)

Certain joints on each of the ribs are formed from bone and cartilage. The cartilage is flexible, allowing movement without the need for fluid-filled synovial membranes.

Most synovial joints are similar to the one above left, but some have an articular disk between the two layers of articular cartilage, as in the joint on the left. These disks occur in joints like the ones between the collarbone and the breastbone and are believed to act as shock absorbers. Both the knee and elbow are synovial joints.

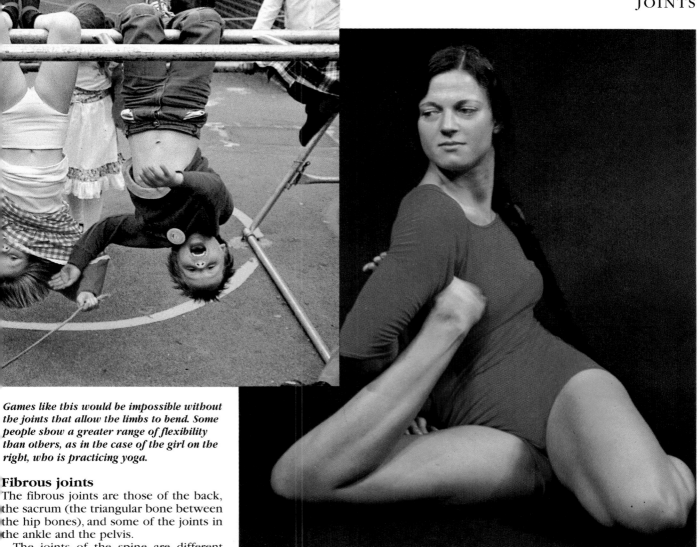

Games like this would be impossible without the joints that allow the limbs to bend. Some people show a greater range of flexibility than others, as in the case of the girl on the right, who is practicing yoga.

John Moss/Colorific!

Fibrous joints

The fibrous joints are those of the back, the sacrum (the triangular bone between the hip bones), and some of the joints in the ankle and the pelvis.

The joints of the spine are different from the other fibrous joints. Besides being joined by fibrous tissue, they are cushioned by a small bubble of jelly called a disk. This capsule of jelly acts as a shock absorber, and there is one between each of the spinal bones (the vertebrae).

If the vertebrae are crushed together, such as during heavy lifting, the jelly bubbles can be forced out through the fibrous tissue (see Back and backbone). When this happens the bubble may push backward and press against the spinal cord or nerve root, causing severe pain. This is called a slipped disk (see Slipped disk). Often the bubble pops back by itself after plenty of rest, or it may have to be helped back by pulling the spinal bones apart during traction in the hospital. Occasionally surgery is needed, and the damaged disk has to be removed from between the vertebrae.

Cartilaginous joints

Some joints in the body are formed between bone and cartilage (see Cartilage). Cartilage is very flexible, and

this allows a good deal of movement without the need for fluid-filled synovium. The joints between the ribs and breastbone at the front of the chest are cartilaginous joints. The joints attaching the ribs to the back are synovial joints. These allow the ribs to move up and down freely when we breathe.

Damage

Damage to the joints may give rise to problems many years later. People who injure their joints regularly are more prone to osteoarthritis. The cartilage is worn away from the end of the bone so that bone rubs against bone. The exposed bone becomes stronger and more dense, but it does not have the same wearing properties as cartilage and, in due course, the joint surface loses its shape, resulting in pain and limited movement.

Treatment

The development of spare part surgery has transformed the treatment of severe

osteoarthritis. At one time the only type of treatment that offered relief from constant pain was aspirin. Now complete replacement joints are fashioned out of plastic or metal, and they will last for up to 20 years or more.

Pain relief is dramatic following joint replacement, and with good physical therapy a full range of movements can be restored. Many joints can be treated in this way, but the hip is by far the most common joint to be treated using a prosthesis (replacement; see Prostheses).

Rheumatoid arthritis is caused by inflammation of the synovium, which itself begins to eat away the cartilage at the end of the bone, leading to an increased chance of osteoarthritis. In severe cases of rheumatoid arthritis, where inflammation cannot be controlled by anti-inflammatory drugs such as aspirin, some relief can be obtained by surgically removing the synovium. This is thought to help slow down the rate at which osteoarthritis develops.

Kaolin

Q My 10-month-old baby sometimes gets bad diarrhea. Could I give him kaolin and pectin?

A Diarrhea in babies and children should always be taken seriously, particularly if it is accompanied by vomiting. This is because they can very easily become dehydrated (short of fluid). The best treatment for your baby is to give clear fluids—such as beef bouillon or flavored gelatin water, but not milk—until the problem settles down. Medicines should only be given to babies and children on the advice of a doctor.

Q I've heard that if you take too much kaolin and pectin you'll become constipated. Is this true?

A Yes. To prevent this from happening, you should stop giving kaolin and pectin at the first sign of the diarrhea drying up.

Q Is there such a thing as kaolin mixed with an antibiotic that you can take if you have diarrhea from a virus?

A Yes, but these preparations should be avoided. If the diarrhea is due to an infection in the intestines that the antibiotic is designed to treat, the diarrhea may disappear before the infection is cured. This can give the false impression that the patient is better, and in this way the infection is more easily passed on to others.

Q Are the narcotics in kaolin mixtures addictive?

A There is absolutely no danger of becoming addicted to narcotics as a result of the amount in such mixtures. However, narcotics in larger amounts can be very addictive. One of the problems addicts suffer from is constipation.

Q Is it possible to become allergic to kaolin lotions?

A No. But, if you have very sensitive skin it is better not to use anything that may aggravate it; just let nature heal the condition.

If you have ever had an attack of travelers' diarrhea on vacation, then you have probably used a kaolin and pectin preparation to control the condition.

Kaolin is china clay that is mined from the ground. It is carefully cleaned and purified before it is made into a medicine and its principal use is as treatment to relieve minor attacks of diarrhea in adults. Kaolin is also occasionally used as a lotion to treat boils, bruises, and other skin inflammations, although the use of antiseptic creams and antibiotics has largely replaced kaolin for this treatment.

Remedy for diarrhea

When kaolin is used in the treatment of diarrhea, it is thought to work by absorbing fluid inside the intestines, causing the diarrhea to dry up.

Kaolin can be combined with other substances. The most familiar mixture is kaolin and pectin, although it can be mixed with peppermint water, chloroform water, and sodium bicarbonate, all of which make it more palatable.

Kaolin may also be used with small doses of narcotics (see Narcotics), which decrease contractions of the intestines. Morphine has been used in this situation, but much more common nowadays are synthetic morphine derivatives such as loperamide and diphenoxylate. Drugs such as atropine, which block the nerves that stimulate the contraction of the intestines, can also be used. However, because it is a liquid remedy, it is messy and less convenient to carry around than tablets in plastic containers.

While all these treatments, including kaolin, are often effective in treating diarrhea, they should not be used when diarrhea is caused by a serious infection, because they may prolong the illness. Signs that a serious infection may be the cause of the diarrhea include high fever or blood in the feces. In such cases, antibiotics may be required (see Antibiotics).

Other uses of kaolin

Kaolin can also be used to treat severe vomiting and other digestive disorders, and its effectiveness relies on the fact that it is such a good absorbent of fluids. For this reason, kaolin is occasionally used as a lotion or dusting powder to keep wounds dry.

Kaolin and kaolin compounds can be given to children on the advice of a doctor to control attacks of diarrhea safely, effectively, and quickly.

Tom Belshaw

Keeping fit

Q I have tried to persuade my husband, who has a sedentary job and is overweight, to diet and exercise, but he says that this is unnecessary. What can I say to persuade him?

A Fit people tend to live longer than those who are unfit. You also feel much healthier when you are fit. You tend to look better, too, so being fit is good for both your health and your ego.

Q My uncle is confined to a wheelchair. How can he keep fit?

A People who are wheelchair-bound can still do vigorous aerobic (heart and lung) exercise. This is particularly important in disabled people like your uncle, who have limited movement. A physical therapist should be able to put together a realistic exercise program for him. This, coupled with a sensible diet that is tailored to your uncle's specialized needs, should keep him fit and in shape.

Q I am 43 and haven't exercised regularly since I was in school. Could I start a fitness program without risk to my health?

A Yes, provided that you do not suffer from a heart condition and your doctor does not advise against exercise. However, it is important to start gradually; the best thing to do is to plan an expanding program of exercise and then stick to it. The only difficult part of getting fit is making yourself exercise, so you should choose an exercise that you are keen to participate in—and enjoy!

Q Bodybuilders look incredibly fit. Could I get fit by a program of lifting weights?

A The simple answer is no. Lifting weights is not an aerobic exercise. Weight lifting and being careful about your diet will certainly trim off excess weight, and so you will look fit, but true physical fitness can only be achieved by exercising the heart and lungs.

Modern life can be the enemy of the body. Inactivity, fatty or processed foods, stress, and smoking all conspire to make our bodies flabby, sluggish, and more prone to disease. But people can all be more fit with a little effort.

Bicycling is a very good exercise and gets you out into the fresh air and sunshine.

Keeping fit can take a good deal of hard work and self-discipline, which may explain why so many people are unfit. However, for those individuals who are willing to make the effort, the benefits soon become apparent; fit people are likely to look better, feel better, and live longer, too.

Getting fit

It is very easy to invent excuses for not keeping fit, such as age, being overweight, or lack of time. However, age is no barrier to keeping fit, nor is weight. Also depending on the chosen program of exercise, it can take as little as 10 minutes a day, and everyone has that much time to spare. In most cases poor health is no excuse either. However, anyone with a preexisting condition, such as a heart complaint, should see their doctor who will find the type of exercise that is most suitable.

The first rule of getting fit is never to throw yourself into a vigorous exercise program without working up to it gradually, particularly if you haven't exercised for a long time. Trying to do too much too soon will lead to discouragement and may be harmful, causing sprains or torn ligaments. Next decide on a program of fitness. Certain exercises are intended to produce specific results—for example, mobility exercises, strengthening exercises, and heart and lung exercises.

Mobility exercises include those exercises that actually move the joints and muscles—examples range from swinging the arms to reaching for the ankles.

Strengthening exercises are designed to build up strength in the arms, abdomen, and legs. Push-ups, sit-ups, squats, and lifting weights from a seated or lying position are just a few of these exercises.

Perhaps most important, however, are the heart and lung exercises. The heart is a muscle and, like any other muscle, it can either be lean and work at a peak of fitness or be flabby and unfit. Fit hearts and lungs do their work more efficiently. The lungs are more efficient in taking in and expelling air, and the heart is more efficient in pumping out oxygenated blood that is then carried to the muscles (and other tissues) to give them energy and nourishment. So the healthier the heart

Q I am a housewife. I read somewhere that housewives walk up to seven miles (11.3 km) a day when doing the housework and shopping. Isn't this sufficient to keep me fit?

A Unfortunately not. Exercise really does have to make you breathless before it does anything for your level of fitness. The most useful form is swimming, which has the highest level of oxygen consumption, followed by running and jogging (although this type of exercise can damage knee joints). Rapid walking is also a very good way of toning up, and has high oxygen consumption.

Q I cycle to work every morning. Are the traffic fumes likely to be harmful?

A The levels of toxic carbon monoxide gas in the blood of cyclists have been measured and it is surprisingly high—sometimes up to 5 percent—but this is only for short periods of the day, and there is no evidence that the exposure will cause illness. Cigarette smokers who regularly expose themselves to carbon monoxide (from automobile exhausts) are at increased risk from coronary artery disease because the nicotine makes their blood platelets more sticky. However, the benefits derived from the regular exercise of cycling to work far outweigh the possible harmful effects of breathing in carbon fumes so that you would be well advised to stick to your bike.

Q I am a 39-year-old married woman with a part-time job and three children, and life is rather hectic. What is the ideal diet to help me keep fit?

A You need a diet relatively low in carbohydrates, but which contains all the essential proteins and vitamins to give you energy. An ideal mixture is fresh salads and vegetables, fruit, seafoods, chicken, and, surprisingly, potatoes. You should cut down on sugar, fatty dairy products, alcohol, and flour. You can increase the bulk of the meals with extra vegetables and fruit, and this will satisfy your hunger without causing weight gain.

and lungs are, the more efficient the intake and circulation of oxygen is, and the more energetic and fit the person can become.

A normal heart beats between 60–80 times a minute. A trained athlete—for example, a runner—might be able to get his or her heart rate up to almost 200 beats per minute, a feat beyond the average individual who may be able to manage 120 beats per minute with great effort. The output of the heart with each beat, called the stroke volume, increases with training (see Heart). This is why physically fit athletes seem to have larger hearts (containing more muscle) than

Cycling machines are an ideal way to get fit. Under medical supervision, they are also an excellent form of physical therapy for patients who have heart conditions.

sedentary people, and larger lungs, so that air can be breathed in and out faster than normal.

Heart and lung exercises range from running on the spot indoors to a variety of outdoor forms of exercise. Swimming and bicycling are the best exercises to take in terms of oxygen consumption. Next comes running. Squash, which is commonly thought to be one of the most demanding sports physically, comes a long way down on the list. This is because it demands quick strenuous bursts of activity, rather than a sustained continuous effort, and therefore it does not exercise the heart and lungs as effectively as the other forms of exercise mentioned.

All of the above activities are called dynamic exercises. However, there are other types of exercise that should also be considered. These are called static

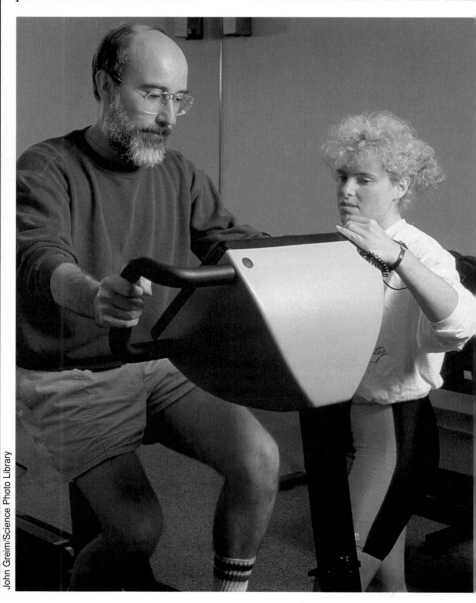

John Greim/Science Photo Library

exercises, or isometrics (see Isometrics). Although isometrics do not increase the efficiency of the heart and lungs, they build up the muscles. One of the best known programs is the Canadian Air Force Pilots' program, for men and women. The exercises, which include repetitive movements performed against the clock, are graded and the program is progressive.

Choosing your exercise

Ideally a fitness program should contain a range of the previously mentioned exercises. However, your time, and your willpower, may be limited, and for this reason it is important to plan a suitable scheme in which all the types of exercises are done regularly—for example, three or four times a week. At the same time it is important that you choose the

Regular exercise does not have to be a chore. A game of tennis (right) not only improves stamina, muscle tone, and health, but can be great fun as well! Of course, regular exercise is good for you whatever your age (below).

Zefa

kind of exercises that appeal to you; if you dislike bicycling but enjoy swimming, you should aim to swim and not worry about bicycling.

For example, it would be wise to spend 10 minutes each day doing some type of dynamic exercise that makes you breathless. Then at least three times a week you should aim to take a period of constant vigorous exercise that makes you breathless, such as running (if this is impractical, a period of digging in the garden or dancing may be substituted). This form of exercise should last for at least 20 minutes each session.

Although this is the goal, it is understandable that not everyone will be

881

What is the right weight for you?

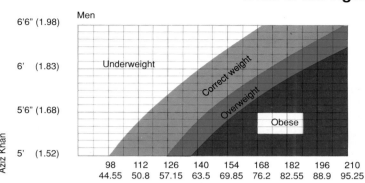
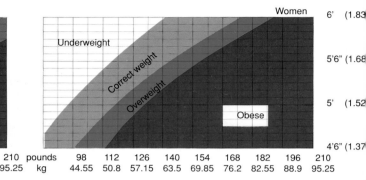

feet (meters)

Men

- 6'6" (1.98)
- 6' (1.83)
- 5'6" (1.68)
- 5' (1.52)

Underweight

Correct weight

Overweight

Obese

| 98 | 112 | 126 | 140 | 154 | 168 | 182 | 196 | 210 | pounds |
| 44.55 | 50.8 | 57.15 | 63.5 | 69.85 | 76.2 | 82.55 | 88.9 | 95.25 | kg |

feet (mete

Women

- 6' (1.83)
- 5'6" (1.68)
- 5' (1.52)
- 4'6" (1.37)

Underweight

Correct weight

Overweight

Obese

| 98 | 112 | 126 | 140 | 154 | 168 | 182 | 196 | 210 |
| 44.55 | 50.8 | 57.15 | 63.5 | 69.85 | 76.2 | 82.55 | 88.9 | 95.25 |

Aziz Khan

able to achieve it. The point is that the exercise should be vigorous: it is the quality and intensity of the exercise, rather than the length of time that you spend doing it, that counts.

Diet and fitness

We all have the capacity to improve our level of fitness. A lack of exercise results directly in a lack of physical fitness and an increase in weight.

An essential part of many fitness programs is losing weight. Very few people who are fit are fat, and excess fat tends to make people much too tired to be very active. Regular exercise is probably the best way to lose weight, but where weight is a particular problem or where eating habits have become irregular and unhealthy, a change in diet is often necessary as well.

The body requires a balanced diet, one that provides a person with sufficient proteins, vitamins, and minerals (and in

the right proportions), in addition to dietary fiber (see Diet). It is advisable to try as far as possible to cut down on foods such as fatty meats and cheeses, and substitute chicken and fish, preferably broiled or baked.

At the same time try to introduce more fiber into your diet, for example, whole grain breads, wheat bran cereals, and fruit and vegetables. You should also try to cut down, but do not completely cut out, all high calorie foods; you still need some of this type of food to provide the body with energy.

Staying fit

Many people embark on a fitness program thinking that a miracle will occur and they will become fit overnight. Unfortunately, as they soon discover, this does not happen. Fitness can only be achieved gradually and with some effort, and the most healthful, effective plan is one that is incorporated life long.

Weigh yourself once a week. Always use the same scales, and weigh yourself at the same time of day, preferably without clothing. Stand evenly on the scales. Keep a note of your weight; this way you can insure that you stay slim.

This is why it is so important to stick to the program, even when there appears to be no change at first. Be patient and results will appear soon enough. The physical rewards will certainly be worthwhile, for when the weight begins to slip away, and the muscles become toned then you begin to feel more energetic your spirits will rise, and your health will greatly improve. Once you get fit and feel great, that will be incentive enough to keep fit in the future.

Eating a well-balanced diet, which contains the required amount of proteins, vitamins, minerals, and fiber, is an important part of any fitness program.

Are you fit?

Someone who is fit will be able to:
- walk up several flights of stairs without becoming breathless
- walk briskly, jog, swim, or bicycle for 20 minutes without running out of breath
- perform normal household chores without getting tired
- recover from fatigue quickly

Simple steps to improve fitness:

If you are not satisfied with your fitness level, and don't feel able to embark on a formal exercise program, there are still some simple things you can do everyday to improve your health:
- walk instead of taking the bus
- walk up stairs instead of taking the elevator and escalator
- join a walking or hiking club

Tom Belshaw

Keloids

Q My mother has had keloids treated in the past and tells me that I may get one if I have my ears pierced. Is this right?

A A keloid may indeed form after an injury, even something as trivial as having your ears pierced. The tendency to form keloids may run in families as well, so there is a real possibility that the procedure may result in you getting a keloid.

Q I have keloids. Does this mean that I may have a tendency to form other types of skin tumors?

A There is no evidence that affected individuals are more likely to form other skin tumors. Why some people have a predisposition to form keloids is not clear, but essentially keloids are an exaggeration of the body's natural response of scar formation.

Q I have a lump on my leg that I believed to be a keloid, but recently it has started to bleed. Is this all right or should I have it seen to?

A Keloids have no tendency to ulcerate and bleed, so the lump on your leg is unlikely to be a keloid. With any lump on the skin, however small, and whether it bleeds or not, it is always wise to let your doctor see it in case it is a sign of a more serious condition.

Q I have a scar on my face that has developed into a keloid. I have been told that it is harmless, but it is unsightly and makes me very self-conscious. Would plastic surgery help?

A If your keloid is causing you distress, then there are several options open to you. Good results are achieved from simpler treatments than surgery, such as freezing keloids off with a cold probe and injecting them with a steroid compound. If these treatments are unsuccessful, then you can have the keloid removed surgically. It may also be necessary for you to have X-ray treatment following surgery to prevent another keloid from developing.

Keloids develop as a result of a disorder in the body's natural healing process that causes excess scar tissue to form. They are harmless, but if they cause embarrassment they can be easily treated.

Keloids are lumps of fibrous tissue that can develop at the site of an injury to the skin, such as a burn or a surgical incision. They may be triggered by severe acne or something as trivial as ear piercing.

Causes and symptoms

Keloids are really just an exaggeration of the normal healing process that results in scar formation after an injury.

After a laceration, for example, the natural healing process causes the breach in the skin to be filled (see Lacerations). Initially a blood clot forms in the wound, and then actively dividing cells and blood vessels grow into the gap. Finally, tough fibrous tissue is deposited in the form of a scar. A keloid develops when this fibrous tissue is laid down in excess, resulting in a raised lumpy area of scarlike tissue (see Scars).

Some people seem to have a tendency to develop keloids, and they usually first appear in childhood or adolescence. Keloids may be the result of an abnormality in the local hormonal or enzyme mechanisms that determine how much tissue formation is appropriate.

In the early stages a keloid appears as a soft pink raised area over the site of a previous wound. In time it becomes whiter and firmer and often forms clawlike projections into the surrounding skin. On the earlobe a keloid may become a pendulous mass of tissue.

Keloids are overdeveloped scars that can appear anywhere on the body, such as the arm (below) or abdomen (inset).

Because keloids are almost always benign, do not spread or bleed, and are rarely painful, medical opinion seems to favor leaving them alone. However, remember that it is important to show any lump on the skin, however small, to your doctor in case it is a sign of a more serious condition.

Over the course of several years, even without treatment, some keloids soften and flatten of their own accord. However, treatment may be required if the keloid is unsightly and causes embarrassment.

A great many keloids are successfully removed by injecting them with a steroid compound. Smaller keloids can be removed using an extremely cold probe (see Freezing). Where such measures are unsuccessful, or where the keloid is very large, surgical removal may be necessary. The problem with surgery, however, is that a new scar may result in the formation of another keloid. This can usually be avoided by postoperative X-ray treatment.

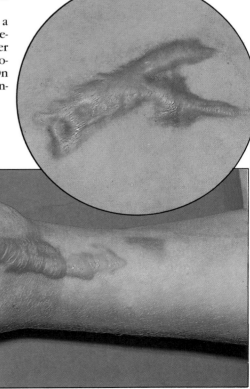

Ketones

Q When I had a stomach upset, my doctor asked for a urine sample so he could test for ketones. Why was this?

A Any illness that causes loss of appetite or vomiting is very likely to result in increased levels of ketones in the blood and urine because the body is breaking down fat to give you energy. A positive test for ketones in the urine simply confirms that such an illness may be present.

Q Whenever I am overweight I go on a crash diet. Will I start to produce ketones?

A Mostly you will lose water. If you do not combine your diet with exercise, your body will metabolize more muscle than fat. A crash diet will slow your overall metabolism; although you eat less, your body will use proportionately less energy and store more fat. If you reduce your glucose intake, your body will metabolize muscles and fat and produce ketones. Long-term diet and exercise produce better results with less drastic measures.

Q My husband has diabetes, and sometimes his breath smells bad. What causes this?

A Ketones give the breath a characteristic sickly odor that some people find unpleasant. In diabetics this is a warning sign of ketosis (the presence of excessive ketones in the body), which may lead to a diabetic coma. This means that there is insufficient insulin to enable the glucose in the blood to be used as fuel. As a result an excess of ketones is released to give energy.

Q I've heard that children are more likely than adults to suffer from an excess of ketones. Is this true?

A Yes. Children often develop ketosis when they are ill, especially if they have been vomiting, but it is usually mild and improves as the illness is treated. It is the body's initial attempt to provide the energy the child needs.

Ketones help us to use our body fat for energy. Too many ketones in the body is dangerous and is a sign of diabetes.

Nearly all our energy reserves are stored in fatty tissue built and maintained by glucose and carbohydrates. We need a constant supply of glucose in the bloodstream to carry out all the body's functions and to supply tissues with energy. When glucose intake is low, for example when dieting, proteins and carbohydrates are broken down to make glucose.

Metabolism occurs in every living cell. Ketones are an intermediary stage of fat metabolism. Insulin made by the pancreas metabolizes ketones into glucose (see Insulin, and Pancreas).

How they work

There are three types of ketones: two ketone bodies (acetoacetic acid and beta-hydroxybutyric acid) and acetone. Acetone, which is a waste product of fat metabolism, is produced at the same time as the ketone bodies but has no useful function. Ketone bodies, on the other hand, are readily utilized by the body as a source of energy.

When glucose is scarce, fatty tissue is broken down into fatty acids and carried in the bloodstream to the liver, where ketone bodies are formed (see Liver and liver diseases). The ketones are then released into the circulation, to be taken up and used for energy by the muscles, the heart, the brain, and the many other tissues and organs.

Ketosis

Ketosis is the potentially serious condition in which there is an abnormal accumulation of ketones in the body due to a carbohydrate deficiency or inadequate carbohydrate metabolism. As a result, fatty acids are metabolized, and the end products, ketones, begin to accumulate.

The underlying causes of ketosis include starvation, alcohol, inadequate intake of protein and carbohydrates (as a result of dieting), and, most commonly, diabetes mellitus (in which lack of insulin prevents glucose from being used as a fuel; see Diabetes). Symptoms include sweet, sickly smelling breath, loss of appetite, and vomiting. Untreated ketosis may lead to unconsciousness and even death.

Pregnant women in labor can often become ketotic. However, high levels of ketones in the blood may delay the progress of labor by interfering with the uterus's ability to contract effectively (see Pregnancy). If necessary, a glucose IV will stop the formation of ketones.

Ketone formation in the liver

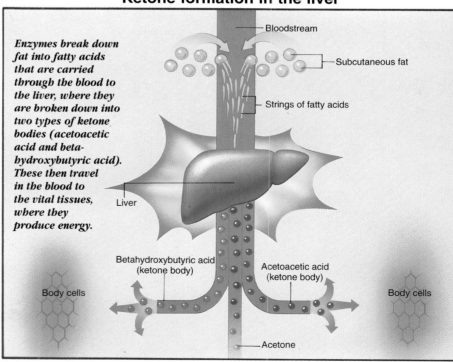

Enzymes break down fat into fatty acids that are carried through the blood to the liver, where they are broken down into two types of ketone bodies (acetoacetic acid and beta-hydroxybutyric acid). These then travel in the blood to the vital tissues, where they produce energy.

Bloodstream

Subcutaneous fat

Strings of fatty acids

Liver

Betahydroxybutyric acid (ketone body)

Acetoacetic acid (ketone body)

Body cells

Body cells

Acetone

Aziz Khan

Kidney dialysis

Q I have been told that I need to go on a dialysis machine. Will I need it all the time?

A This is likely unless a suitable kidney can be found for transplantation. However, some people find they can adapt their way of life to accommodate the treatment and prefer dialysis to a transplant.

Q Does a person on dialysis need a special diet?

A Because the kidneys can no longer excrete excess minerals, retained salt in the blood raises the blood pressure and may cause fluids to seep into organs such as the lungs. As a result, some patients on dialysis need to be careful about the amount of salt they take, particularly those with high blood pressure. They are also advised to eat relatively small quantities of protein so as to create less urea for the kidneys to excrete.

Q If I am on a renodialysis machine, will I ever be able to go on vacation?

A A lack of mobility has always been a problem for patients on dialysis. In some countries home dialysis machines are available, which makes traveling less of a problem. Many patients on peritoneal dialysis can travel with their machines.

Q My 12-year-old son has to go on dialysis. Will he have time left for his home work?

A Discuss the situation with your son's teacher. It may be possible for someone to go through your son's studies with him while he is actually connected to the machine, thus using the time well.

Q My sister has to go on dialysis. Will she feel depressed? How can I help her?

A The way that patients come to terms with the psychological problems of dialysis will depend on their temperament, their job, and most important of all, the amount of family support that they receive.

Kidney dialysis is carried out by a renodialysis machine that can perform many of the functions of a real kidney. This means that those suffering from kidney failure can lead active lives with the help of regular dialysis.

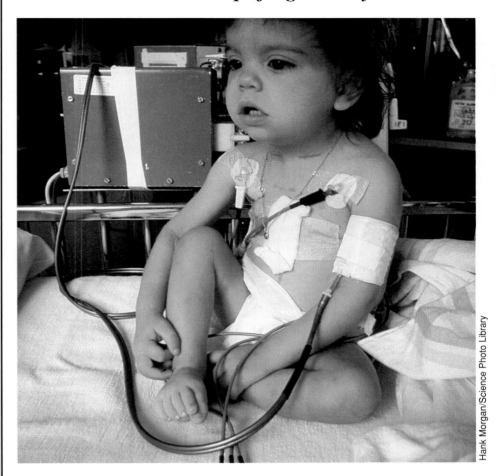

Hank Morgan/Science Photo Library

Even a very young child with kidney failure can have dialysis on a renodialysis machine while awaiting a kidney transplant.

The kidneys filter the blood and remove impurities that would become poisonous if they were allowed to accumulate. The kidneys do this in two stages. First, blood is coarse filtered by a structure called the glomerulus. Second, a fine adjustment takes place in the tubules (small tubes in the kidneys) whereby important nutrients that have also been filtered out are reabsorbed. The renodialysis machine that carries out dialysis imitates the glomerulus, but it cannot perform the function of the tubules (see Kidneys and kidney diseases).

There are two common methods of dialysis that are used today. The first, hemodialysis, relies on a renodialysis machine to filter the blood. This is the usual form of dialysis, and it is common for dialysis patients to need three or four long sessions of hemodialysis each week.

The second form, peritoneal dialysis, works in the same way as hemodialysis, but instead of using a machine, the peritoneum (the membrane lining the patient's abdomen; see Peritoneum) is used as the dialyzing membrane. Patients are therefore not dependant on a machine. Although peritoneal dialysis is more efficient than hemodialysis, there is always a danger of developing peritonitis (infection of the peritoneum).

The renodialysis machine
The basic principle on which a hemodialysis machine works is very simple. A very thin membrane is placed between the blood and the cleaning fluid (called

KIDNEY DIALYSIS

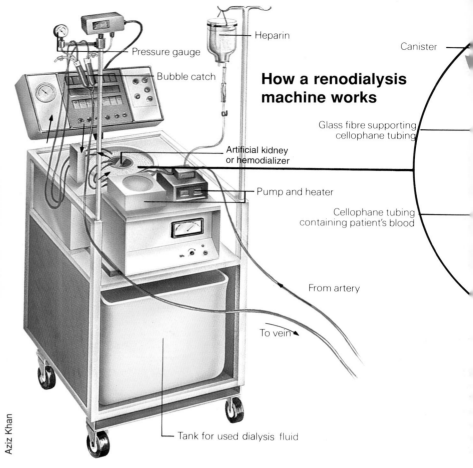

How a renodialysis machine works

Labels: Heparin; Canister; Pressure gauge; Bubble catch; Glass fibre supporting cellophane tubing; Artificial kidney or hemodialyzer; Pump and heater; Cellophane tubing containing patient's blood; From artery; To vein; Tank for used dialysis fluid; Aziz Khan

Q My grandmother is suffering from kidney failure. Would she be eligible for treatment on a renodialysis machine or is she too old?

A Age itself is no barrier to being placed on a dialysis program. Each case is evaluated on an individual basis; age as well as general health, lifestyle, and where your grandmother lives will be taken into consideration. After the doctors have considered all these factors, they can decide whether your grandmother is eligible for dialysis.

Q I have heard that doctors can perform dialysis by inserting a tube into the stomach. Is this method ever used today?

A Yes. This procedure is called peritoneal dialysis. It uses the membrane lining the patient's abdomen as the dialyzing membrane. The dialysis fluid is poured into the patient's abdominal cavity through a plastic tube. The abdomen can take up to 5 to 7 pt (2 to 4 l) at a time. After this has been left for a suitable period to balance with the blood salts, as in a renodialysis machine, the waste is drained out of the same tube. This can be done on a continuous basis, freeing the patient from his or her dependence on the normal hemodialysis machine. It often produces a better therapeutic effect with greater clearance of wastes. There is, however, some danger of peritonitis developing.

Q My 18-year-old brother has had kidney trouble for some time. Now he has been taught how to use a renodialysis machine for dialysis at home. I have heard that patients in this situation often get infectious hepatitis. Is there any risk to other members of the family?

A The risk has been reduced considerably by screening of blood for dialysis for hepatitis B. Now that there is a vaccine against hepatitis B, protection should be complete. A sterile technique should still always be practiced during dialysis, however.

dialysis fluid). The kidneys filter blood with a high concentration of certain impurities (e.g., urea, excess sodium, potassium, and other minerals; see Excretory system), whereas the dialysis fluid is low. This results in a concentration gradient, whereby molecules flow from an area of high concentration (the blood) to an area of low concentration (the dialysis fluid). The size of the holes in the membrane determines the size of the molecules that may pass across. The smallest molecules pass most readily, and larger molecules cannot pass at all.

It is not only the size of the molecules that is important but the speed at which they pass. Molecules with a very low molecular weight have a high rate of clearance from the blood, while those with a high molecular weight have a low rate of clearance. Therefore it is necessary to have the largest area of membrane or sieve possible, together with a good supply of blood to run across the membrane.

In the past flat sheets of cellophane were used as the dialyzing membrane in renodialysis machines, and blood was pumped over one side while the other side was bathed in dialyzing fluid. These Kil plates, as they were called, used up a lot of space, making the renodialysis machine very unwieldy. Today more compact coils of membrane are used, so ren-

odialysis machines are smaller and patients can now undergo dialysis in their own homes. Dialysis membranes used to be cleaned and reused, but disposable units are now available, reducing the risk of infection.

To carry out hemodialysis an adequate and ready supply of blood is necessary and this is taken from a large blood vessel, usually an artery in the forearm.

There are two ways that this can be done. The first, which is a temporary arrangement, involves inserting one little plastic tube into an artery and another into a vein in the forearm, then connecting these with more tubing to the renodialysis machine. This is called a shunt. When it is not being used for dialysis, the tube in the artery is connected up to the tube in the vein, so that the blood continues to flow around the body.

A more permanent arrangement is called a fistula (see Fistula). For this a small operation is performed, in which an artery is joined to a vein under the skin surface. After about six weeks the vein wall thickens and can withstand repeated puncturing with a needle. At each dialysis a double needle is inserted and connected with plastic tubing to the renodialysis machine. Good maintenance of the fistula is essential to the patient's well-being.

To stop the blood from clotting in the

Blood for cleansing flows from the patient's artery into the hemodialyzer, then through two coils of flat cellophane tubing immersed in a canister through which the dialysis fluid is pumped, thereby washing out waste products from the blood. Purified blood returns to the patient's vein.

emodialysis machine, the anticlotting substance heparin is used. It is very important that no air bubbles get into the blood and pass back into the patient, because these could block the capillaries (small vessels) in the lungs. A special bubble detector insures that the blood is free from air bubbles. A pump is required to drive blood through the machine, and the necessary fluids must be warmed. Cold blood going back to the patient would cause hypothermia in a relatively short space of time.

Patients are taught exactly how to take care of themselves during home dialysis. For example, the shunt or fistula must be kept clear of blood clots by flushing it through with blood thinners from time to time, and the skin over the area needs to be kept scrupulously clean to avoid any risk of infection.

Drawbacks

The frequency with which a patient needs to be connected to the dialysis machine depends upon the severity of his or her kidney disease and the quality of the shunt. An efficient shunt will enable the blood to be cleared of impurities

This man has a fistula (an artery joined to a vein) and has been shown how to insert the needle for dialysis at home.

more rapidly than would a poor shunt. It is common for patients to need three periods of three-hour dialysis treatments each week.

All patients with chronic renal failure become anemic and dialysis does not correct this. At least one of the causes of this anemia is a deficiency of a stimulant to blood production in bone marrow (a hormone called erythropoietin that is made in the kidneys). The anemia can be treated by blood transfusion, but this does not remove the problem and when the transfused cells die off in about 50–60 days, the anemia must be treated all over again (see Anemia). To treat the anemia, all dialysis patients are given erythropoietin and occasional blood transfusions.

Raised blood pressure can sometimes be a problem, and there is a higher incidence of heart attacks and strokes among patients on dialysis than in those whose kidneys function normally. It may be treated with conventional drugs, but more often the doctor attempts to reduce blood pressure by lowering the amount of body salt. This is done either by restricting salt in the diet or putting less salt in the dialysis fluid (see Blood pressure).

Because the kidneys are no longer filtering well, patients with chronic renal failure are more prone to infection than others. Chest and urinary infections cause most trouble. Much more hazardous, particularly for the staff looking after such patients in the hospital, used to be the risk of viral hepatitis, which is transmitted in the blood. Outbreaks of hepatitis used to occur in dialysis units from time to time and this sometimes resulted in fatalities. Fortunately, with the advent of a vaccine for viral hepatitis, patients and workers in dialysis units can now be completely protected from this danger. However, good practice is still necessary; blood dialysis fluid is handled with great care, gloves and masks are worn at all times, and any spillages of fluid are cleaned up immediately.

Outlook

Although dialysis is a life-saving procedure, it is a full-time job relying upon impeccable hygiene. Home dialysis has gone a long way to reducing the inconvenience of regular admission to the hospital, but the stress it places on the patient's family cannot be underestimated. A patient may easily become depressed, however, the support and encouragement of a patient's partner and family can do much to alleviate this.

Dialysis is usually a second choice to a kidney transplant and is often used only until the time when a suitable donor kidney becomes available.

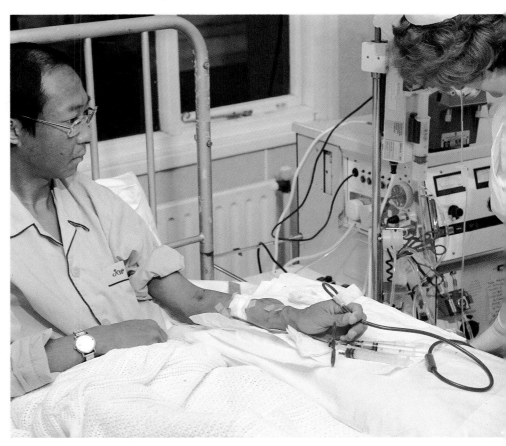

Kidney transplants

Q Can kidneys from donors that become available for transplant be stored in some kind of tissue bank?

A They can be stored, but not for more than 48 hours. Clearly it would be a great advantage if it were possible to store kidneys for a longer period of time, because such a bank of kidney tissue would mean a greater choice of potential recipients and better timing of the transplant operations.

Q My brother has to have a kidney transplant operation, and I have been told that my kidney would be a good match. If I gave one of my kidneys, would this mean that I would have to be extra careful about my own health in the future?

A You should always be careful about your health. However, the remaining kidney will be perfectly capable of doing a good job for the rest of your life. Indeed, our kidneys have three or four times as much filtering capacity as they actually need.

Q Are there any special things that people with a new kidney have to do to stay healthy and fit?

A At the present time it is necessary for the patient to stay on a type of drug, called an immunosuppressant, probably for the rest of his or her life. The dose the patient needs to take will depend upon how well the tissue of the donor kidney matched the tissue in the recipient's body. People on these drugs do have to be careful about exposing themselves to infections.

Q My father has had a kidney transplant, but his body has rejected it. Is it possible for him to have another transplant operation?

A Yes, it is, but it is more difficult. Usually, after rejection, patients have to go back to dialysis on a kidney machine.

Kidney transplants mean that it is possible for patients with kidney failure to be given a healthy new kidney from a donor. So how do the risks involved with the procedure compare with the benefits to the patient?

The first successful kidney transplant was performed in the mid-20th century, when a kidney was transplanted from one identical twin to another. However, it was not until the development of powerful immunosuppressive drugs (drugs that control the rejection of transplanted tissue by the recipient's body) had progressed sufficiently that implantation of tissues from an unrelated donor became a possibility (see Donors).

Patient selection

Unfortunately there is a limited supply of suitable donor kidneys. On the other hand, dialysis (using a kidney machine) is successful in prolonging life and machines can be used at home, so many factors go into the selection of a suitable recipient. Age alone is not a factor, but it [is] important to consider the patient's qual[i]ty of life. It is known that very young an[d] very old people are less suited to tran[s]plants than others. Other medical cond[i]tions that may make patients ineligibl[e] include cancer, mental illness, active infe[c]tion of the kidneys, certain heart cond[i]tions, and blood vessel disease.

Surgeons would also be less inclined t[o] advise transplants for patients with di[a]betes and generalized diseases involvin[g] the kidneys. They would also be relucta[nt] to operate on a child under eight yea[rs].

Surgeons performing a kidney transplant. Before the operation the donor must be matched for compatibility with the recipien[t] or else the kidney will be rejected.

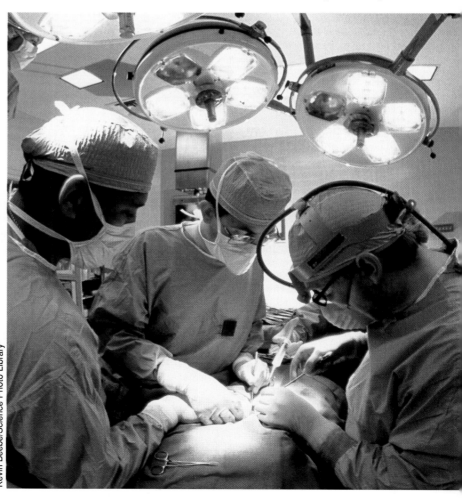

Kevin Beebe/Science Photo Library

...ld because of the size of the kidney and the subsequent growth of the patient. The patient must be made as fit as possible for the operation, and this usually means a period of time on dialysis (see kidney dialysis).

Suitable donors

Anyone under the age of 65 with normal kidneys and no history of cancer is a suitable kidney donor. The problem lies in persuading people that holding a kidney donor card does not mean that doctors will not do their utmost to help them if they have a serious accident. Most kidneys used in transplants are removed from people suffering from severe head injuries, usually caused by road traffic accidents but sometimes the result of brain hemorrhage. A kidney is never removed without the consent of the next of kin unless the patient is carrying a kidney donor card giving permission for use of their kidneys.

It is modern practice now to remove kidneys from patients who are brain-dead, even though some living donors are willing and prepared to allow surgeons to remove one of their kidneys for trans-

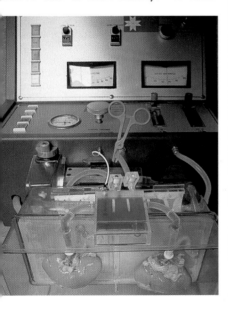

Donor kidneys (above) are preserved in a machine that will keep the organs viable until they can be transplanted into a suitable patient.

The donor kidney (top right), which is stored for less than 48 hours, still retains as much of its own ureter and blood vessels as possible. The new kidney (below right) is put in place. The renal artery is stitched to the recipient's internal iliac artery and the renal vein to the iliac vein. In the technique illustrated here, the ureter (inset) is stitched directly to the recipient's bladder.

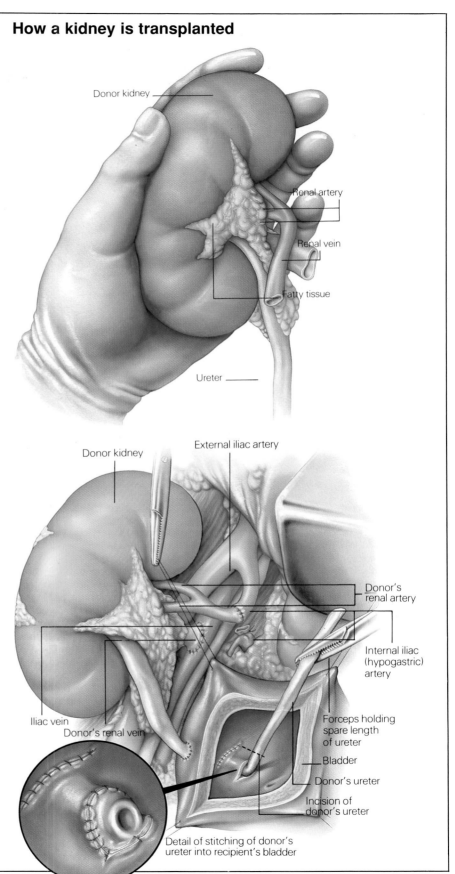

How a kidney is transplanted

Donor kidney

Renal artery

Renal vein

Fatty tissue

Ureter

Donor kidney

External iliac artery

Donor's renal artery

Internal iliac (hypogastric) artery

Forceps holding spare length of ureter

Bladder

Donor's ureter

Incision of donor's ureter

Iliac vein

Donor's renal vein

Detail of stitching of donor's ureter into recipient's bladder

Frank Kennard

Bill Petch

Rejection

Nowadays, however, immunosuppressive drugs are efficient enough at suppressing the immune system's response to foreign tissue to allow donor tissue that is not an absolutely perfect match to be used in transplants. This is a great advantage because it means that a larger number of kidneys will suit a potential recipient (see Immunosuppressive drugs).

Acute rejection symptoms almost always occur, usually several times in the first few months following a transplant. After this things begin to settle down. During the rejection process blood tends to clot in the small capillaries of the vessels supplying the kidney (see Capillaries). As a result the urine output tends to fall and a natural waste product called creatinine increases in the blood. Doctors have devised all sorts of tests to try to get advance warning of rejection, but urine output and creatinine in the blood are still considered to be the best signs. When rejection starts the doses of immunosuppressive drugs need to be increased temporarily and some doctors prescribe blood thinning pills, called anti coagulants, as well.

Because rejection episodes are so common, patients with kidney transplants need careful medical attention and nursing. A more accurate guide to the state of the transplanted kidney can be obtained by means of a kidney biopsy (removal of a minute piece of kidney for examination: see Biopsy), which is a simple procedure performed under local anesthetic.

Complications

Rejection is perhaps the most common early complication. Sometimes the stitching done during surgery is not perfect and urine leaks. This can easily be corrected by further surgery. More than 75 percent of patients become susceptible to infections; this is a potentially hazardous situation for those on immunosuppressive drugs (who have poor defenses against disease due to their immune system's response being repressed by the drugs). Regular checking of the urine and the use of antibiotics is essential for these patients. Raised blood pressure may also cause problems, but the condition can be treated.

Outlook

Over 90 percent of patients are back at work within three months of a kidney transplant. These operations have been a great success, and many doctors believe it is preferable to treatment by renal (kidney) dialysis. With the development of new immunosuppressive drugs like cyclosporine A, the rejection of transplanted kidneys has become less common.

plant. This latter type of operation is most often performed when close relatives are involved. However, unless the tissue match is absolutely perfect, it makes little difference to the survival of the transplant whether the kidney comes from a close relative or from someone who is not related to the patient.

Donated kidneys can be kept on ice for up to 48 hours. They are stored in a special oxygenated salt solution that is kept at around 50°F (10°C). Generally speaking the longer the kidney has been kept, the less well it performs following an operation. The best results are achieved by transferring the kidney at or very near to the time of death. However, storage of kidneys for a short period allows surgical teams time to prepare for the operation and gives the patient time to be admitted to the hospital prior to surgery (see Transplants).

Tissue matching

The body is protected from any invading foreign tissue or germs by the system of immunity (see Immune system). This sys-

After a successful kidney transplant, patients can return to a normal life.

tem enables the body to recognize foreign tissues or germs and then to make antibodies to destroy them. This system is vital in enabling the body to fight disease. But it has considerable disadvantages when it comes to transplants because transplanted tissue is likely to be rejected, just as the body will reject other foreign tissue and germs.

The parts of the donor tissue that are recognized as foreign by the recipient are called antigens, and these are found stuck to the surface of the donor kidney cells. So if transplanted antigens are not recognized as compatible with the body's own antigens, then rejection will take place and the transplant will not take.

Tissue compatibility is a very complicated area of research, and this is the reason that it is so difficult to find an exact match between donor and patient. It has been estimated that the chances of finding a perfectly compatible donor are up to one in a million.

Kidneys and kidney diseases

Q I know that alcohol causes damage to the liver, but does drinking have any effect on the kidneys? And how much fluid should I drink each day?

A Alcohol tends to have no detrimental effect on the kidneys. The amount of fluid you need to drink each day depends on how much you lose and the amount of physical work you do, since this will increase the volume you lose in sweat. Even office workers should drink at least 2.12 pt (one l) of fluid a day. People with urinary infections are encouraged to drink large quantities of water so that the infection is flushed out.

Q My mother suffers from high blood pressure. Will this harm her kidneys?

A High blood pressure causes the small blood vessels to thicken. This causes damage to the filtering units in the kidneys (nephrons), and as these are lost the ability of the kidneys to remove waste products is hampered. This will result in kidney failure unless the condition is treated.

Q If one kidney fails can the other one cope on its own?

A Yes. In fact, we have so many nephrons in each kidney that we can quite easily do without not just one, but almost half of the other kidney as well. For this reason it is perfectly reasonable to remove a kidney from a healthy person and donate it to someone else. The donor can live with one kidney for the rest of his or her life, provided that it remains healthy.

Q Do some forms of sexually transmitted disease (STD) lead to kidney trouble?

A STDs are a rare cause of kidney disease, although occasionally gonorrhea can lead to kidney infection by spreading up the ureter from the bladder. A much more common cause of kidney trouble is bacterial, fungal, or viral infection, or infection of the urinary tract.

The main purpose of the kidneys is to extract impurities from the system. They are amazingly efficient, and because there are two it is possible to live normally if one fails.

The kidneys contain a complicated system of filters and tubes. Apart from their main function of filtering impurities from the blood, the kidneys also absorb many essential nutrients back into the bloodstream from the tubes. Another important function that is performed in the tubes is balancing the amount of salt and water that is retained.

The kidneys lie on the back wall of the abdomen. A tube called the ureter runs from the inner side of each of the two kidneys down the back of the abdominal cavity and into the bladder. The tube leading from the bladder is called the urethra. In women its opening is in front of the vagina, and in men it is at the tip of the penis. The urethra is much shorter in women than men, therefore women are more prone to bladder infections than are men (see Cystitis).

Functions

The kidneys contain thousands of tiny filtering units or nephrons. Each nephron can be divided into two important parts; the filtering part (glomerulus) and the tubule, where water and essential nutrients are extracted from the blood.

The glomerulus consists of a knot of tiny blood capillaries that have very thin walls. Water and the waste dissolved within it can pass freely across these walls into the collecting system of tubules on the other side. This network of blood capillaries is so large that at any one time it may contain almost a quarter of the circulating blood, and it filters about 4.4 fl oz (130 ml) from the blood each minute.

A baby needs fluid to keep his kidneys flushed, so give him drinks of cooled boiled water between feedings.

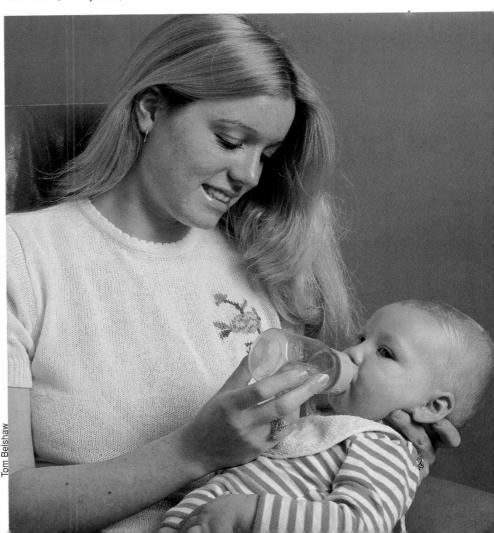

Tom Belshaw

The kidney's filtering system

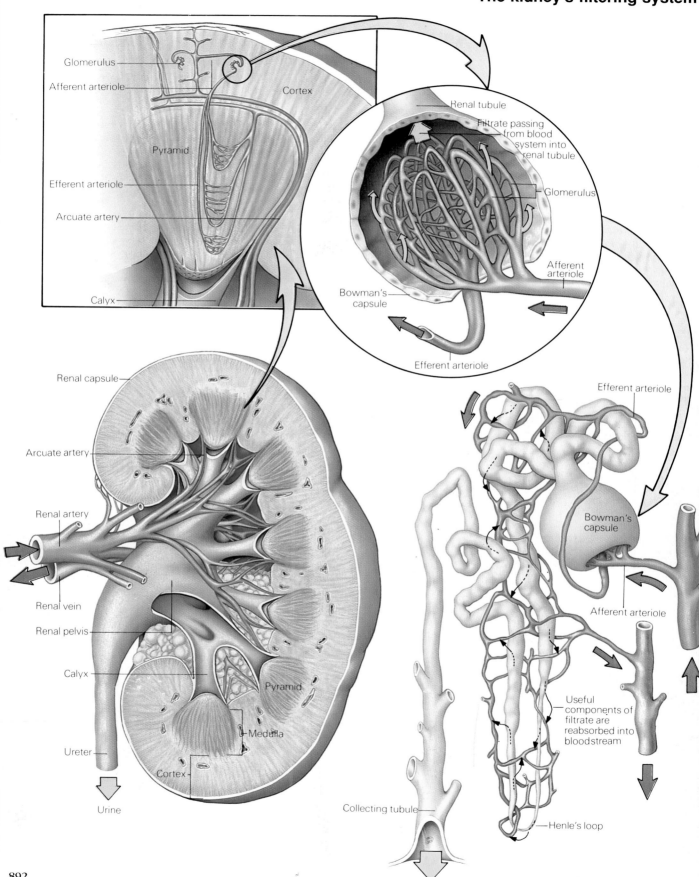

Glomerulus

Afferent arteriole

Cortex

Pyramid

Efferent arteriole

Arcuate artery

Calyx

Renal tubule

Filtrate passing from blood system into renal tubule

Glomerulus

Afferent arteriole

Bowman's capsule

Efferent arteriole

Renal capsule

Arcuate artery

Renal artery

Renal vein

Renal pelvis

Calyx

Pyramid

Medulla

Ureter

Cortex

Urine

Efferent arteriole

Bowman's capsule

Afferent arteriole

Useful components of filtrate are reabsorbed into bloodstream

Collecting tubule

Henle's loop

Frank Kennard

892

agnified view of a kidney (left), showing s different components and how they work. he renal artery carries blood to the kidney, plitting into arcuate arteries and finally to afferent arterioles. Each of these ends a glomerulus (inset). As blood passes rough the glomerulus, it is filtered rough the glomerular wall and enters the nal tubule. The basic components of blood asma, protein, red and white corpuscles, d so on) are too large to cross the mipermeable membrane of the glomerulus, it most of the other material (e.g., water, lts, and hormones) that the blood carries ound the body can pass across it. The xt stage is called selective reabsorption, hich is seen in the detailed enlargement elow). Materials essential to the body are absorbed into the efferent arterioles, ross the tubule wall. Once the blood has en thoroughly filtered and all the required aterials have been reabsorbed, the blood aves the kidney in the renal vein while aste products are excreted in the urine via e urethra.

The holes in the capillary wall form a biological sieve and are so small that molecules beyond a certain size cannot pass through. If the kidneys become infected, the glomeruli inflame and the sieve fails to be so selective, allowing larger molecules, such as proteins, to escape into the urine. One of the smallest protein molecules to find its way into the urine is albumin (the main protein in the blood). When your doctor tests your urine for protein, he or she is checking to see if the kidneys (and liver) are working properly.

The tubules run between the glomeruli to a collecting system that ultimately drains into the bladder. Each glomerulus is surrounded by a structure called the Bowman's capsule, which is the beginning of its tubule. It is here that almost all the filtered water and salt is reabsorbed so that the urine is concentrated. To reabsorb all this water, the body has a highly sophisticated system in which a hormone secreted into the blood from the pituitary gland in the brain changes the permeability (ability to reabsorb water) of the tubule (see Hormones).

While the hormone is in the blood, the tubule allows a great deal of water to be reabsorbed. When the hormone is turned off, however, the tubule becomes less permeable to water and more is lost in the urine; this is called diuresis and the hormone concerned is called antidiuretic hormone (ADH). In certain conditions, such as diabetes insipidus (not to be confused with sugar diabetes or diabetes mellitus), this hormone may be totally lacking. When this happens the patient cannot conserve water and thereby loses large quantities in the urine, which have to be replaced by drinking.

Another hormone, aldosterone, secreted by the adrenal glands just above the kidneys, is responsible for exchanging sodium salt for potassium salt—thereby helping to control blood pressure and the balance of salt in the body. Parathormone, a hormone made by four small glands buried behind the thyroid gland, regulates the reabsorption of the essential mineral calcium, from which our bones and teeth are made (see Thyroid).

Kidney disorders

Once a nephron is destroyed it seldom regrows. From birth onward we gradually lose nephrons. Fortunately we have so many that this seldom becomes a problem. Indeed, about a third of all our nephrons do very little. These redundant nephrons are gradually brought into use as wear and tear takes its toll.

Doctors can get a good idea of the number of nephrons working by measuring the level at which certain waste substances are present in the blood and removed in the urine. One such waste product is called creatinine. Its level is kept very low in the blood, rising when the blood becomes concentrated, as it does when we are thirsty. When doctors see a rise in the level of creatinine in the blood, it is a warning sign that the kidneys are failing. The rate at which creatinine can be removed from the blood is a better indication of renal (kidney) function. If a patient's kidneys fail to clear more than 0.34 fl oz (10 ml) of blood of creatinine each minute, the assistance of a dialysis machine, or artificial kidney, will be needed before long.

Inflammation of the glomerulus leads to sudden kidney failure. The early signs are the appearance of the protein albumin in the urine and sometimes particles of red blood cells. If your urine becomes pink or rust in color you should see your doctor as soon as possible. In kidney fail-

People living in hot climates need to drink more to replace the fluid lost in sweat.

Q Are there are any drugs that are likely to cause damage to the kidneys?

A Yes. There is a dangerous form of kidney disease caused by certain drugs that results in damage to the duct system. Phenacetin has been linked with this kind of kidney disease, but there is reason to believe that other anti-inflammatory drugs, like acetaminophen and aspirin, may also cause trouble if large amounts are taken regularly. Thus the people most at risk are those who take tablets of this type habitually, especially if they live in hot climates where the amount of the drug concentrated in the urine is likely to be high, making kidney problems more probable.

Q My father's doctor has told him he needs an IVP. What is this, and how is it carried out?

A IVP stands for intravenous pyelogram, and it is a test done in the hospital to check the function of the kidneys. A dye that concentrates in the kidneys is injected into the bloodstream. By taking an X ray soon after the injection, the kidneys can be seen outlined by the dye, giving doctors a good idea of their size. When the dye is excreted, the position of the ureters and the bladder can be seen. Patients suffering from an enlarged prostate tend to be unable to empty their bladders completely, so any residual dye left in the bladder will show on the X ray and confirm the diagnosis conclusively. This test is painless.

Q The doctor has told me that I have bacteria in my urine and have to take antibiotics. Why does this happen, and is it easy to cure?

A The urine is normally sterile. However, some people shed bacteria in their urine, and this is a sign of infection somewhere in the urinary tract. As long as the bacteria persist, you have the chance of developing acute inflammation of the kidney. Doctors may switch from one antibiotic to another over several weeks until the most effective is found and the infection is completely cleared.

Various types of kidney stones, including the strange stag's horn formation.

ure excess water and salts cannot be excreted and so collect in parts of the body, either at the base of the spine in patients who are lying in bed, or around the ankles in patients who are up and about, causing swelling (see Edema).

In most cases acute kidney inflammation clears up completely and full recovery is normal. Rarely, however, damage to the glomeruli is progressive, and the patient gradually develops renal failure. This is called chronic glomerulonephritis. The most common cause of this condition is an allergy to the streptococcus bacteria. In the days before penicillin, streptococci caused epidemics of sore throats followed by acute glomerulonephritis, and a high proportion of these victims developed chronic renal failure. However, this type of disease is seldom seen today (see Penicillin).

Inflammation of the kidneys, usually caused by infection coming up the ureter from the bladder, is the most common cause of tubular disease. Repeated infections caused in this way can ultimately result in the destruction of sufficient nephrons to cause kidney failure. A telltale sign is the appearance of pus in the urine. In the early stages of disease, the patient's urine may appear quite clear, and a microscopic examination is needed to spot the white cells that make up pus, but later the urine becomes cloudy. There are a number of other causes of cloudy urine. The first amount urinated in the morning may be cloudy because it contains a deposit of undissolved salts that have collected overnight; however, if you are worried, see your doctor.

Inflammation of the kidneys due to infection is called pyelonephritis, and this usually responds very well to treatment with antibiotics (see Antibiotics).

Kidney stones, called calculi, are composed of the salts of calcium and phosphorus. The two main causes of kidney stones are infection and an excessive amount of calcium in the blood. Stones associated with infection are more common in women, and can reach very large sizes so that they cannot pass down the ureter. They lie inside the kidney, and as they grow they take on the shape of the collecting duct system in which they lie. When an X ray is taken, they show up as a branched lump of chalk, looking similar to the antlers of a stag. Smaller stones may be passed down the ureter, causing colic and severe pain.

High blood pressure

The kidneys regulate the amount of salt in the body and produce a hormone called renin. The level of renin depends on the level of salt, which in turn is controlled by the action of the adrenal hormone aldosterone on the tubules (see Salt). Renin activates another hormone called angiotensin. It is the activation of this hormone that causes a rise in blood pressure (see Blood pressure).

See your doctor if:
- Your urine is discolored, particularly if it is red
- You have pain on urinating, lasting more than two days
- You urinate frequently for more than three or four days
- You have accompanying pain in the loin or abdomen
- Your ankles are swollen

Kleptomania

Q Is kleptomania really more common among women than among men?

A Yes, but the reasons are probably cultural. Women usually do the shopping and are therefore exposed to temptation more than men, so for this reason it is associated more with women than men. Stealing because of depression is also more common in women, because the incidence of depression is higher in women than in men. However, true kleptomania is very rare.

Q My son is going through a phase of taking money from my purse. Is this kleptomania, and what should I do about it?

A It is very unlikely to be kleptomania. Many children go through this phase; they do it for sheer gain, to see if they can get away with it, and to test their own and their parents' sense of what is right and what is wrong. Punish your son in exactly the same way as you would for any other naughtiness. He will almost certainly grow out of doing this.

Q Why does it always seem to be rich people who are involved in kleptomania?

A Not all shoplifting is kleptomania. However, because the paradox of rich people stealing small objects, generally when they have large amounts of money on them, is worth reporting in the newspapers and on TV, it is easy to get the impression that wealth and kleptomania go together. In fact, true kleptomania is not particularly associated with any social class or culture.

Q Is kleptomania a form of hysteria?

A It was thought to be in the past, but it is now officially classified as an obsessive-compulsive neurosis. This reclassification probably helps, for neuroses can, in general, be treated. Hysteria is not a medical term and does not refer to a specific condition (see Hysteria).

A kleptomaniac is someone who is a compulsive stealer of all sorts of objects of little value that they do not need, often being no more than a can of fruit. They appear to get a buzz from the act of stealing, which points to a psychological problem that can be treated.

Kleptomania is a neurosis that takes the form of a compulsive and recurring desire to steal. It is not a hidden desire to acquire wealth; the articles stolen are seldom of value, and the person stealing them often has the money to pay.

Neither is the person a hoarder, in the way that some people amass piles of old newspapers or other worthless objects. The true kleptomaniac seldom makes any particular attempt to keep the stolen object once they have it. It seems that it is the act of theft itself that is compulsive and, like most compulsions, it is not

The compulsive stealing of objects of very little value, by someone who has no need of them, is the sign of true kleptomania.

something that just happens once but occurs over and over again (see Complexes and compulsions).

Causes

There are different opinions as to the causes of kleptomania. Some agree with the theories of the famous psychiatrist Sigmund Freud that the cause is a repressed sexual conflict within the individual, and the objects stolen have sexually satisfying qualities. However, since almost any object can be given a sexual symbolism if one tries hard enough, this theory is indeed very difficult to prove.

Others see kleptomania as an act of revenge against society, a symbolic way of asserting one's authority, or a compensa-

tion for material or emotional deprivation during childhood. However, even if good evidence could be produced to support such theories, it still might not help much in treating the condition.

Symptoms

The sign of true kleptomania is the repetitive taking of objects that are of little value to the kleptomaniac and that are usually different with each theft.

This means that a single act of theft committed by an individual is not classed as kleptomania, although the theft may well have a psychological reason behind it. Similarly, the compulsive stealer of a particular type of item, such as the man who steals women's underwear off clotheslines, is not a kleptomaniac because only one type of article is taken.

It is often said that a kleptomaniac does not know what he or she is doing when the theft is being committed, but this is not always true. Some know very well and even experience some distress when they feel the compulsion to steal. Others create a fantasy rationalization of what they have done. They may say the stolen object was given to them or that they paid for it on a previous visit to the shop.

These are not just excuses to get the person out of trouble; the kleptomaniac believes them, at least at the time of the event, even if no one else does.

In other cases the person is aware of what he or she is doing, but seems totally unaware of the consequences of the act.

Treatment

Kleptomania is a comparatively rare condition, and because of this it has not been possible to discover one treatment that is always appropriate, especially because kleptomaniacs are often reluctant to accept the need for treatment.

One common treatment that has the advantage of working quite quickly if it is going to succeed at all is called aversion therapy, or covert sensitization.

The patient imagines the act of stealing in as much vivid detail as possible, then with the therapist's help visualizes the chain of consequences of that act—being caught, being taken to court, having the crime reported in the newspapers, and so on. The therapist piles on the agony by painting as dark a picture as possible of the reactions of family and friends, so that the act of theft is associated in the person's imagination with as much anxiety as possible.

The repeated association builds up an aversion within the person that helps to stop him or her from repeating the behavior ever again. If this technique seems to have no effect, then further investigations may be made to find out why the behavior has persisted.

Kleptomaniacs are often unable to stop themselves from stealing, even if detection is likely.

Kleptomania is associated with apparently purposeless stealing. Other conditions can also produce a temporary compulsion to steal, but this behavior is not true kleptomania.

Small children often steal, partly for gain but also because of imperfectly formed ideas of what is "mine" and "not mine." Their moral sense is surprisingly poorly developed before the age of 10. Slightly older children sometimes steal because they are unable to control the desire to possess things.

Adolescents may go through periods in which they steal. This can be either simply to prove their own ability to go against adult wishes, or to win approval from their friends.

Depression, especially in middle-age, also causes episodes of theft, almost as a cry for help or attention. It is probably this phenomenon that has linked kleptomania, quite wrongly, with the image of the middle-aged or elderly woman standing dazed in the manager's office of the local supermarket, accused of stealing for the first time in her life.

None of these are instances of true kleptomania, and the treatment, if required, will usually be different.

Knee

Q Why do I get a tender swelling in front of my knee after kneeling to wash the kitchen floor?

A This is a form of bursitis, an inflammatory swelling of the bursae at the front of the knee. You have probably noticed that the inflammation dies down with rest but flares up again whenever you kneel for any extended period of time. Try not to aggravate the condition, and when you do any work that involves kneeling, use rubber kneeling pads or towels to ease the pressure on your knees.

Q My son injured his knee while playing football at school. It swelled and became very stiff. Why was this?

A The inflammatory response to injury involves a large outpouring of fluid into the tissues, resulting in a swollen joint and stiffness. This condition can often be improved by a doctor draining some of the fluid.

Q Sometimes my knee will not straighten out. I am told I have a loose body in the joint. What does this mean?

A Any solid material in a joint can limit its range of movement. In the case of the knee, the loose body can be a bit of cartilage, or a chip of bone that may have broken free. Diagnosis is made by X-ray examination and arthroscopy. Surgery may be necessary if the loose body does not get reabsorbed naturally.

Q When I had a checkup, the doctor tested my knee reflexes. How do they work?

A The tendon over the kneecap has tension-sensing nerves in it. These run up to the spinal cord, but not the brain, then directly down to stimulate the muscles in the thigh. This feedback insures that the nerves work properly. If the tension is suddenly increased by tapping the tendon below the kneecap, the muscles will contract automatically, producing the knee jerk.

Because the knees are so important to movement, any injury or disorder can render a person immobile. Fortunately, with modern surgical and medical treatment, permanent disability is rare.

The knee is the joint situated between the thighbone (the femur) and the shinbone (the tibia). It is designed to allow great flexibility of movement, yet still be strong and stable enough to hold the body upright.

Structure and function

To allow easy movement, the knee joint is constructed like a hinge. The end of the femur is smoothly rounded off and rests comfortably into the saucer-shaped top of the tibia. The surfaces of the bones are covered with a shiny, white, and hard substance called cartilage (see Cartilage).

To stabilize the joint further, yet still allow flexibility of movement, two leaves of cartilage lie in the joint space on either side of the knee. These are the bits of cartilage that get torn in sports injuries and may be removed in a cartilage operation on the knee. Without them the knee can still function, but wear and tear seems to increase so that a person may develop arthritis later on in life (see Arthritis).

To lubricate the joint the surfaces are all bathed in a very slippery liquid called synovial fluid (see Joints). This is made, and held, in the joint by a capsule that surrounds the whole knee area. There are also additional bags of fluid called bursae that lie in the joint and act as cushions against severe stresses.

Strength and stability are provided by fibrous bands called ligaments (see Ligaments). Without hindering the hinge movement of the knee, these ligaments lie on both sides and in the middle of the joint and hold it firmly in place.

The movements of the knee joint are governed by muscles within the thigh (see Muscles). Those at the front pull the knee straight and those at the back hinge it backward. At the top these muscles are attached to the hip and the top of the thighbone (the femur). Farther down the leg they condense into fibrous tendons that cross over the knee (see Tendons) and are then attached to the shinbone (the tibia).

Front view (left) shows the bones of the knee joint. The section (right) shows the structure in detail, including the bursae.

Structure of the knee

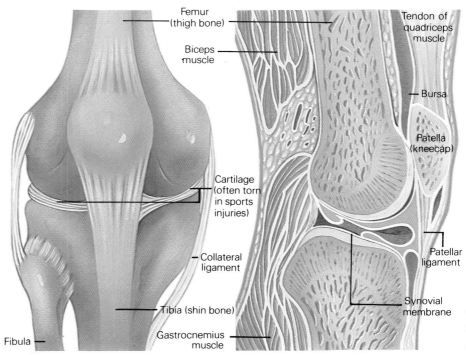

Femur (thigh bone)

Biceps muscle

Cartilage (often torn in sports injuries)

Collateral ligament

Tibia (shin bone)

Fibula

Gastrocnemius muscle

Tendon of quadriceps muscle

Bursa

Patella (kneecap)

Patellar ligament

Synovial membrane

Sue Dandre

KNEE

To prevent the tendon at the front from rubbing the joint as it moves, a bone has been built into the tendon. This bone is called the kneecap, or patella, and lies on the tendon itself; that is, it is unattached to the rest of the knee. The kneecap runs up and down the bottom of the femur in a cartilage-lined groove and is lubricated by synovial fluid. There are also two additional bursae that act as the shock absorbers for the kneecap.

The knee joint is traversed by blood vessels that nourish the ligaments, cartilages, capsule, and bones. Also, as with all important structures, nerves run to the knee so that the brain can know the exact position of the joint to coordinate balance and movement (see Balance).

The knee is important principally for locomotion (see Movement). At every step it bends to allow the leg to move forward without hitting the ground, otherwise the leg would have to be swung outward by tilting the pelvis, as in the typical stiff leg walk. To complete the step, the knee is straightened and the foot brought back to the ground by movement at the hip.

Treatment of injuries

Twists and sprains are common knee injuries caused by excessive forces stretching the knee joint ligaments. The knee swells, becomes stiff, and the injured ligament feels tender. On the whole sprains get better by themselves with rest and gentle remobilization (see Sprains). An elasticized bandage, applied in a figure eight (see Bandages), will give good support to the knee initially, and a walking stick can help take the weight off the leg. In a severe ligament injury, the knee may need to be put in a plaster cast.

Either of the two leaves of cartilage in the joint space may get torn by a sudden twist of the knee; the knee locks, will not straighten, and also tends to give way. Nature often sorts this problem out, but if the symptoms persist or recur, the doctor will refer the patient to an orthopedic specialist (see Orthopedics). In the hospital the diagnosis is usually confirmed by arthroscopy (see Endoscopy). An arthroscope is a fine telescope that is actually fed through a small cut into the joint. The torn cartilage can be seen through it and minor repairs can be performed by remote control. For more serious injuries it may be necessary to remove the cartilage completely. However, the muscles will gradually strengthen to compensate for this loss.

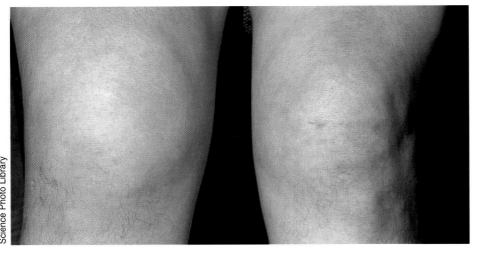

Increased fluid in the knee (far left), called knee effusion, often affects those who play contact sports, such as football players (below). There may be swelling of the joint and loss of bone tissue around the kneecap.

Dislocation of the kneecap may result from a sideways knee injury. The kneecap is pulled out of its groove and the patient is unable to straighten the knee (see Dislocation). Treatment consists of pushing the patella back into place, followed by a period of rest. However, the dislocation may recur with only minor stresses on the joint, in which case surgery may be necessary.

Severe injuries can break the bones at the knee, with the result that the knee cannot bear weight and is very swollen and painful. The definite diagnosis is made by X-ray examination (see X ray). Surgical correction may be necessary, followed by a prolonged period in a cast.

Prevention

In view of the knees' importance for mobility, it is not surprising that knee injuries are very disabling, and it makes sense to take precautions to avoid them.

Before any sporting activity is undertaken, it is essential to warm up by stretching the major muscle groups before starting each exercise program. Jogging or bicycling—small distances at first—are good for building up the knee muscles. Although jogging can put incredible stress on the knees, the risk of injury can be minimized by a very gentle build-up to the exercise.

Other problems

As opposed to the sudden loss of function following injury, many people find their joints getting stiff and painful with progressing age. In general, stiffness is a sign that the muscles need to be stretched. Morning stiffness that improves as the day progresses is typical of rheumatoid arthritis (see Rheumatoid arthritis). It may also be caused by a previous injury.

Anti-inflammatory drugs should relieve pain, but if the arthritis becomes crippling, a knee replacement operation may be necessary (see Joint replacement).

After persistent, unexpected activity the bursae may get inflamed, a condition called bursitis (see Bursitis). The knee swells in the area of the affected bursae. Fortunately bursitis settles with rest, but it does tend to recur from time to time.

Injury or surgery will put the knee out of use for a time, with the risk of muscle wasting. Thus physical therapy forms an important part of aftercare. It is this aftercare, together with advances in orthopedic surgery, treatment, and diagnostic instruments that makes it unnecessary to be permanently disabled by a stiff knee.

The fine motor skills used in ballet depend on the smooth movement of all the joints, especially the knees. Injuries must be treated promptly, followed by physical therapy.

Zefa

Lacerations

Q My husband had his spleen removed after a laceration in a car crash. Why wasn't the laceration just repaired?

A It is easier and safer to remove the organ than to try to repair a laceration. However, the spleen plays an important role in immune protection. Removal of this organ could cause a fatal infection that would otherwise have been prevented.

Q I lacerated my hand and severed a nerve. The surgeons stitched the nerve together but there is still a numb area. Why is this?

A When a nerve is completely severed, only the most central portion of it, with a cell body, survives. New fibers will grow out from this living portion, and the severed nerve ends are stitched together to guide these new fibers down the course of the old nerve. This is a slow process, and it may be months before the fibers grow all the way and sensation returns.

Q I am expecting my first baby soon. I have heard that an episiotomy is almost routine now. I don't like the idea of having one. Is this procedure absolutely necessary?

A An episiotomy (a surgical incision at the opening of the vagina) is by no means routine, but is done only when necessary. The object is to prevent vaginal tearing, which, in a tight delivery, may be more extensive and damaging than the controlled incision of an episiotomy. You should discuss this with your obstetrician.

Q When I hurt my hand while gardening, my doctor said I must have an antitetanus shot. Why was this?

A The organism that causes tetanus (*Clostridium tetani*) is found in soil. It causes disease by producing a toxin that affects the nervous system, and it tends to grow in deep wounds or those in which there is a large area of damaged tissue.

Lacerations are wounds where the skin is torn rather than cut. As it takes great force to tear the skin, lacerations are often serious. Internal organs can suffer laceration, too. First aid and prompt medical treatment are essential.

Wounds (see Wounds) are traditionally divided into five kinds—scratches, abrasions, cuts, lacerations, and puncture wounds. The distinction between cuts and lacerations is often unclear, but in general a cut is a neat incision through the skin, usually caused by a sharp object, such as a knife or piece of broken glass, whereas a laceration is usually caused by a blunt instrument, leaving a ragged wound with crushing and bruising of the surrounding tissue. However, many doctors use the word *laceration* to describe all sorts of cuts.

The damage a laceration inflicts depends on the area of the body involved. Lacerations of the hand, for instance, frequently involve damage to the tendons or nerves. On the arms and legs, the impact that causes a laceration may be enough to break a bone. This sort of injury needs immediate medical attention, because if

bone is exposed to the air it can become infected, making the injury worse.

Scalp lacerations bleed profusely because of the rich blood supply to the head, but this good blood supply also means they tend to heal more quickly. Lacerations involving the eyelids or lips need careful treatment not to spoil the person's looks.

Internal damage

The term *laceration* is also applied to the damage sustained by internal organs in major injuries, lacerations of the spleen and liver, for instance. Such lacerations may occur in one of two ways. A violent compression, such as a kick in the abdomen, can cause a ragged tear and

The blood vessels near the surface of the skin are badly crushed, so there is little bleeding from this laceration.

A skin laceration

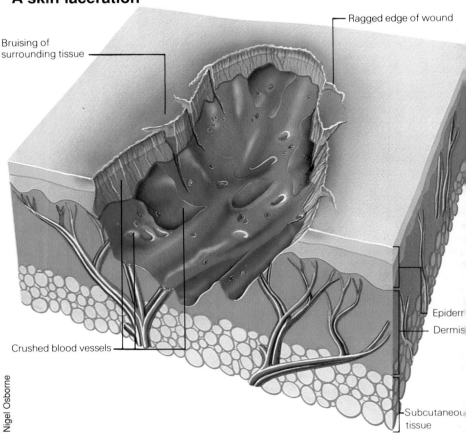

Bruising of surrounding tissue

Ragged edge of wound

Crushed blood vessels

Epidermis

Dermis

Subcutaneous tissue

Nigel Osborne

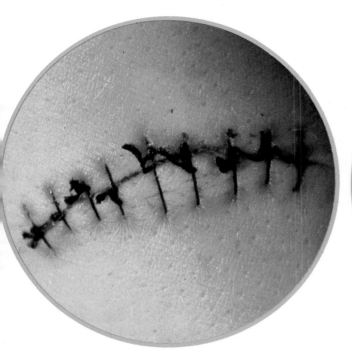
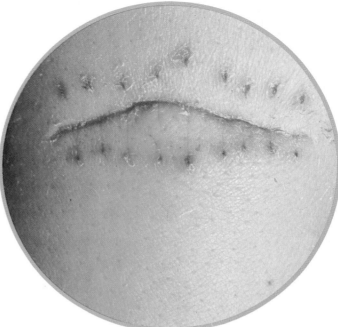

rofuse internal bleeding. A forceful
mpact, as in a car collision or a fall from
height, might well produce severe lac-
rations of major organs.

Lacerations of the vagina can occur
uring a difficult birth, if it is a breech
feetfirst) birth, for instance. If an epi-
otomy (a surgical cut across the muscle
urrounding the opening of the vagina;
ee Episiotomy) is not done, the risk of
aceration increases.

Lacerations usually have a ragged edge,
nd the surrounding skin is bruised. They
ay bleed less than expected, however,
ecause blood vessels are crushed.

Slanting blows may raise a flap of skin;
is is particularly likely to happen on the
calp. Lacerations on the hands are likely
o involve nerves or tendons, and this will
e indicated either by a loss of some
ovement, by a loss of some feeling, or
y a pins and needles sensation. Prompt
eatment is essential to restore function
nd avoid disability.

Liver and spleen lacerations are usually
dicated by a severe and constant pain
the abdomen, and in the case of a lac-
ation to the spleen there may also be a
ain in the shoulder. If the lacerations
e severe, there will be internal bleed-
g, and the patient will be in a state of
ock—the skin becoming cold and
ammy, and the pulse rapid and weak.
nmediate treatment with a blood trans-
usion is needed (see Hemorrhage).

In childbirth any laceration of the vagi-
a becomes evident immediately after
e delivery, with bright red bleeding
om the vagina. Vaginal tears are usually
paired immediately, and there are few
tereffects. However, if the cervix is
rn, this usually only requires repair if
e bleeding persists.

*This laceration needed stitches to close the
edges. A neat scar was left when the stitches
were removed 14 days later.*

TAKE CARE

What to do

- Call the local emergency service immediately
- Minor lacerations can be cleaned at home with antiseptic
- Take care not to do more damage. If bleeding is profuse, direct pressure over the wound with a gauze pad or other clean cloth for at least 10 minutes will usually control it (see Dressings)
- Avoid using a tourniquet; only use one when direct pressure on the wound makes no difference to the rate of blood loss
- Foreign bodies, such as grit or broken glass, are best left where they are for a doctor to treat
- If a fracture is suspected, cover the wound and keep the limb still until emergency services arrive
- Laceration of internal organs is usually indicated by a severe pain in the abdomen. If suspected, call an ambulance immediately. The patient should not have anything to eat or drink since an anesthetic may be needed

CAUTION: Do not try this without first consulting a doctor unless you are properly trained

---

Treatment

When no important structures have been
damaged, minor lacerations can be treated at home with an antiseptic solution,
insuring that any dirt is removed. A simple dry dressing is best, because antiseptic ointments left on the wound may
make it soggy and delay the healing
process (see Dressings).

If the laceration is more serious, the
patient should see the doctor at once, or
go to the local hospital's emergency
room. There the wound will be examined
to see if any underlying structures have
been damaged. If they are not the wound
will be cleaned and foreign material
removed. Stitches may be needed.

Where important areas have been damaged, the repair will be carried out in the
operating room. Sometimes lacerations
involve a considerable loss of skin, and a
skin graft may be needed to cover the
defect at a later date (see Grafting).

If internal injuries are suspected, an
intravenous infusion may be set up in
case a blood transfusion is needed.

Sometimes an abdominal tap will be
performed. A special needle is inserted
into the abdominal cavity to take a fluid
sample. Liver or spleen lacerations usually produce a bloody tap.

Outlook

Most surface lacerations heal within two
weeks. Some scar tissue is inevitable, but
usually this tissue becomes as strong as
intact skin, though it may take several
months to do so.

The outlook for internal lacerations
depends on the seriousness of the injury
and how quickly it is treated. Blood transfusion and early surgery to stem the
bleeding will prevent shock setting in.

Laparoscopy

Q What happens to the gas that is used to distend the stomach to give the surgeon carrying out a laparoscopy a good view of the internal organs? Where does it go?

A Most of the gas is allowed to escape through the place in the abdominal wall where the laparoscope was inserted. Any remaining gas will be rapidly absorbed into the bloodstream.

Q I have heard that intrauterine contraceptive devices are sometimes removed with a laparoscope. Surely they are normally removed through the vagina?

A Occasionally the device may burrow through the wall of the uterus into the pelvic cavity. When this happens it may be removed with a laparoscope.

Q Can a laparoscopy be performed on a man?

A Yes, if one is needed to view the gallbladder or the liver. However, its most common use is in gynecology.

Q Will a laparoscopy upset my periods?

A It can affect them for a short time, especially if performed at the same time as a D&C (dilatation and curettage).

Q I have been told that I must have a laparoscopy for a suspected ovarian cyst. Will it leave a scar?

A Yes, but since this is usually only about 0.75 in (2 cm) long and situated at the navel, it will probably be almost invisible.

Q I read that certain people are unsuited to this technique. Is this true?

A It can be difficult to carry out this operation on very fat patients, on patients with scars on their lower abdomen, or if the patient has a large mass of tissue, such as fibroids, in the abdomen.

The technique of laparoscopy makes it possible for a surgeon to view the inside of the abdomen without major surgery. Its most common use is in gynecology.

Laparoscopy is a technique that was developed relatively recently. It involves viewing the inside of the abdomen through a rod-shaped instrument called a laparoscope; this contains lenses attached to a light (see Endoscopy).

This instrument has gradually become more sophisticated, so that surgeons are now able to pass fine instruments through the laparoscope to perform small abdominal operations. It is most commonly used in gynecology, although it is sometimes used in other branches of surgery (see Gynecology).

Laparoscopy allows a very clear view of the fallopian tubes, uterus, and ovaries. This has made it very useful in diagnosing various gynecological diseases, such as pelvic infection and ovarian cysts, thus enabling correct treatment to be given. It is also invaluable as a means of checking that gynecological complaints, such as endometriosis (tissue resembling the lin-ing of the uterus that grows outside the uterus; see Endometriosis) and ovarian cancer, are responding to treatment.

As a test for infertility caused by blocked fallopian tubes, it is also possible to send dye into the uterus to see if it spills out of the fallopian tubes into the abdominal cavity. (If it does it can be seen to do so through the laparoscope, and this means that the passages that allow the egg and sperm to meet are open; see Infertility.) At the same time a specimen of the lining of the uterus can be removed by D&C (see Dilatation and curettage) and examined under a microscope to see if the woman is ovulating.

There are three other common reasons for carrying out a laparoscopy. These are

The abdomen is inflated with gas (top), then the laparoscope is inserted (below) to illuminate the reproductive organs. (The operating table is tilted at this stage.)

Laparoscopy in progress

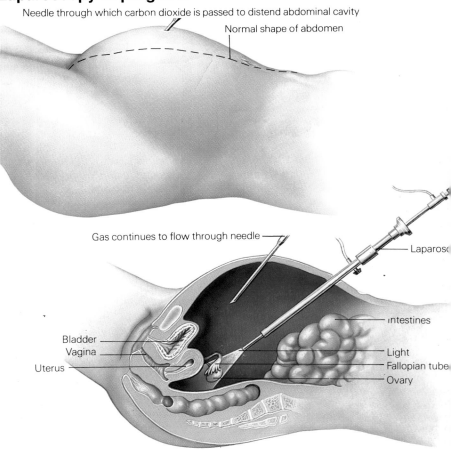

Needle through which carbon dioxide is passed to distend abdominal cavity

Normal shape of abdomen

Gas continues to flow through needle

Laparosc

intestines

Bladder

Vagina

Uterus

Light

Fallopian tube

Ovary

Uses of laparoscopy in gynecology

Problem	Causes	Use of laparoscopy
Endometriosis (tissue from the lining of the uterus growing in other parts of the abdomen)	Not fully known	To see if this condition has been cured by hormone treatment. If deposits are small they can be removed by means of the laparoscope
Infertility	Abnormal reproductive organs	Gives a view of reproductive organs so that they can be checked for abnormality
	Failure to ovulate	Check can be made on whether the egg has been released from ovary
	Blocked or damaged fallopian tubes	Dye can be passed through the neck of the uterus to check whether the passages that allow egg and sperm to meet are open. Eggs to be fertilized may be aspirated (sucked out) through the laparoscope for in vitro fertilization (test-tube baby)
Lower abdominal pain or pain during intercourse	Ovarian cyst	If uncomplicated cyst may be drained through the laparoscope
	Pregnancy outside the uterus	This shows up through the laparoscope
	Infection	Shows up through the laparoscope
Ovarian cancer	Abnormal increase in rate of cell division results in tumor	A check can be made to see if operation to remove tumor has been successful and that no new tumor has formed
Reversal of sterilization (assessment procedure)		To check whether entire fallopian tube has been removed and whether it is possible to rejoin the tubes
Sterilization		The laparoscope can be used to burn a portion of the fallopian tubes or to place clips on them

the navel. The laparoscope illuminates the cavity and makes it relatively easy to inspect the contents.

Some laparoscopes contain a small side channel through which fine surgical instruments can be passed to allow minor operations to be performed. For instance, where a certain type of infertility is involved, scissors may be passed down the laparoscope and used to divide any filmy bands of tissue that may be preventing the eggs from moving down the fallopian tubes. In other cases a needle may be passed through the instrument to suck fluid out of simple cysts in the ovary. For sterilization, forceps may also be passed into the cavity and used to grip the fallopian tubes. It is then possible to send an electric current down the forceps and thereby cut the tubes. Clips can also be used to separate the tubes. Using the same technique it is possible to remove small portions of abnormally situated uterine cells (endometriosis) that may have caused pain in the lower abdomen.

When the laparoscope does not have this side channel to allow these small operations to be carried out, a second small incision may be made in the abdominal wall and another small hollow tube inserted, through which operating instruments can be passed. In either case the surgeon can view the operation as he or she performs it.

After the operation has been completed, the patient may feel bruised around the abdominal area, but this usually lasts only a short time. The patient generally feels fit enough to return to normal activity after about 48 hours.

o determine the cause of pelvic pain without performing a major exploratory operation; to investigate the cause of absent periods; and to perform sterilization operations.

What is involved

Laparoscopy is usually performed under general anesthetic, although occasionally only a local anesthetic is administered (see Anesthetics).

After the anesthetic has been given, a needle is inserted into the front of the lower abdominal wall, and carbon dioxide is passed through this to distend the abdominal cavity. The operating table on which the patient is lying is then tilted, in order that the patient is lying head downward. This means that most of the abdominal organs find their way into the upper part of the gas-enlarged cavity, where they are not in danger of being pierced by the laparoscope and do not obstruct the view of the pelvis. The laparoscope is then inserted through a small incision at

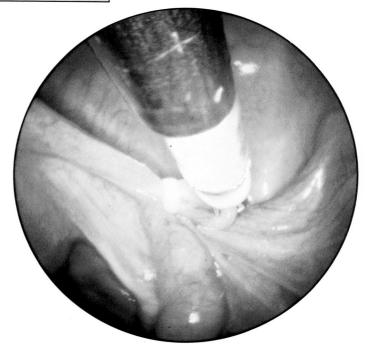

What the surgeon sees through the laparoscope. This magnified view shows the clear illumination of the patient's fallopian tube and also a part of the ovary.

Laparotomy

Q How large is the cut in a laparotomy? I am worried about the size of the scar that will be left.

A Surgeons always take great care to keep scars as small as possible. However, the incision must be large enough for the surgeon to get his or her hand into it and reach into all parts of the abdominal cavity, so very tiny scars are not possible. Generally laparotomy scars are about 4–8 in (10–20 cm) long.

Q I don't like the idea of somebody probing about in my inside and chopping bits out without my permission. Can I refuse to let them do it?

A Your surgeon will discuss with you in advance what he or she thinks your problem will be and what must be done to correct it. Based on this discussion you will be asked to sign a consent form giving him or her permission to do as much, or as little, as you choose. He or she will do no more than you allow, and you do retain the right to refuse permission for any procedure. You should always get a second opinion before consenting to any major operation.

Q I have heard that a patient is automatically put on a catheter to get rid of urine after a laparotomy. Is this true?

A No, it isn't. If the necessary surgery is restricted to organs such as the spleen, gallbladder, or stomach, in the majority of cases a catheter (a tube passed into the bladder to drain it) will not be necessary. However, if the kidneys, bladder, or pelvic organs are involved, a catheter may temporarily be necessary.

Q Is it safe to carry out a laparotomy on a child?

A In general, laparotomy is needed less frequently for children than it is for adults. When it does have to be carried out, the risk is little different from that involved in any abdominal operation, nowadays very low.

This procedure enables a surgeon to see and feel a patient's internal organs and thereby make an accurate diagnosis of what is wrong.

A laparotomy is the procedure in which a vertical incision is made through the wall of the abdomen into the abdominal cavity. It enables a surgeon to investigate or explore a patient's symptoms. The procedure is only resorted to when all the other less invasive procedures that do not require an operation, such as an X ray examination or a blood or urine test, have failed to reveal what is wrong with the person concerned.

Once the internal organs have been exposed to view, and the trouble has been identified, the necessary surgical treatment, usually a matter of repair or removal, is carried out immediately. This will often save the patient a second operation. Surgery may involve repairing a hole in an organ, removing a diseased area that is beyond repair, or disposing of a cancerous growth.

Although all laparotomies start off in broadly the same way, they can involve a wide range of surgical procedures.

When a laparotomy is needed

Persistent or repeated attacks of abdominal pain is the most common symptom that may make a laparotomy necessary. Other reasons for it may be recurrent vomiting, nausea, intestinal upset, or an unexplained abdominal swelling that could be due to a cancerous growth.

Abdominal emergencies

When the abdomen has been badly injured, perhaps by a severe blow in a traffic accident, there is a possibility of internal bleeding or of serious damage to an internal organ; a laparotomy is often carried out to assess the extent of the damage, seal off torn blood vessels, and to remove any tissue damaged beyond the possibility of repair.

When a patient develops severe abdominal pains, and possibly other symptoms of serious internal trouble, and the likely cause—appendicitis, a burst peptic ulcer, or a gynecological condition, for example—is not apparent, an operation is necessary to discover what is wrong and to correct it before there is further deterioration. A large number of operations in which the appendix is removed start off as laparotomies (see Appendicitis).

In some cases a laparotomy may be no more than a relatively minor procedure. In other cases it may turn into major surgery, followed by a blood transfusion and a period of intensive care. The long term outlook will, of course, depend on what the laparotomy reveals.

When pain and other internal symptoms do not provide unmistakable clues to the cause of a disorder, a laparotomy makes detailed internal investigation possible.

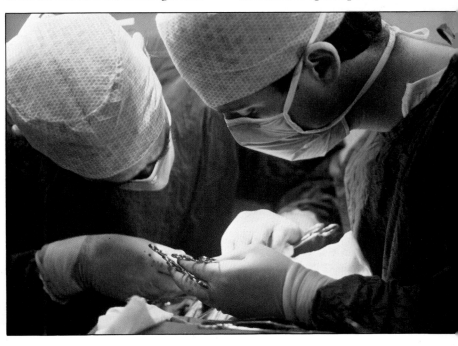

Larynx and laryngitis

Q My husband keeps coughing and clearing his throat. He says it is a smoker's cough, but he is also hoarse. What should he do?

A It sounds as if your husband has chronic (long-term) laryngitis from smoking. He should cut down on smoking, and preferably give up altogether, if there is to be any improvement. Because he has had the condition for some time, it is essential that he see a doctor. It is possible he is developing cancer of the larynx, and to postpone treatment is to risk the spread of a disease that is curable in its early stages.

Q I've just heard a person who had his larynx removed talking on the radio. How can he manage to speak?

A He is using what the experts call esophageal speech. The esophagus is the tube that takes food down to the stomach, and what this person does is swallow air, so that it passes down to the stomach, then belch it up, controlling the amount released, and the sounds produced, by means of the esophagus. With practice people can become skillful at this type of speech and can express themselves clearly, although they do have a rather unusual voice.

Q Can my larynx get tired? My voice seems to crack after a lot of conversation.

A The larynx does get tired, like any other organ, especially if overused. This means shouting, screaming, or singing for too long, or talking for hours on end, particularly in a dry or smoky atmosphere.

In fact, what you describe is a mild laryngitis or irritation of the vocal cords within the larynx. The cure is to stop talking completely for a few hours. You could also try inhaling steam, with a soothing aromatic preparation added. Boil the kettle, then pour the hot water into a jug or bowl. Don't try inhaling steam directly from a kettle; you could burn your mouth and throat.

The larynx contains the vocal cords, so any disorders will affect speech. However, most conditions of the larynx can be completely cured by early treatment.

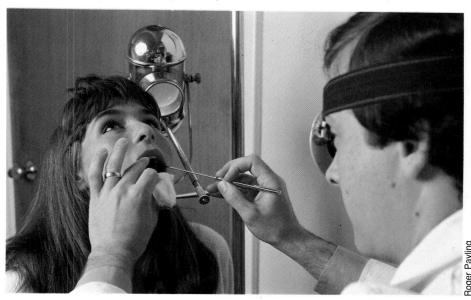

Roger Payling

The larynx cannot be seen easily because of its position in the throat. Doctors use a special technique in order to view it.

The larynx, or voice box, contains the vocal cords that vibrate to produce speech. As such it is an extremely delicate instrument. Together with the epiglottis it also guards the entrance to the lungs.

When we eat or drink, the epiglottis closes tightly over the opening to the larynx so that food or liquids slide over it down into the esophagus, which leads into the stomach (see Hiccups). When we breathe, the larynx is, of course, open.

Position and structure

The larynx is placed at about the center of the neck, at the top of the windpipe (trachea), out of sight around the corner of the back of the throat.

The larynx is essentially a specialized section of the windpipe with an external sheath of cartilage. Positioned over it is the epiglottis, the flap-valve that comes down from the back of the throat to cover the opening into the larynx, called the glottis. The action of the epiglottis is automatically controlled by the brain, but it sometimes fails, and then liquids or food particles go down the wrong way. Unless a lump of food is so large that it sticks in one of the passages below the larynx, it will be coughed up.

The voice

The vocal cords are mounted on specially shaped pieces of cartilage within the larynx. Air breathed out over them makes them vibrate, which produces sound. The cartilages move in order to tighten or relax the cords, producing high- or low-pitched sound (see Vocal cords).

However, the quality of sound produced is also strongly influenced by the nature and action of the tongue, lips, and jaw, because the sound waves resonate (bounce) around the adjacent passages.

Injury to the larynx

If the larynx is injured, by a blow or a knife wound, for example, it may become blocked; similarly, scalding liquids or poisons can burn and irritate its lining, which may in turn cause swelling and blockage. The difficulty in breathing and the pain of such injuries usually disable the patient severely.

In such cases it is vital to restore the airflow to the lungs, and this is usually done in the hospital. It may be possible for a tube to be passed down the windpipe (trachea), creating a new artificial passage; or it may be necessary to make a hole in the trachea below the larynx so that air can pass directly to the lungs. This procedure is called a tracheostomy (see Tracheostomy).

Acute laryngitis

Acute laryngitis means inflammation of the larynx caused by an infection, such as

a cold or influenza, or by overuse of the voice (typically shouting or singing), or by irritation, usually through smoking.

The sufferer either has difficulty speaking and has a hoarse and throaty voice, or else the voice disappears completely. There is pain in the larynx, and tenderness is often felt in the region.

It is an irritating but not dangerous condition, and it passes if the voice is given a complete rest, which means no speaking for as long as it takes for the condition to correct itself (normally a day or two). Inhaling hot steamy air with a soothing additive can help; antibiotics help only rarely.

Chronic laryngitis

Chronic laryngitis is laryngitis that occurs over a long period of time. Its cause is always irritation, mostly of the sort caused by violent shouting. Tobacco smoke and dust and overuse of the voice are also common causes. Continued hoarseness may also be a symptom of cancer of the larynx. However, whatever

Mild laryngitis can be relieved by steam inhalation from a soothing preparation in boiling water, with the head covered.

Disorders of the larynx and their treatment

Disorder and cause	Symptoms	Treatment
Injury by any of the obvious causes, particularly burns from scalding liquids	Sudden pain; difficulty in breathing; harsh, hoarse cough or croup	Urgent medical attention. Tracheostomy (an opening made in the windpipe) may be needed to save life in severe cases
Acute laryngitis (short-term hoarseness and soreness) caused by bacterial or viral infection	Sore larynx; difficulty in speaking or loss of voice	Strict voice-rest; steamy inhalations; possibly antibiotics
Chronic laryngitis (any hoarseness that lasts more than 10 days), usually caused by too much smoking, or dust, or overuse of voice	Hoarseness; constant frog in the throat; occasionally tenderness in the larynx or adjacent areas	Specialist examination to exclude the possibility of cancer; strict voice-rest; removal of the irritant
Diphtheria (the severe, mainly childhood disease that has now been virtually eliminated by mass vaccination)	Sore throat, fever, coughing; the tell-tale sign is a web over the larynx, caused by white blood cells and other substances produced in response to inflammation	If severe a tracheostomy is required; antibiotics. Immunization would have prevented the disease
Laryngotracheobronchitis. Caused by a virus or bacteria, or occasionally by an allergy	The larynx suddenly becomes swollen; severe cough or croup; difficulty in breathing	Urgent hospital treatment; possibly antibiotics; steamy inhalations and moist atmosphere; tracheostomy in some cases
Benign tumor (a lump or growth that will not spread). These are described as polyps or nodes, and their cause is abuse of the voice—too much singing, shouting, or even loud talking, as, for example, in teaching	Hoarseness that develops gradually	Removal of polyp or node. This provides a complete cure, but speech training may be required to prevent recurrence
Cancer of the larynx. The majority of cases are males aged between 50–69, and a high proportion of them are heavy smokers	Hoarseness becoming progressively worse over several weeks. Difficulty in breathing or swallowing. Coughing blood and often a sticky mucus that necessitates constant clearing of the throat. Pain in the throat, ears, and enlarged glands in the vicinity of the larynx occurs when the condition is established	Radiotherapy, or surgery if the case requires it. Recovery excellent; speech therapy, if the larynx is removed, will be needed to teach the patient to speak with the esophagus (the tube leading down to the stomach) and to breathe through a tracheostomy

Roger Payling

he cause, chronic laryngitis should lways be reported to a doctor.

Cancer of the larynx

This type of cancer is 10 times more common in men than in women, and most common in heavy smokers.

It arises in the cells of the larynx, and ts initial symptom is hoarseness lasting everal weeks. A dry cough follows, and occasionally coughing up flecks of blood, followed some weeks later by swallowing and breathing difficulties.

Untreated, this can end in death. If detected soon enough, it can be completely cured by radiotherapy (see Radiotherapy). More severe cases require removal of the larynx. The patient learns o speak again using his or her esophagus, and to breathe with the help of a permanent tracheostomy. Alternatively an lectronic artificial larynx may be used.

Polyps and nodes

Polyps are tiny lumps attached to tissue by a stalk, similar to a berry. If they develop on the vocal cords as a result of long-term vocal abuse, they cause hoarseness and a breathy quality of the voice. Vocal cord nodes (sometimes called singer's or

Front and side views of the larynx (right). The tracheostomy (below) is an emergency operation that restores breathing. An incision is made in the larynx and air pumped into the lungs.

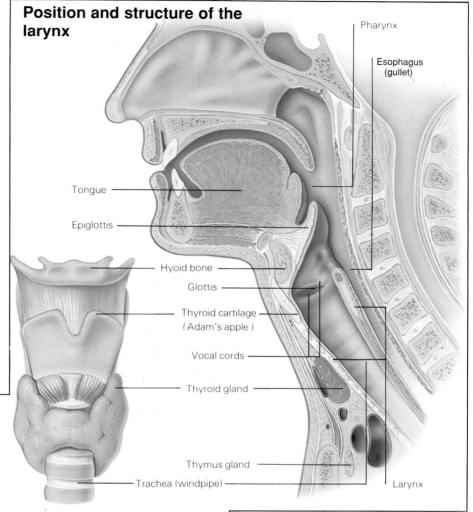

Position and structure of the larynx

Pharynx

Esophagus (gullet)

Tongue

Epiglottis

Hyoid bone

Glottis

Thyroid cartilage (Adam's apple)

Vocal cords

Thyroid gland

Thymus gland

Trachea (windpipe)

Larynx

Mike Courteney

A tracheostomy

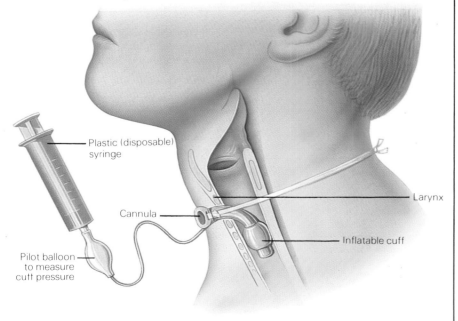

Plastic (disposable) syringe

Cannula

Pilot balloon to measure cuff pressure

Larynx

Inflatable cuff

teacher's nodes) are also lumps, and develop from long-term abuse. They both need to be removed surgically.

Laryngeal diphtheria

Diphtheria used to be greatly feared, but today it has been almost eradicated by vaccination (see Vaccinations). However, it can still occur, particularly among young children, and is extremely contagious (see Diphtheria).

If contracted, diphtheria tends to spread via the throat, which, with the larynx, becomes sore and inflamed. In response to the inflammation, a sticky, grayish, false membrane or skin forms across the larynx and obstructs the airway.

Without an emergency tracheostomy and appropriate antibiotics given urgently, death can occur from suffocation caused by obstruction to the airway.

Laryngotracheobronchitis

This is the technical name for croup, the dry, distinctive-sounding cough caused when inflammation narrows the larynx.

Q Is it true that cancer of the larynx can now be completely cured?

A Indeed it is. If the cancer is detected early enough, it can be cured with radiotherapy. This is a controlled dose of radioactive rays delivered to the area of the cancerous tumor. This kills the malignant cells and, provided the cancer has not spread too far, this treatment can effect a complete cure. In these cases there is no need to remove the whole larynx unless the condition is comparatively advanced.

Q My neighbor's three-year-old contracted croup the other day and was rushed to the hospital, because it was feared he would be unable to breathe. Why was this?

A Your neighbor's child was almost certainly rushed to the hospital because he was so young. In children under the age of five, croup can be dangerous because the larynx is so small. If it becomes inflamed, which is what happens in croup, the airway narrows, and there is a danger of suffocation. This is why emergency treatment is needed.

Q My husband's doctor has referred him to the hospital for a specialist examination of the larynx. Why should this be necessary when the doctor said that he had laryngitis?

A Your husband's doctor was acting properly. Laryngitis is not a serious condition and usually clears up of its own accord if the voice is rested. However, its initial symptom, hoarseness, is the same as that of cancer of the larynx.

Although a serious disease, this can be cured completely if diagnosed early. However, this involves examining the larynx closely. Since the organ is situated out of sight around the corner of the throat, a special technique is required to view it, and specialist skill. Sometimes, too, a person cannot tolerate anything near the back of the throat, in which case an anesthetic may be required if the larynx is to be seen at all.

Such inflammation is frequently caused by bacteria, but it may also be caused by a virus. The larynx, trachea, and bronchi (the airways leading to the lungs) become so inflamed and swollen—and a sticky, heavy mucus is formed—that the air supply is in considerable danger of being cut off.

If the case is severe, a tracheostomy is once again necessary. Milder cases respond to oxygen, antibiotics, and insuring that the atmosphere around the patient is warm and humid to soothe the inflamed areas.

Hoarseness

The nerve serving the vocal cords travels down into the chest before ascending to the larynx. So injury or disease affecting the chest can paralyze the vocal cords or produce hoarseness. For this reason hoarseness is a symptom that may be difficult to interpret, and you should not be unduly alarmed if your doctor refers you to the hospital for simple tests.

The number of disorders involving the larynx is relatively high, but today they can all be cured if their main symptom, hoarseness, is recognized early enough. For this reason any hoarseness lasting more than 10 days should be reported to your doctor without delay.

People who use their voices a great deal, like singers or teachers, are likely to get laryngitis or, in some cases, to develop polyps or nodes (tissue lumps) on their vocal cords.

Home treatment of laryngitis

If you are suffering from a short-lived hoarseness, loss of voice, or from pain felt deep in the throat:

- Don't speak any more than is absolutely necessary. Rest your voice; carry a notepad and pencil with you, and write messages to people, rather than talk to them
- Avoid dusty or smoky atmospheres. If you smoke, give it up, if possible for good
- Try inhaling steam from hot water in a jug or bowl (don't inhale directly from a boiling kettle since this could burn). An additive, such as lemon or honey, may make this more pleasant. A pharmacist will advise on other preparations available
- If you have been hoarse for more than 10 days, report this to your doctor without delay

Lasers

Q If I needed some form of laser treatment, could I be sure of getting it?

A Laser surgery is still in its relatively early stages, with one exception—the use of lasers to treat diabetic eye disease. If you are diabetic you could be fairly certain of receiving laser treatment if you needed it. Other forms of laser operation are rare, and since the operations can all be carried out in conventional ways, you will almost certainly be given conventional treatment unless you happen to go to a hospital where experimental laser work is being done. As lasers become more versatile and more compact, however, they will also become more generally used in hospitals.

Q Do all diabetics need to have laser treatment for their eyes?

A No. Only a small proportion will need this treatment. Diabetics have regular checkups, partly to keep abreast of any trouble with their eyes. As a result the treatment is usually started in good time, with excellent results.

Q Are the lasers used at pop concerts and other shows harmful to health?

A No. They are low-energy lasers and not harmful unless directed straight into the eyes at eye level.

Q I've heard that I could have the tattoo on the back of my hand removed using a laser. Is this correct?

A Yes, removing tattoos is one area in which lasers are of proven value.

Q If I have an operation on my ulcers carried out by laser is it likely to have any long-term effects?

A Aftereffects are rare and in any case are no different to those that may follow an operation carried out with conventional equipment.

The use of lasers in medicine and surgery is an exciting new development, still relatively experimental. Laser treatment of diabetic eye disease, however, already has an excellent success record.

A laser is a special type of light beam. All light carries energy, which in this scientific sense means the power to do work, typically by making heat. Laser beams are essentially light made to carry a great deal more energy than it does from conventional sources, such as the sun or domestic lamps.

Most of the lasers used in medicine are created in gas-filled tubes, working on a principle roughly similar to that of the fluorescent lamp.

Uses

All the different applications of lasers in medicine are made possible because the beam can be precisely directed onto a tiny area. Also of great importance is its ability to heat a tiny area without damaging a larger surrounding area.

This may sound disturbing but it is exactly what is required in the many

Laser treatment of diabetic eye disease (below) is now routine. The beam, directed onto individual diseased blood vessels on the retina (right), seals them as it cuts (seen here as separate spots).

instances where tissue is diseased. It is often far less drastic and less risky than cutting away tissue in the conventional medical way, using a scalpel or surgical knife (see Microsurgery).

Different types of laser are used on different types of tissue and for different surgical jobs. One form, called the argon laser (after the gas used in its production), specifically affects the red pigment in blood. This means that it can pass through certain tissues without damaging them, but if it encounters blood vessels, it heats them to the extent that they coagulate or harden.

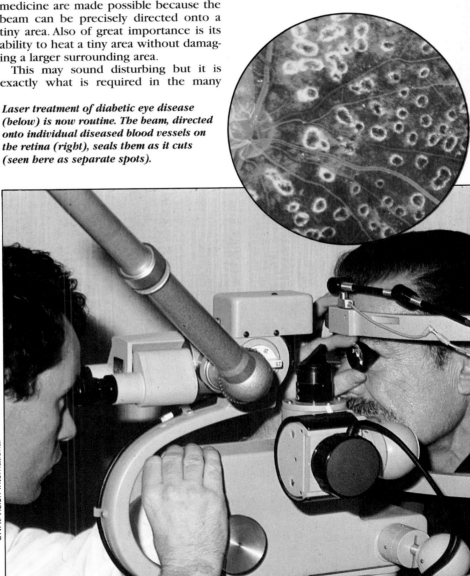

How a laser works

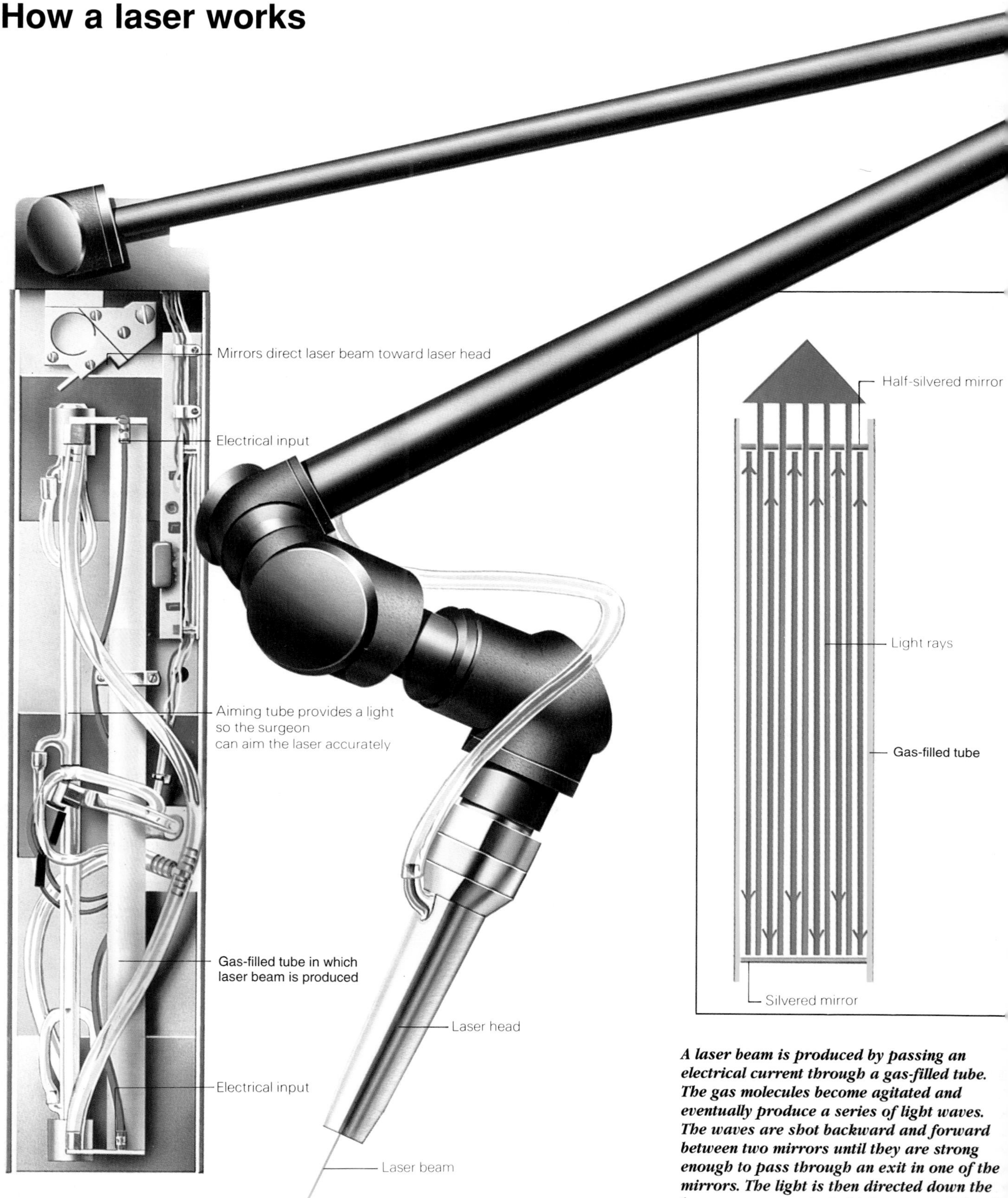

Mirrors direct laser beam toward laser head

Electrical input

Aiming tube provides a light
so the surgeon
can aim the laser accurately

Gas-filled tube in which
laser beam is produced

Electrical input

Laser head

Laser beam

Half-silvered mirror

Light rays

Gas-filled tube

Silvered mirror

*A laser beam is produced by passing an
electrical current through a gas-filled tube.
The gas molecules become agitated and
eventually produce a series of light waves.
The waves are shot backward and forward
between two mirrors until they are strong
enough to pass through an exit in one of the
mirrors. The light is then directed down the
laser arm, concentrated into a powerful and
fine laser beam by a mirror, and then
emitted from the laser head.*

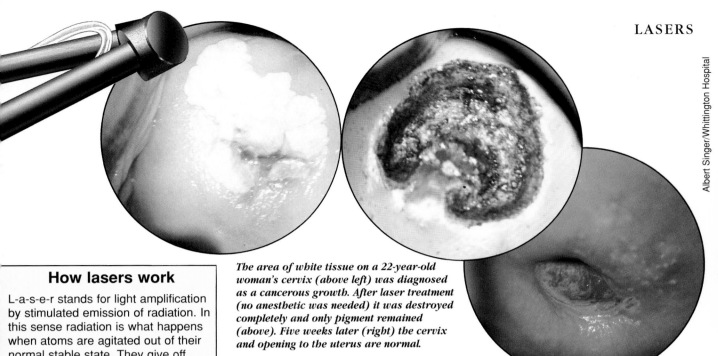

Albert Singer/Whittington Hospital

How lasers work

L-a-s-e-r stands for light amplification by stimulated emission of radiation. In this sense radiation is what happens when atoms are agitated out of their normal stable state. They give off some of their stored energy in the form of rays or waves.

In lasers, light is agitated or stimulated to produce radiation. For most medical lasers a gas-filled tube is used. An electric current passed through it agitates the gas atoms, just like in a fluorescent lamp. A domestic lamp produces ordinary light, while the type of gas used in a laser gives radiated light of a different nature, and indeed different properties according to the type of gas used. Carbon dioxide and argon are the principal gases used in medical lasers, but others are following fast.

The radiated light is reflected back and forth in the tube by a mirror at each end so that it collides with further gas atoms and stimulates them, too. The radiation is amplified in intensity, and escapes in a controlled beam through an exit in one of the mirrors.

All the radiated light so produced has a uniform wave pattern, with troughs and peaks of the waves in phase (lined up). This is a basic reason for the laser beam's tremendous strength.

Diabetic eye disease

The use of coagulating lasers is now well established in eye surgery, particularly as a means of treating the potentially serious eye problems suffered by long-term diabetics. In time the disease causes a deterioration in the blood vessels at the back of the eye. The danger is that these will start to bleed, in turn impairing or destroying the eyesight (see Diabetes).

The area of white tissue on a 22-year-old woman's cervix (above left) was diagnosed as a cancerous growth. After laser treatment (no anesthetic was needed) it was destroyed completely and only pigment remained (above). Five weeks later (right) the cervix and opening to the uterus are normal.

An argon laser shone through the lens of the eye, which has no blood vessels and thus remains unharmed, is directed onto the affected blood vessels. The blood within them coagulates and the bleeding stops, or is prevented from starting, and danger to the sight is averted.

This technique, called photocoagulation, affects the vision only in the restricted areas of the eye where the laser has done its work, and skillful use of the instrument usually leaves the patient's general vision intact.

Gastroscopic laser coagulation

Bleeding ulcers in the stomach and duodenum (the portion of intestine below the stomach) are a common medical problem (see Ulcers). They often occur in people whose health is generally not good, not least because of blood loss, and who would find a full operation under general anesthetic hard to tolerate.

The best treatment for these patients is a laser used in conjunction with a fiber-optic tube (see Endoscopy). This instrument, which is made of flexible material, can transmit either light or a laser beam along its length. The tube is passed down into the patient's stomach or duodenum via the throat, which can be done under only mild sedation. The surgeon can then locate the ulcer visually and direct the laser beam precisely onto it, coagulating the blood, and stopping the bleeding.

The laser knife

The other major type of laser used in surgery is the laser knife. This is produced using the gas carbon dioxide, and the resulting beam is capable of cutting through the cells that make up the skin and muscle tissue.

There is nothing new about using an instrument other than a knife to cut tissue; surgeons have been using a technique called diathermy for many years. This works by passing a high-frequency current through tissue that coagulates the ends of blood vessels as it cuts to reduce bleeding.

A laser is even better in this respect, because it affects less tissue around the cut. This means that, in removing an area of skin for example, a bed with plenty of healthy undamaged blood vessels is left around the affected tissue, which is essential for skin grafting (see Grafting).

Perhaps the most intriguing use of the carbon dioxide laser is for removing unwanted tattoos, which is achieved with minimum inflammation (see Tattooing). It is also effective in removing certain birthmarks and cancerous moles.

There are several other applications of the carbon dioxide laser under development, including mastectomy (removal of all or part of a breast), curing nearsightedness, and the vaporization of cervical cancer in its earliest stages.

Outlook

Naturally surgeons need to be certain that using a laser is better than the conventional method of incising (cutting) tissue. It is for this reason that lasers have not yet become fully established in surgery. Their main disadvantage is that the equipment tends to be bulky, and using laser light can damage the eyes if certain safety precautions are not taken. This aside, lasers remain an exciting and rapidly developing, but still largely experimental, field.

Laxatives

Q I am pregnant and I get terribly constipated. Should I take a laxative?

A No. First try increasing the amount of fiber in your diet; often this will do the trick. You should also increase your fluid intake and eat plenty of fruit. If this doesn't work, you should discuss the problem with a doctor when you visit the prenatal clinic.

Q Can you get addicted to taking laxatives?

A Yes. Doctors call this laxative abuse. Although it is not very common, it does tend to occur in younger and middle-aged women who start taking laxatives as a dieting aid. It is a dangerous practice because it may result in a disturbance of the body's chemistry. Patients do not usually admit to laxative abuse and this makes it difficult for the doctor to diagnose; consequently patients may harm themselves further.

Q My three-year-old son has discomfort when defecating and then he passes very hard feces. Should I give him a laxative?

A No. Laxatives should not be necessary for children, even if they are suffering from a little constipation as your son seems to be. In toddlers the best way of dealing with this problem is to increase the amount of fruit in their diet, and perhaps add some more roughage in the form of bran to what they are already eating.

Q My grandfather has been taking laxatives for years and now finds it difficult to defecate. Why is this?

A The laxatives most people take act by stimulating the intestine to contract. Over a prolonged period this may have the effect of poisoning the nerves in the intestine wall so that eventually it becomes very lazy. Your grandfather should see his doctor who may prescribe a remedy to soften the feces and therefore help relieve this problem.

Vast quantities of laxatives are taken by people living in Western society. However, it is better to treat constipation by including more roughage, such as bran, in the diet.

Laxatives are used in the treatment of constipation (see Constipation). With a balanced diet they should not be needed, and if taken for too long, may have serious side effects. It is important to remember that you do not have to defecate every day to maintain good health.

Bulk laxatives
Bulk laxatives are designed to increase the amount of vegetable fiber that passes through the intestines. The best example is bran, which comes from wheat germ.

It is now believed that intestinal problems, such as constipation and diverticular disease (inflammation of the intestine; see Diverticulitis) are related to a lack of fiber in the modern Western diet. Bulk laxatives help increase fiber intake. They can be taken as tablets or granules, or simply by eating whole grain bread, and by adding bran to breakfast cereals.

Ironically, commercial bulk laxatives are an expensive way of doing what could be done just as effectively by a change in diet.

Nonbulk laxatives
There are three types of nonbulk laxatives.

Stimulants such as castor oil and senna act on the nerves in the intestine wall and increase the power and frequency of peristalsis (see Alimentary canal). They can sometimes cause abdominal cramps and may permanently damage the intestine if used for too long.

Fecal softeners, such as mineral oil, soften the feces and make it easier and less painful for feces to pass through the rectum. Fecal softeners may sometimes irritate the anus and inhibit vitamin absorption for two reasons: they move the food through the intestines too quickly to be absorbed; and fat-based softeners inhibit absorbtion of fat-based vitamins.

Finally there are the osmotic laxatives, such as magnesium sulfate and Epsom salts, which work by drawing water into the intestine, thus making the feces softer and bulkier. These laxatives may cause stomach upsets in elderly people and in those suffering from kidney diseases.

All nonbulk laxatives should only be used on a doctor's recommendation.

Dangers
Nonbulk laxatives that stimulate the colon (large intestine), and are taken over several years tend to poison the nerve fibers in the

colon. As a result, the colon is unable to produce muscular contractions and move feces onward. Further stimulation is useless, and bulk laxatives only make matters worse. Osmotic laxatives may help.

Uses
When a patient has a painful anal condition, such as hemorrhoids and fissures (ulcers or lacerations of the skin), fecal softeners or osmotic laxatives can be of some use, though the long-term objective should be to increase fiber in the diet. Nonbulk laxatives are also used in forms of heart disease, such as angina, to prevent straining to defecate (see Heart disease).

Constipation and serious illness
Many drugs make people constipated, including powerful painkilling drugs, such as methadone. Also, being immobilized through illness, particularly when in the hospital, may induce constipation. Laxatives can be useful at these times.

Laxatives may also be used to clear the intestine before examinations, such as a barium enema (see Barium liquids), a colonoscopy (see Colon and colitis), before childbirth, and to prepare people for intestinal surgery.

Don't
- ever give a laxative to a constipated child: a change in his or her diet is often sufficient to relieve constipation
- ever use laxatives as dieting aids; they are of no value and may be addictive
- ever try to keep your intestines regular with such mixtures as senna pods in boiled water; like other drugs derived from plant sources, senna is potent and potentially dangerous
- ever use nonbulk laxatives, except on a doctor's advice
- ever use any laxative over a long period because it can have harmful consequences
- change to a diet that is high in fiber, if constipation persists. Ask your doctor's advice, particularly if other symptoms are present

Types of laxatives

Type	Action	Examples	Problems
Bulk laxatives	Act by making the feces more bulky; feces are passed more often and are easier to pass. A diet containing whole grain breads and similar foods has the same effect	Bran and other bulk fiber	Flatulence and abdominal distension may occur, but this usually settles down as the intestine becomes used to fiber
Nonbulk laxatives Stimulants	(take only on doctor's advice) Act by stimulating the nerves in the intestine wall	Senna; cascara; castor oil; figs, prunes	May cause abdominal cramps. Prolonged or regular use probably damages the intestine permanently
Osmotic	Act by drawing water into the intestines and therefore keeping the feces fluid	Magnesium sulfate (Epsom salts) and other magnesium salts; lactulose	Magnesium salts may upset the chemical balance in the bodies of older people or those with kidney disease
Fecal softeners	Soften the feces, making it easier to defecate	Mineral oil	May irritate anus and cause anal seepage. May also cause a lipid pneumonia and interfere with vitamin absorption

Laziness

Q My husband and I love to take part in all sports but our son is not in the least interested in them. Does this mean that it is his nature to be basically lazy?

A Not necessarily. Some people are naturally less interested in sports than others and prefer to put their time and energies into other things. It may also be that your son is a loner who will take to mountaineering or parachuting, or something of that sort, rather than to team sports.

Q My elderly father seems to have given up all interest in life. Has he just gotten lazy or is it a part of growing old?

A Old people are naturally less interested than they were in leading a highly active life, and are sometimes physically less able to do all that they used to do. Often, however, an underlying condition, such as arthritis, shortness of breath, or even unrecognized malnutrition, is limiting their activities unnecessarily and could be corrected. You should encourage your father to see his doctor for a routine checkup.

Q I am a 45-year-old housewife and I don't seem to be able to do nearly as much as I did 10 years ago. The family thinks that I have just gotten lazy. What can I do to resolve this problem?

A It may be that you have become lazy, but there are several other much more likely possibilities. You should first of all go to your doctor so that he or she can see if there is any underlying disorder, such as anemia, that is responsible for your lack of energy, and then correct it. Or it may be that you are beginning menopause and would benefit from HRT. It might also be a good idea to point out to the family that 20 years or so of housework and motherhood is hard work and that some extra help from them wouldn't hurt! Perhaps the laziness is in your family rather than in you!

When it is just a temporary disinclination to do anything active, laziness is an enjoyable restful, state. However, persistent laziness can be a sign of a physical or emotional problem, and it then has to be considered as a symptom of something, not merely a pleasure.

Laziness is often confused with both lethargy—which is actually drowsiness or sleepiness and lack of energy (see Lethargy)—and lassitude, which is fatigue and exhaustion (see Fatigue). Laziness as a disease, rather than a way of living, hardly ever exists on its own; it is usually part of a more widespread condition.

Views of laziness
Laziness means different things to different people. Each of us has our own view of what is an acceptable level of activity in both work and leisure and therefore our own definition of laziness. Most of us tend to regard it as something that affects other people: few admit to being lazy themselves! To someone who works a 20-hour day, almost everyone else is lazy. To the person who can carry on working, talking, or dancing until four in the morning, anyone who is flagging by midnight seems lazy rather than quite reasonably fatigued. Children who fail to come up to their parents' expectations are all too often labeled lazy without anyone trying to find out why it is that they do not achieve what is expected of them.

Laziness and relaxation
Pure laziness, or the sheer disinclination to do anything other than just lie around, does exist and almost everyone experiences it at some time. As an infrequent passing thing it is nothing to be worried about and requires neither investigation nor treatment. It is probably the body's natural way of putting on the brakes and making a person rest and relax when, perhaps without realizing it, he or she has been overdoing things and is in danger of becoming physically or mentally exhausted (see Relaxation).

Laziness as a symptom
Persistent laziness does not often exist on its own or develop without some underlying cause. In many instances what appears to be laziness is really the most obvious outward sign of one of a wide range of illnesses. So the first thing to be decided is whether the supposed laziness is simply a disinclination to work or, in reality, a severe lack of energy, excessive fatigue, actual drowsiness, or an inability to concentrate (see Depression).

Laziness may, for example, be associated with a continuing infection somewhere in the body that causes lack of energy but is not severe enough to cause an outright illness such as infectious mononucleosis or tuberculosis.

To people who like being busy all the time, inactivity almost always looks like laziness. However, there are times when being lazy—doing nothing and enjoying it—can be restful and relaxing and so a positive contribution to good health.

Jerry Harper

Other common causes of laziness are anemia, due possibly to persistent loss of blood (in heavy periods, for example); inadequate nutrition—a problem that affects old people and those suffering from anorexia nervosa (compulsive self-starvation); chronic liver or kidney disease; and some hormone disorders, such as diabetes or thyroid disease.

Obesity is often accompanied by what appears to be laziness. Conversely when someone who seems lazy is losing appetite and weight, the condition should be investigated without delay, because the symptoms taken together all point to the possibility of cancer.

Chronic heart or respiratory disease accompanied by shortness of breath make exertion something to be avoided. Many disorders of the nervous system diminish mental and physical activity and result in what appears at first to be laziness; so too do some of the drugs taken regularly as part of the treatment for a chronic condition, and an excessive intake of alcohol.

In other instances the trouble of which laziness is a symptom is emotional or mental rather than physical; some form of depression, boredom, fear of failure, or a conflict of interest or loyalty are particularly common underlying causes.

Laziness in children

Many parents worry that their baby, especially if it is their first, is lazy or spends too much time drowsing or actually sleeping. It is important to realize that young babies naturally need to spend most of their time asleep and that this is no cause for alarm; nor is the fact that the actual amount of sleep that individual babies need varies quite widely from one to another (see Sleep and sleep disorders).

Laziness over crawling, standing, walking, talking, and other activities is different. It is almost always due to slow development rather than to any real disorder. It is important for parents to remember that the time range for normal development is wide and that there are enormous differences in the rates at which perfectly normal children may progress (see Growth).

A child at school who gives the impression of either laziness or underachievement is likely to be given special tests of intelligence, sight, and hearing, because difficulties in any of these areas may produce behavior that gives the appearance of laziness.

Unhappiness or problems either at school or at home can also give rise to laziness. Undue concern, criticism, or pushiness on the part of parents over a child's level of attainment or apparent lack of interest in work may actually increase the difficulties. Once it has been established that there is no underlying disease and that the child has adequate sleep and nourishment, the best way of dealing with the problem is usually by encouragement and reward.

Laziness in adolescence

Adolescents, as well as feeling rebellious and anxious about the future, can also have particularly stubborn bouts of laziness. Usually, showing a sympathetic understanding of the conflicts that give rise to them will probably do more good than irritable criticism (see Adolescence).

Laziness in later life

Laziness as a problem of middle age has several common causes. The enthusiasm and ambitiousness of earlier life have probably passed, and when people find themselves disappointed and perhaps mildly depressed at what has become of their lives, they become prey to boredom, settling for a quiet life and the laziness and lethargy that often go with it. Physically, too, they may be in less than good shape, and too much food and drink and too little exercise will all contribute to their laziness (see Exercise).

In women the onset of menopause may add to their feelings of tiredness, depression, and disinclination to attempt anything needing much effort. This is a time when hormone replacement therapy, given on the advice of a doctor, may be a great help (see Menopause).

However, laziness in later life is fortunately not irreversible; indeed, it is vital to be free of it to go on living a healthy full life. The first step is to recognize the problem and understand it, then to realize that middle age can be a time not for sitting back and letting things slide but for making new beginnings and taking fresh paths, with the determination not to fall prey to flab and sloth.

Lazy eye

Q I heard recently that my young cousin has a lazy eye. Is this painful?

A No. A lazy eye is totally painless because the brain is completely ignoring it. If pain were felt it would indicate that there is some other problem, such as infection or injury.

Q My teenage daughter's hairstyle completely covers one eye. I am worried this may cause her to develop a lazy eye. Could this happen?

A No. A true lazy eye can only develop in early childhood. Covering an eye once vision has fully developed will only cause temporary ignoring of the input from that eye.

Q My father had a lazy eye when he was a child. Is this condition hereditary?

A The underlying cause can be inherited. However, provided you keep a vigilant watch for signs of the eyes deviating and take your child to the doctor if and when amblyopia does appear, then treatment can be started early and no harm will occur.

Q My son has developed a squint. Will it correct itself in time?

A No. If you notice any sign of a squint, however slight, you should take your child to the doctor as soon as possible. A lazy eye can be the end result of squinting and quickly becomes irreversible if it is left untreated.

Q Originally my son's left eye was lazy, but after treatment his right eye seemed the worst of the two. Why was this?

A Obstructing the vision of the good eye can often lead to a temporary shift of brain effort away from that eye. Fortunately once the patch covering the good eye has been removed—the length of time this is left in place varies from person to person—normal vision will soon return.

Lazy eye, or amblyopia, is a common eye complaint among young children and is often the result of weakness of the muscles surrounding the eye. Prompt treatment is needed.

A lazy eye can still work, but the brain has chosen to ignore it. Initially sight in the affected eye becomes poor, then as the problem gets worse the eye ceases to follow objects and looks lazy because of its sluggishness and poor responses. Finally the brain suppresses its signals altogether and the eye is effectively blind.

Causes

The medical term for lazy eye is *amblyopia ex anopsia*. Factors such as squint, cataracts, and other optical abnormalties impair the normal use of the eye, especially during infancy. This condition will eventually prevent the formation of a normal image on the retina (see Eyes and eyesight). For example, a farsighted child will strain his or her eyes to focus properly and so make the eye turn inward.

Normally the two eyes are moved by their muscles so that the images formed in the brain are identical. With amblyopia ex anopsia, however, the two eyes do not work in conjunction, and a double image will be formed in the brain. Because this is unpleasant the brain ignores one image

Glasses that have a frosted or covered lens over the good eye will make the lazy eye work and thereby correct the condition.

and concentrates on the other. A single image results but at the expense of the sight of one eye, which becomes lazy.

Any disease that affects only one eye will also lead to the visual supremacy of the other eye and hence to a lazy eye.

Treatment and outlook

The aim of treatment, which must be carried out under the supervision of a qualified ophthalmologist, is to encourage the brain to use the lazy eye and to correct the defect causing the problem. Glasses that have a frosted or covered lens over the good eye will force the lazy eye to work. This will be adequate for most cases of lazy eye. In severe cases, however, surgery may be necessary.

As long as the underlying problem is sorted out before the age of seven, a lazy eye will usually respond fully to treatment. After this age the damage is likely to be permanent because the brain has stopped laying down new nerve pathways, and if a source of information has been suppressed nothing can be done to reverse it. Therefore any abnormality that impairs the vision of a child, however slight, should be brought to the doctor's attention immediately because the child will not outgrow it.

Lead poisoning

Q My daughter likes to suck on pencils. Could she get lead poisoning?

A No. Pencil lead is not actually lead, but a harmless carbon compound.

Q Can lead be absorbed into the body through the skin?

A No. Lead enters the body either by inhalation, as in breathing in gasoline fumes, or by ingestion, for example, from eating lead-contaminated food or sucking toys made of lead or painted with lead-based paints.

Q I've heard that adults can suffer from permanent damage due to lead poisoning. Is this true?

A Yes. Lead may affect the nerves that control the hand muscles, causing a characteristic wrist drop that may be permanent.
In children, however, lead poisoning is more serious, and can lead to damage to the nervous system that causes mental retardation.

Q My son is slow and he behaves very badly at school. Could he be suffering from lead poisoning?

A This is unlikely. Such symptoms are much more likely to be indicative of one of a number of other conditions. You should have your son see a doctor, a school counselor, or a therapist as soon as possible.

Q I live in an old house where the pipes are lead. Should I change them to copper?

A Usually, the tap used for drinking water comes almost straight off the mains, so there is not much opportunity for lead to dissolve. If you are concerned, it is easy to test your tap water for lead.

Q Can gasoline be made without lead?

A Yes. It has to be made lead-free in many countries, but it does cost more.

One of the biggest concerns today is lead pollution. Everyone is likely to suffer from its effects, but the greatest dangers are to children. So how can we protect ourselves from lead poisoning?

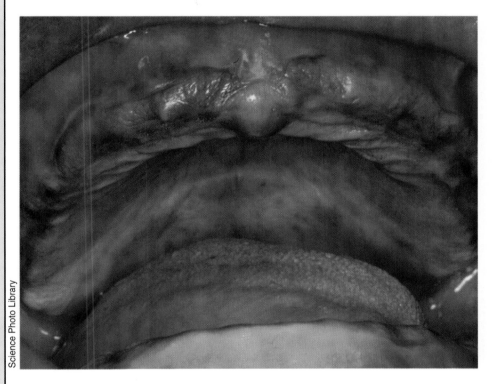

Science Photo Library

The mouth of a person suffering from chronic exposure to high levels of lead: the palate takes on a gray appearance.

Lead in the human body is always a poison. It serves no useful function and it may have serious effects.

In the past most of the lead that found its way into people's systems came from lead plumbing in houses, lead-containing paint, and lead used in industry. Although these sources of lead may still cause worry, most of the concern about lead today is over the amount that is released into the air from the burning of gasoline by automobiles and other vehicles.

Causes

The dangers of full-blown lead poisoning are greatest in people working with industrial processes that use a lot of lead. This includes metal smelting, where there is contact with molten lead, and battery making. Industrial plants that use lead in their processing may be a danger to the surrounding neighborhood, and in most places careful checks are kept on the environmental effects of these processes.

In the past it was always painters who were associated in doctors' minds with lead poisoning, because most paint used to contain lead. However, it is now unusual for paint used for ordinary domestic purposes to contain lead, although paint in old and dilapidated houses may contain an unhealthy level. Children, who often put things in their mouths and suck on painted toys, are more susceptible to the effects of lead and for them it presents the most dangers.

Lead in plumbing

The word *plumbing* comes from the Latin word for "lead" because up until the 20th century water-carrying pipes were usually composed of that material. Nowadays pipes are usually made of copper. Lead that is dissolved off the walls of old lead piping is a major cause of contamination and poisoning.

Domestic water varies in its content, depending on its treatment. When it contains lots of calcium and magnesium, it is called hard water, when it does not it is called soft water. In soft water areas larger

TAKE CARE

Protecting children

Roger Payling

- Never let children suck older painted toys unless the paint is lead-free
- If you are living in a house with flaking paint that a child can eat, for safety's sake redecorate
- In industrial areas remove the outer leaves of vegetables before eating
- Use the prescribed safety precautions if you are working in an industry that uses lead

- Where possible, replace all lead pipes that carry drinking water with copper pipes. If you are worried about the lead content of your tap water, use a lead-testing kit
- If symptoms of lead poisoning appear in your child, particularly in the form of disruptive behavior and obvious slowness in school, take him or her to see your doctor without delay

Treatment

The treatment depends on the source of the lead that has caused the trouble. Often it is enough simply to remove the cause. In industry, especially, safety procedures have been introduced to minimize the effects.

Once lead has gotten into the body it becomes incorporated into the bones which then act as reservoirs of lead, allowing it to escape back into the bloodstream even after the source of the poison has been removed.

Lead in the bloodstream can be eliminated from the body by means of the kidneys. It is possible to improve the rate of excretion of lead by using drugs that make more of it dissolve in the blood and therefore help to clear the reservoir of lead in the bones.

Outlook

The outlook for children who have definitely had lead poisoning is not good. This is because the developing brain is more sensitive to the effects of lead than the fully developed adult brain. As many as 40 percent of affected children are left with seizures and mental retardation. It is impossible to say whether children who have suffered full-blown lead intoxication can ever achieve their full mental potential. Adults fare less badly.

amounts of lead are likely to be dissolved in drinking water than in hard water areas, because the scaling that hard water leaves on the inside of the pipes may prevent the lead from becoming dissolved in it.

Removal of domestic lead

Lead abatement, the removal of lead-containing paint from homes, is becoming popular and is a big business in the US. It is the responsibility of landlords to provide a safe environment for their tenants and this includes safe levels of lead.

However, it may be questioned whether the removal of lead in old houses is a good idea. In the US children living in houses that contain lead paint are usually tested for blood lead levels. If they are not suffering from lead poisoning to begin with, then scraping lead paint from the walls is likely to release more lead dust into the environment unless it is done carefully.

Symptoms

Lead poisoning can produce a complicated mixture of symptoms. It may affect the nervous system, producing general ill-health, fatigue, and disturbed sleep. There may also be a disorder of the nerves themselves after they leave the spinal cord. This is called peripheral neuropathy. When it is due to lead it is likely to affect those nerves controlling the muscles that straighten out the hand and wrist after one has made a fist; this causes the wrist to drop.

Lead poisoning may also cause abdominal pains and constipation. There is usually also a loss of appetite, and patients may complain of a metallic taste in the mouth. In the long term, it may also produce kidney disease. The proper formation of blood cells is another process that is poisoned by lead. Anemia usually results.

In children the same symptoms may occur. However, seizures, weight loss, and poor coordination of movement are more common. There are also behavior disturbances, however the most serious problem is the risk of permanent mental retardation.

Lead pollution and food

■ Inner leaves
■ Outer leaves

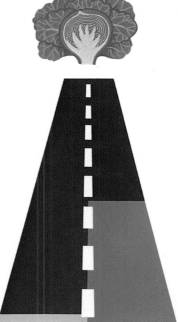

John Hutchinson

Rural   370 ft (113 m) from residential road   350 ft (107 m) from major road   670 ft (204 m) from highway interchange

Location of cabbages

Zefa

Our most direct source of lead is polluted food. In tests it has been found that cabbages have different levels of lead on the outer leaves, depending on their proximity to a highway. The heavier the traffic, the higher the contamination (above). Even crops grown alongside rural roads (left) will have traces of lead contamination.

Damaging levels

The most important question about lead is whether it is indeed heading toward dangerous levels in the environment. There is evidence that governments are taking the warning signs seriously; unleaded gasoline has been introduced in the United States as well as in many European countries, and new automobiles are being designed to use it.

The reason that there is widespread concern is the growing amount of evidence that lead levels that were once regarded as safe in children are now being associated with small but significant impairment of mental development.

One study which was performed in the US measured the amount of lead in the first teeth of children after they had been shed. Since lead is incorporated into teeth in the same way that it is incorporated into bone, this provided a much more accurate way of assessing lead exposure over a long period of time than simple blood levels would have done. It was found that those children who had the greatest tendency toward disturbed behavior had the greatest amount of lead in their teeth. There was also a clear difference in IQ of four to five points between the children with the lowest level of lead, who had the highest IQs, compared with children with the highest lead levels. These were all normal children, the vast majority of whom had blood levels of lead that were then considered to be within normal range.

The future

Many historians believe that the Roman Empire collapsed partly due to the Romans themselves. Many citizens suffered from lead poisoning because of the high lead level in the water of the plumbing system that the Romans invented.

Some respected authorities believe that there is a chance of modern civilization going the same way because we are poisoning the developing brains of our children with lead released from the exhaust pipes of automobiles and other vehicles and from industrial processing. It is therefore to be hoped that the results of research into lead poisoning and contamination will stimulate the governments of the world to act wisely, especially to protect the younger generation.

Learning

Q Why is it that some people are poor learners while others learn rapidly?

A To some extent learning ability depends on a person's general level of intelligence. However, whatever the intelligence level, different people learn different things at varying speeds. For example, people who have trouble learning dates or mathematical processes may be very quick at learning how to repair motorcycles. Other people can learn the lines of a play easily but cannot learn how to run a washing machine. Little is known about why these differences occur, but they may have to do with different levels of development in separate parts of the brain.

Q My son has had poor report cards from school. They say he learns slowly, yet at home he seems really quick and intelligent. Is he choosing what he learns?

A This may be the case or, alternatively, he may be reacting badly to the particular teaching method used at the school or even to some of the teachers. It is worth talking to his teachers to find out whether he is falling behind because of such difficulties or some other problem, such as dyslexia.

Q After a bad car accident my father has had to learn to walk again. Why is it so difficult to do this in middle age?

A Assuming that your father's physical condition is normal once more, there may be difficulty because brain cells that have been damaged cannot regenerate themselves in the way that other cells in the body can.

By the time a person reaches middle age, most of the brain's cells are already locked into miniature computer programs that deal with the many tasks that are performed almost without thinking. As we age, the brain takes longer to create new programs because there is not much adaptable capacity to fit in a new program.

From the moment of birth an individual begins to learn, and continues to do so throughout his or her life. The way in which a child learns affects his or her whole approach to the future. So how does the learning process work?

Learning is not just about schoolbooks and study, demonstration, and practice. It covers a wide range of processes, beginning with the childhood skills of learning to walk, talk, and deal with the physical world. It progresses to learning facts and figures, job skills, and the skills of living on a daily basis. Included at every stage is the wider task of learning how to interact with other people and cope with the ways in which they behave.

You are never too young to learn. From an early age, children can acquire all kinds of skills that allow them both to acquire new knowledge, and to learn interpersonal skills

Ways of learning
The learning process can work in a variety of different ways. The most simple of these different methods are learning by association, learning as the result of reward, and learning by the imitation of others.

Roger Payling

An example of learning by association might be a situation in which a child places his or her hand on a hot stove, which makes the child pull its hand away in pain and fright. The parent has previously warned the child not to touch the stove because it is hot, and the child has now learned this by experience. From now on the child will associate touching a hot stove with pain, and usually will not continue to touch the hot stove.

In the same way, a child can learn about softness, hard surfaces, roughness, and smoothness from touch. Gently taking a child's hand and placing it on each of the surfaces, explaining the word as you do it, is very beneficial in teaching the child to understand the tactile world around it.

Visual experiences also help a child to learn. Watch a young child play with brightly colored toys and you will discover which color he or she prefers.

Children can be taught lessons in many different ways. Loving and caring for a pet, such as a rabbit, helps a child to learn about responsibility when the pet's well-being is entirely dependent on him or her.

Showing a child the color spectrum through items such as toys or illustrations in a book makes it easier for him or her to learn the names of colors. Different sounds can also be taught in this interactive way. If the learning

Q Can we really learn while we are asleep?

A No. For some time it was thought that if you left a tape recorder playing something like a piece of poetry while you slept, you would awake having learned the poem. This is just not true—research shows that people learn absolutely nothing while asleep.

Q I remember reading somewhere that there is a chemical you can take that helps you to learn things more quickly. Is this true?

A Some experiments have shown that ribonucleic acid, which acts as a messenger controlling cell activity, can speed up the rate at which rats and mice learn simple tasks like balancing on a rod. Other drugs can also help slow down the rate of memory loss in older people. However, we are not yet at the stage where taking a pill can drastically increase our ability to learn things more rapidly.

Q My father is fond of saying that we learn more from our mistakes than from our successes. Is this right?

A Yes and no. Mistakes are often more dramatic than successes, so our level of arousal becomes higher when we make a mistake and we remember the mistakes vividly. On the other hand, while mistakes alert us to what we should not have done, they don't tell us which of several alternatives we should try the next time we find ourselves in a similar situation.

Q If it is so much trouble to learn things, how do people ever manage to learn habits that are harmful to them?

A Very often they learn by imitation. For example, young people may start smoking because they see their parents smoking or to keep up with friends who smoke. Once they become dependent on the nicotine in cigarettes, the habit cannot be broken easily and may by this stage have become a harmful addiction.

Pictor International

process is a pleasurable one, the child will learn, for instance, that the sound of a certain piece of music brings a feeling of happiness.

A surprising number of social habits are also acquired through learning by association. People often begin to feel hungry just from hearing the sound of the table being set or seeing a clock registering that it is lunchtime.

Rewarding behavior

Learning by being rewarded is an obvious way of acquiring the desired behavior. Unfortunately, people seldom realize just how powerful the tiny rewards of smiling, nodding, and showing interest are when it comes to influencing not only the behavior of a child, but also that of an adult. It is logical that if a certain type of behavior brings a positive response from someone, then that behavior will be repeated. This can be applied to many areas of daily life; for instance, when choosing a restaurant for dinner, or a store to buy household items, people naturally tend to return to somewhere they have been made to feel welcome before.

For young children in particular, rewards of praise and the occasional candy can quickly establish toilet-training habits, encourage the correct social behavior, and help produce good schoolwork. However, it is not a good idea to make promises along the lines of "If you help me tidy up, I'll give you some candy," because this encourages the child to weigh the trouble of helping against the reward of candy, and he or she may decide that no tidying up and no candy is preferable. Instead, if the child is rewarded immediately, he or she

Acquiring job skills is one way in which learning can change a person's whole approach to life.

may eventually do a little voluntary tidying, and the habit is reinforced and becomes established, with only an occasional reward. However, some children will respond more easily and readily than others to this type of conditioning, while some other children never seem to learn.

Learning by reward can be just as powerful a stimulus for altering the behavior of even the most intelligent adult—one class of students conducted an experiment to influence their psychology teacher by arranging so that the left side of the class would constantly frown at him, while the right side smiled. The professor soon stopped his normal habit of pacing up and down lecturing the whole class, and instead addressed only the smiling students while completely ignoring the frowning half of the class.

Imitation

Imitation is another extremely powerful influence on learning. Many of the noticeable similarities between a child and his or her parents are due not to heredity, but to the way in which the child unconsciously picks up its parents' habits and mannerisms.

Adolescents are particularly likely to learn by imitation. At an age when their changing status in the world produces some uncertainties that they need to resolve by adapting their lifestyles, imitation of their peer group and other role models allows them to experiment with aspects of adult behavior.

ormal learning

he amount and rate at which a person earns is influenced by a wide range of ctors, including the strength of their ish to learn, the strength of their habit f learning, the rewards they get from earning, and the vividness and clarity of e material that is presented to them uring the learning process.

Once a person is old enough to rapid- grasp new concepts and ideas as they ppear, the pressure on them to learn as uch and as soon as possible can ecome immense. In a society dominat- d by information and knowledge, arents naturally tend to feel that the ore their offspring learn and the more ey can get ahead of their fellow stu- ents, the better equipped they will be get a good job and survive in today's orld when they leave education.

However, too often the limitations of omeone's inherited intelligence and e type of knowledge and skills that ey find it easiest to acquire are

Zefa

At school, these young students may encounter pressure to do well, both from teachers and parents. But everyone develops intellectually at his or her own pace, and it is important to nurture this so that each child can realize his or her full potential.

ignored. This can badly affect a student's intellectual development by putting the wrong pressure on him or her at the wrong time.

Rather than pressuring students it is better to encourage their natural curiosity and interest, which will give them a desire to learn. Parents can encourage the habit of learning by supporting the school system, providing a quiet place where homework can be done, and, if possible, helping their children in subjects when they have difficulties, having consulted the teachers involved. Good progress by a student at school should be rewarded with praise and encouragement, even if it is only a small improvement.

Discovery learning

Everybody's powers of observation are increased by introduction to new experiences, such as visits to places of interest, or simply having some unusual item pointed out while on a walk. This natural human urge to learn is used in

Discovery learning encourages self-education through problem solving. People tend to remember far more of what they actually do than of what they are told.

discovery learning, a system that encourages students to learn by a series of problem-solving exercises. The questions and problems are often provided by the students themselves, with minimal guidance from their teachers. Discovery learning is based on the maxim: "I remember 10 percent of what I hear, 50 percent of what I see, but 90 percent of what I do."

In the past few decades, there has been a certain trend in schools toward using the discovery method, because it gives students a greater ability to learn about the world outside of school. However, there is now a countertrend that includes the greater use of traditional methods of learning. It is clear that education has to make use of many learning techniques and teaching methods in order to encourage students' abilities.

Learning difficulties
Learning problems at school can have many causes, and some of them have nothing to do with learning itself. In the beginning there may be an actual fear of going to school, which may stem from shyness, or a fear of other students, unfamiliar surroundings, or new routines.

School phobia can usually be avoided if parents explain to their child beforehand what will happen, stressing the opportunities to form new friendships, do new and exciting things, and that Mom and Dad will be interested to hear all about it when the child comes home. It is important not to place emphasis on being good and doing what the teacher says, since performance anxiety would make anyone more anxious (see Anxiety).

Other anxieties can interfere with a child's ability to learn. At about nine or 10 years old, a child begins to realize that school is partly a competitive place with tests and assessments and that he or she cannot succeed by charm or obedience alone. Bad grades can cause intense anxiety that interferes with learning.

There can also be hidden physical barriers to learning, such as undetected impaired vision or poor hearing. It is important that a child with poor learning abilities should have his or her eyes and ears checked out by a doctor before anything else is done. Children can also show signs of word-blindness (see Dyslexia), quite independent of

actual learning ability. In this case, special help will be sought by the school. Teachers are always on the alert for these types of difficulties, and extra remedial help with reading and writing can often be obtained.

Rates of development
The rates at which students develop vary, and progress at school is partly a matter of natural maturing as well as of learning. A child of seven or eight who does not yet read is often merely a slow developer. It does not mean that he or she is lazy, unintelligent, or unable to

concentrate, but that his or her growth rate is slower than average. Similarly, students who struggle through junior high and high school often later find careers and environments which allow them to succeed. Development rates cannot be forced and the child must be allowed to continue at his or her own pace. This approach often produces unexpectedly gratifying results, because many people have a late learning spurt and catch up easily later on. Anxiety induced by too much external (or self induced) pressure to succeed is the only thing that stands in the way.

Legionnaires' disease

Q A friend of mine just came back from vacation, and his doctor thought he had Legionnaires' disease, but it was the flu. Is this disease easily confused with other illnesses?

A Yes. The start of the disease is like any other flulike illness that would make you feel generally off-color. These symptoms are then followed by a pneumonia that may not have any particularly remarkable features. Legionnaires' disease can be confused most easily with pneumonias that are caused by the mycoplasma group of organisms; blood tests are used to try to distinguish between the two types of disease. The antibiotic erythromycin is used to treat both.

Q Are there any types of people who are likely to get Legionnaires' disease?

A Yes. Like so many of the rarer infections, Legionnaires' disease is more common in patients whose immune systems are suppressed, either by a disease or by a treatment like the one given to prevent rejection of kidney transplants. Also men are three times more likely to get the disease than women, and it mostly affects people in their mid-50s.

Q Is it possible to get Legionnaires' disease in any country?

A Yes. There have been a number of outbreaks in countries outside the United States, especially in hospitals that have air conditioners. But it does seem to be more common in warmer climates, although this may be because air-conditioning is used more often, which makes outbreaks more likely.

Q Is it true that you can disinfect water to prevent Legionnaires' disease?

A Yes. The bacterium that causes the disease is sensitive to disinfectants, and these are now used to prevent the disease from becoming established in air-conditioning systems.

Although Legionnaires' disease is mainly associated with hotels, it can occur in any air-conditioned environment where the infecting organism is present. It is easily prevented if the right precautions are taken.

How the Legionnaires' bacterium is spread

Jim Marks

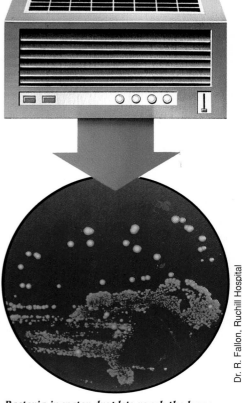

Dr. R. Fallon, Ruchill Hospital

Bacteria in water droplets reach the lungs via an air-conditioning unit.

Legionnaires' disease is a specific form of pneumonia. It first appeared in July 1976 in Philadelphia, Pennsylvania, during an American Legion convention, and the disease got its name from this outbreak. No less than 182 people, all of whom merely entered the lobby or stood near the entrance of the hotel where the convention was held, were affected by Legionnaires' disease. A total of 34 of the people died.

Identifying the organism

These people were infected with a previously unknown organism, which was subsequently named *Legionella pneumophila*. Once it had been identified, experts determined retrospectively that a previous epidemic, which had occurred in 1965 in a psychiatric hospital in Washington, DC, and had involved 81 patients and 15 deaths, had been caused by this same organism.

Today it is estimated that 10,000–25,000 cases occur in the United States every year. Many outbreaks of *Legionella* pneumonia have also occurred throughout the world. The disease can appear in the form of a single sporadic case or as a minor epidemic.

Causes

Legionnaires' disease is caused by the *Legionella pneumophila* bacterium. *Pneumophila* means liking the lungs, and an infection of the lungs is characteristic of the disease (see Lung and lung diseases).

This organism is difficult to culture but will grow slowly on a special culture medium containing charcoal and yeast (see Bacteria). Between three and six days are required for the formation of colonies, and the best temperature for growth has been found to be 95°F (35°C). (Most organisms will form colonies in 24 hours and will grow best at the normal body temperature of 98.6°F [37°C].) These circumstances have made the condition much more difficult to diagnose, investigate, and deal with than most infections. In addition at least nine different strains of *L. pneumophila* are known to exist, and there are at least 43 different species of the *Legionella* genus. The disease is acquired by the inhalation of aerosols that have been contaminated with the organisms.

LEGIONNAIRES' DISEASE

Locations of the organism

The *Legionella pneumophila* bacterium lives freely in the environment, particularly in water, but it is also found in mud and soil. Because it lives in water, the organism is likely to be found in air-conditioning systems and humidifiers.

This is because the air coming into these systems is filtered for dust and at the same time it is cooled by passing through water vapor. Any bacteria in the water are taken up into the air as if in an aerosol and disseminated through the building's air-conditioning system.

Spread of the disease

It is not absolutely clear how the disease is spread, but it may possibly be spread from person to person, although no such cases of this type of contamination have been reported. It is also possible for an individual to be exposed to the disease without displaying any symptoms, this is called subclinical infection.

Legionnaires' disease is known to have been spread from contaminated water used for drinking, bathing, hot tubs, jacuzzis, and even from cleaning medication inhalers or nebulizers.

The disease is an important cause of hospital-acquired pneumonias. Several hospitals have been found to have *Legionella* organisms in their water supplies. The current recommendations are that such hospital water supplies should be heated periodically to a temperature of 170.6°F (77°C) to destroy these organisms. Chlorination of the water is also very effective.

Symptoms

The incubation period varies between two and 10 days. The first signs are flu-like symptoms—a headache, aching muscles, and a general feeling of illness—but without the usual cold and sore throat.

After a day or two the patient develops a high fever, which is often accompanied by uncontrollable fits of shivering and a dry cough. Diarrhea, vomiting, and abdominal pain usually occur, and in addition sometimes there can be sleepiness and confusion. X rays of the chest usually show areas of solidification of the lungs that can affect one or more lobes, which are typical of the disease (see X rays).

Dangers

The severity of the illness can vary from a minor chest infection to a severe pneumonia with disturbance of the intestines, nervous system, and kidneys. The mortality rate in severe cases is high.

In the initial Philadelphia outbreak, 16 percent of the people affected suffered severe and extensive lung involvement, progressing rapidly to respiratory failure, shock, and death. In those patients who were less severely affected, the symptoms improved suddenly on or near the eighth day of the illness. A few days later the X-ray appearances also began to improve. Some people who survive an attack develop scarring in the lungs, known as pulmonary fibrosis.

Further complications

Although pneumonia is the most obvious feature and is present in nearly all cases, many patients suffer more from effects outside the lungs. Involvement of the nervous system, the digestive system, and the kidneys are especially common.

In addition some patients have eye or heart involvement; abscesses within the abdomen; peritonitis; skin and wound infections; severe muscle damage; a reduction in red and white blood cell counts. It is even possible for implanted devices, such as heart valves, to become infected.

Diagnosis

Unfortunately the clinical appearances and radiologic findings in a sporadic case of Legionnaires' disease are not sufficiently different from those in some other forms of pneumonia to allow for a positive diagnosis to be made (see Pneumonia).

Blood tests will show a moderate rise in the levels of white blood cells. The rate of settling of the red cells, called the erythrocyte sedimentation rate, is also increased.

The urine may contain blood and protein, which indicates at least a degree of kidney damage. None of these signs are, however, specific to the condition.

The organisms are difficult to isolate but can be found if the sputum is cultured using the special medium. An antibody test on the sputum, known as the immunofluorescent test, will establish the diagnosis in about 20 percent of all cases of Legionnaires' disease.

DNA testing

A test that identifies DNA prepared from the RNA of the *Legionella* organism has been developed, and identification kits that use the radiolabeled complementary DNA that have been prepared in this way are commercially available.

Monoclonal antibodies to *L. pneumophila* are currently being researched and developed, and once these become available in large quantities, diagnosis of the disease will be easier.

Treatment

Once the disease has been diagnosed, the treatment is with an antibiotic called erythromycin, administered either orally or by injection (see Antibiotics).

The *Legionella* organism is susceptible to a number of other antibiotics, including tetracycline, rifampin, and the fluoroquinolones. However, erythromycin still appears to be the treatment of choice among physicians.

In patients who fail to respond to erythromycin alone, a combination of rifampin and erythromycin is usually given. This combination is considered especially important in people with immune system deficiencies who are severely affected. In severe cases it may be necessary to support the lungs with artificial respiration.

Outlook

The outlook for people who develop Legionnaires' disease will depend on the seriousness of the symptoms and the background of each individual case.

Once the recovery process has begun the recuperating patient should continue to improve in a satisfactory manner. However, the lungs may take up to two months to return to normal, and care should be taken to avoid overexertion until the patient feels completely well.

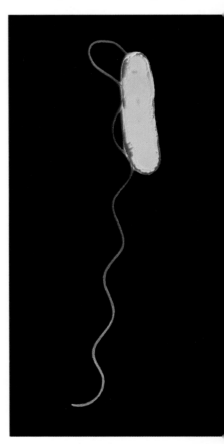

An electron micrograph of the bacterium **Legionella pneumophila**, *the organism that is responsible for Legionnaires' disease, showing its long single flagellum (tail).*

Leprosy

Q My husband and I are going to Uganda for a year. Are there any precautions we can take against leprosy?

A You should certainly have all the usual immunizations, but there is none, unfortunately, against leprosy. You can find out from local doctors the extent of the disease in the community; then, provided that you don't live in intimate or close quarters with an infected person, you will run no risk of infection whatsoever.

Q Is it possible to catch leprosy without knowing it by touching someone who has the illness?

A Leprosy can only be transferred from one person to another through very close contact over a long period. The condition is usually transferred in families; just touching someone will not put you at risk.

Q Are there types of leprosy that look horrible but are not infectious?

A All types of leprosy are infectious, but only after prolonged contact with the infected person. The disfigurement usually results from unnoticed damage to anesthetized (numb) skin, so that an infection occurs on top of this and gangrene (decaying tissue) sets in. Such cases are no more infectious than others, although where the nose is affected it is possible that transmission could take place through the tiny exhaled droplets of moisture that pass from the lungs out through the nose.

Q Can leprosy be passed on at birth?

A The leprosy bacteria are unable to cross the placenta and enter a growing fetus, so a newborn baby can never develop the infection. Infection is almost always transmitted by close family contact between an affected mother and the young child. If the mother is treated early, the child will remain free of leprosy.

Leprosy was once regarded as a dreaded disease, and its sufferers were treated as social outcasts. However, leprosy can now be cured, and it is no longer necessary to isolate patients from their communities.

Leprosy, also called Hansen's disease, is caused by the bacterium *leprae*. The bacterium attacks the skin and the nerves, resulting in loss of sensation, and in severe cases, disfigurement.

The disease was once in evidence in all countries but is now almost always confined to humid, tropical, and subtropical regions, where the most susceptible people are those who are malnourished or starving. There are an estimated 15–20 million sufferers throughout the world, with approximately 200,000 new cases discovered each year.

Causes

The bacterium that causes the disease can be transferred from one person to another by skin-to-skin contact, and possibly also through nose droplets. Transference by insects, unsterilized tattoo needles, and hypodermic syringes has also been reported. Although it is an infectious disease, the chances of catching it are minimal unless there is close contact over a long period; hence leprosy is most likely to affect families.

Leprosy comes in two forms. In both, the symptoms appear after a long incubation period, often two to three years.

Tuberculoid leprosy (so called because it resembles some facets of tuberculosis) is a milder form of the disease. Most commonly affected are the nerves of the face behind the ear and the ulnar nerve, which supplies part of the hand. There is a slow onset of numbness and a loss of sensation in the peripheral nerves (running from the spinal cord to the body's surface). The ulnar nerve behind the elbow feels thick and inflamed, and the skin develops a rash that looks like a tea stain. Damage is caused by the lack of sensation, which allows minor injuries and infections to pass unnoticed.

In lepromatous leprosy the damage caused by the bacterium is far more widespread and malignant. The first symptoms are a thickening, raising, corrugating, and numbness of the areas of skin due to the inflammation beneath. In its most severe forms, all of the skin is involved, but in less severe cases the face and ears are more commonly affected. The face takes on a lionlike appearance. Soft nodules develop on the ears, nose,

Children who are recovering from leprosy receive normal tutoring at this special leprosy hospital in India.

Leprosy worldwide

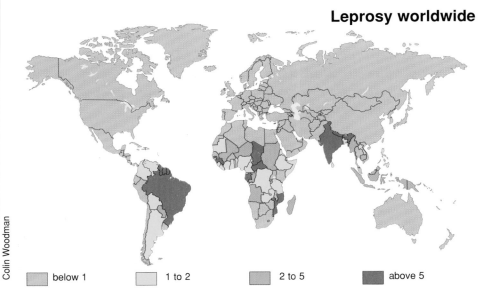

Colin Woodman

| below 1 | 1 to 2 | 2 to 5 | above 5 |

The bacterium that causes leprosy (seen through a microscope, right) is usually, but not exclusively, found in countries with hot, tropical climates, where incidences of the disease are therefore highest (above).

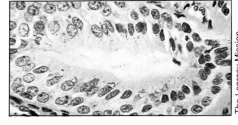

The Leprosy Mission

and cheeks; these often become infected with other bacteria as wounds and ulcers open, causing gangrene. Additionally there is damage to the peripheral nerves of the body, with large areas of patchy anesthesia (numbness) and paralysis. This may affect a whole arm or leg.

Without the proper treatment leprosy is progressive. Numb areas are easily damaged, the injuries go unnoticed, and therefore become infected and sometimes gangrenous; this causes them to become useless and makes fingers and toes likely to fall off.

Infection of the nerves leads to paralysis of peripheral muscle groups so that the wrist or foot becomes paralyzed. At least 25 percent of those who go untreated have either facial disfigurement or some serious disabling deformity.

Because of the tradition of isolating patients, sufferers do not ask for treatment and leprosy spreads through a community. However, patients who have started treatment are no longer infectious; therefore isolation is unnecessary.

Treatment

Treatment is with the sulfone drug dapsone (DDS), which is taken daily by mouth for years and sometimes for life. Occasionally, when dapsone cannot be tolerated, other compounds (such as cofazimine and rifampin) can be given. Often patients develop hepatitis (see Hepatitis) or anemia as a reaction to the drug and are given iron and vitamin supplements (see Anemia).

Physical therapy can be given to rehabilitate affected muscles, although sensation cannot be recovered in damaged nerves. Surgery can also be performed to remove gangrenous areas and reconstruct severely affected parts of the face.

Outlook

The skin test, called the lepromin test, is used to determine the amount of resistance a patient has to leprosy. When resistance is high, as occurs in cases of mild tuberculoid leprosy, the disease can disappear on its own or with a few months of drug treatment. When resistance is low the drug treatment may limit the spread but drugs may need to be taken for life because the condition tends to recur.

Untreated leprosy rarely shortens a patient's life. Since it is slowly progressive, leprosy will cause increasing disability and disfigurement over time. However, if it is caught early, these distressing effects can be prevented by drugs.

This patient has minimized his disability by designing a pen and bolder to write (right). A nerve conduction study (left) determines the extent of the damage.

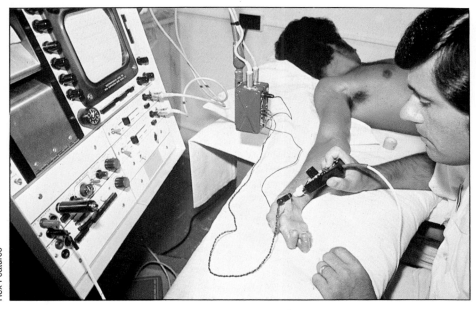

Rex Features

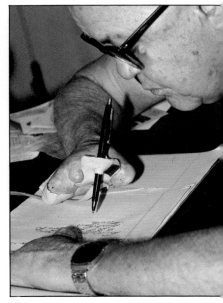

Lethargy

Q I am feeling very lethargic and am putting on weight. Could it be my glands?

A It is very unlikely, but in rare cases lethargy can be a symptom of some diseases of the endocrine glands. The most common is myxedema, which is a failure of the thyroid gland to produce enough thyroid hormone. In such cases the lethargy is usually accompanied by a weight gain and the menstrual cycle is often disturbed. When lethargy is due to a disturbance of the hormone glands there are usually other symptoms that point to this as a cause. You should check with your doctor.

Q At least once a month I feel really lethargic. Is this part of my biorhythm?

A There is no doubt that people's moods vary from time to time. This is particularly obvious with the menstrual cycle in women, but men also show rhythmical variations in their feelings of well-being. Those who believe in biorhythms claim to be able to predict the dates on which a person feels most dynamic and effective. However, these claims have not been scientifically proven.

Q Can I expect to grow more lethargic as I grow older?

A No. You may well find that your physical capacities grow more limited, as a result of the aging process, but you should not suffer from lethargy. It is a question of having plenty to do and getting enough exercise to keep your body in good shape. Keeping up your interest in all aspects of life is a good way to ward off lethargy.

Q I suffer from migraines, and I find that after a headache I feel very lethargic for the next 24 hours. Is this normal?

A Yes. Migraines are often associated with nausea, vomiting, and a headache that may last for 24 hours or more. As the headache wears off, tiredness and lethargy are usual.

Lethargy is a common physical and psychological state. Usually it wears off very quickly, but when it is persistent it can be a symptom of a present or impending illness.

Camera Press

Tiredness is natural, but a lethargic child who is interested in nothing and becomes ill should be taken to a doctor.

Everyone feels lethargic at some time in their life; lethargy is what a person experiences when he or she is lacking in energy and feels exhausted and without a purpose. It is often a short-lived and perfectly natural state, which can be brought on, for example, by eating a very large meal, or by a lack of sleep. However, lethargy can also persist for a few days, over several weeks, or sometimes even for months.

Lethargic people appear lazy, a wholly different condition which implies an uncooperative state of mind rather than a condition which the sufferer feels unable to control. The problem is that it is sometimes very difficult for the onlooker to distinguish laziness from lethargy, especially in an uncooperative teenage son or daughter (see Laziness).

A feeling of lethargy that persists for more than a week or two and that does not stem from an obvious cause, for example stress (see Stress, and Stress management), may occasionally be due to a condition that requires medical treatment. Lethargy may also be a symptom of certain illnesses.

Causes and symptoms

Although lethargy can be, and often is, a symptom of an organic disease, it is important to recognize that in a large number of cases lethargy is purely psychological in origin.

Sometimes the lethargy is caused by a specific psychological condition, such as depression (see Depression), posttraumatic stress disorder (see Posttraumatic stress disorder), chronic fatigue syndrome (see Chronic fatigue syndrome), alcohol- or drug-related social problems (see Alcoholism, and Drug abuse), or anorexia nervosa (see Anorexia and bulimia). However, in many cases the cause is less specific, less serious, and perhaps less obvious.

Lethargy is a feature of persistent fatigue (see Fatigue). In this context fatigue does not mean the sleepiness that implies lack of sleep or the feeling of exhaustion that follows sustained heavy physical exertion. It is used to describe a feeling of extreme tiredness that is unrelated to work of any kind or any other obvious factors.

Physical fatigue is brought about by the accumulation in the muscles of the breakdown products of fuel consumption and energy production into lactic acid, which affects the ability of the muscles to continue to work normally (see Muscles). In high concentration the lactic acids can even cause pain. However, a brief rest will allow time for the normal blood flow through the muscles to carry away these substances. Fatigue from lack of sleep is also a physiological problem and is readily corrected by resuming a regular sleeping schedule (see Sleep and sleep problems).

In many cases of lethargy, however, purely mental fatigue can occur. While it seems to have most of the features of physical fatigue, it has nothing to do with any physical exertion. Indeed, ironically, physical fatigue can often be abolished by a period of brisk physical work or exercise (see Exercise).

It is true that a sustained period of intense intellectual work will produce a sense of fatigue that demands a period of relief from the work. However, most cases of nonphysical fatigue are not caused by overuse of the mental faculties. They can often be the result of boredom, frustration, disinclination to perform a particular type of work, overlong concentration on a single task, anxiety, or sometimes fear. The cure for lethargy induced in this way is to find work that is rewarding, or to challenge one's self to do unrewarding work as quickly as possible and then take steps to set up the likelihood of doing more rewarding work in the future.

Lethargy in women

The changes in chemical balance experienced by women during the monthly cycle can cause mood changes (see Menstruation). The result can be lethargy together with a tendency to be easily upset, irritability, depression, anxiety, headaches, an increase in weight, swelling of the ankles, and a bloated feeling. These are all common symptoms and are known collectively as PMS (see Premenstrual syndrome).

Lethargy is especially common in the early weeks of pregnancy, usually until about 14 weeks. The early days and weeks after the birth of a baby can also be very stressful, partly because of the demands of the baby and lack of sleep but also because the hormonal balance of the mother's body is adjusting after the birth (see Pregnancy). All of this can cause extreme tiredness and may also play a part in postnatal depression.

Many women also complain to their doctors of feeling tired all the time, and are often worried that they may be anemic (see Anemia). Anemia is certainly a cause of lethargy in women, and it

---

How to avoid lethargy

- Keep cool in hot, humid weather. Wear loose-fitting cotton clothes, drink plenty of liquid, and take a little extra salt, unless your doctor advises against it
- Eat regular meals with fresh foods, whole foods, and only small amounts of starchy or sweet foods
- Avoid getting too little or too much sleep

- Stop at intervals when driving long distances. Get out of the automobile, snack, and stretch your legs
- Avoid taking alcohol with other drugs or in excessive amounts
- Exercise regularly. This will tone your body, improve your circulation, and give you a sense of well-being. Exercises can be done at home or in a local exercise or aerobics class

Repetitive work can produce lethargy. Many companies now see the value of giving workers short breaks for refreshments, and some provide gyms for after-work exercise.

ways worth seeing the doctor if anemia suspected.

Depression

More than many of the above factors, however, the presence of fatigue is a common indicator of depression, which may be mild, moderate, or severe. Although it is not unusual for women to experience depression as part of PMS, other people who develop depression may also feel extreme lethargy, together with symptoms such as poor sleep and loss of appetite. It is a curious fact that in depression people feel very tired but frequently have great difficulty in getting to sleep. They may wake very early in the morning, too, and be unable to get back to sleep. This leaves them feeling lethargic and unrefreshed in the morning but still unable to sleep well the following night.

Infections

It is very common for people to feel exhausted after a viral illness such as influenza. This lethargic state may be accompanied by feelings of weakness and depression and can, in some cases, last for several weeks after the illness itself (see influenza). Infectious mononucleosis (glan-

dular fever), an infection that often affects teenagers, is a particularly debilitating illness (see Infectious mononucleosis).

Anyone with a raised temperature will feel lethargic, and lethargy may also be the main symptom of other infections, such as tuberculosis (see Tuberculosis). Therefore having a medical checkup if you are feeling lethargic for any length of time is a good idea.

Many people experience lethargy on hot humid summer days. Overheated places of work without air-conditioning can cause extreme lethargy, especially when the tasks being carried out are repetitive and there is a background hum of machinery. These conditions can be extremely dangerous, because the speed of the worker's reactions is usually reduced, particularly if he or she also happens to be taking tranquilizing drugs (see Tranquilizers).

Similar conditions arise in an automobile on a warm day, especially when traveling at constant speed on a long straight highway. It is well known that drivers occasionally fall asleep at the wheel if they do not break a long journey.

Elderly people in cold surroundings who develop hypothermia (abnormally low body temperature) feel lethargic.

This is particularly dangerous because the lethargy means that the elderly person will move around less and less and as a result will become colder and colder. Friends and relatives should therefore visit regularly to insure that elderly people keep warm and eat sensibly (see Hypothermia).

A large number of drugs are known to produce fatigue and drowsiness in the patient. Sleeping pills are obviously taken to induce sleepiness, but with some types the effect continues the next morning, like a hangover (see Hypnotic drugs).

Tranquilizers that are prescribed to reduce anxiety and to help the patient relax can frequently cause lethargy. Some pills taken for high blood pressure also have this effect. The doctor should be informed if any prescribed drug causes lethargy and fatigue.

The most striking example of lethargy from organic causes is the disease encephalitis lethargica. This was first described by the Austrian neurologist Constantin von Economo (1876–1931) and is now known as von Economo's disease. Thousands of cases of this distressing disorder were reported following the influenza pandemic that occurred at the end of World War I.

The symptoms included extreme long-term lethargy and somnolence; a variable degree of paralysis of the eye movements; and, in many of those who survived the disease, the delayed development of the trembling disorder Parkinson's disease. Fortunately it appears that the virus that caused these serious complications quickly mutated and no new cases occurred after about 1930.

Among the other organic causes of lethargy are:
- poor oxygen supply to the brain
- influenza
- brain inflammation (see Encephalitis)
- infectious mononucleosis
- Marburg and Ebola fevers
- blood poisoning (septicemia)
- poisoning, especially from sedative and antipsychotic drugs
- hydrocarbon poisoning
- metallic poisoning
- altitude sickness
- sick building syndrome
- severe malnutrition
- malabsorption syndromes
- low blood calcium levels from disease
- low adrenal steroid production (Cushing's syndrome)
- short-bowel syndrome
- viral and other forms of hepatitis
- liver failure
- heart block or other causes of very slow pulse
- beta-blocker drugs (see Heart disease)
- rheumatic fever
- fibrosing lung disease
- lung cancer
- respiratory failure
- kidney failure
- leukemia (see Leukemia)
- brain tumor
- meningitis (see Meningitis)
- muscular dystrophy
- brain infection with HIV (see AIDS)

It should be emphasized that lethargy is by no means the principal symptom of any of these conditions, and it would therefore be incorrect to assume that the presence of lethargy alone implies that a person is suffering from any of them. They all have a number of other symptoms and signs.

Lethargy in children
Lethargy in a child is unusual, and it probably means that he or she is sick

A quality controller must concentrate for long periods of time on a single task—unless he or she has regular short breaks, lethargy may be a real problem.

from something, for example, a cold or measles. If a child is lethargic for more than a day or two, it is a good idea to take him or her to the doctor.

Drowsiness and lethargy often occur after a head injury. A child will fall asleep after a bad bang on the head, when he or she has become exhausted from crying. The child should be allowed to sleep, provided that he or she had not been knocked out at the time of injury. However, if there is any doubt about this, make sure that he or she can be roused from sleep (see Unconsciousness).

If someone loses consciousness as a result of a head injury, it is essential that he or she is taken to the hospital for treatment as soon as possible (see Head and head injuries).

Treatment
Usually lethargy is a temporary condition that has an obvious cause. However, when the lethargy persists for some time and seems to have no obvious cause, it is always a good idea to see the doctor (see Tiredness).

Lethargy due to boredom implies a lack of interests, either at work or at play, and this can always be overcome if the cause is recognized and a serious effort is made to correct it. Sustained interest in a subject area is an essential ingredient of contentment. It is a product of knowledge, and of education in its widest sense.

There are endless and varied opportunities for the stimulation of interests, for example at night school, libraries, music groups, craft and art classes, World Wide Web forums, sports clubs, and social clubs. Many other sources of new interests are always available and offer rewarding alternative to idleness and lethargy.

Some women whose lethargy is caused by their monthly menstrual cycle find that taking the contraceptive Pill (see Contraception) helps ease the symptoms. Depression can be treated with antidepressive drugs, and it helps, too, if the sufferer receives understanding and sympathy from his or her family and friends.

Where lethargy follows an illness, recovery can be speeded by encouraging the patient to rest, to eat a nourishing diet, and to get fresh air.

Lethargy that is brought on by the environment, whether it be an overheated workplace or a stuffy automobile, can often be helped immediately by a number of measures. Try taking plenty of short breaks, preferably outside in the fresh air, and refreshments. It is also a good idea to refrain from drinking alcohol, particularly during the day, and especially when other drugs are being taken, as this often causes lethargy, as well as impaired judgment. These simple measures will all help ease the lethargy.

Robert Isear/Science Photo Library

Leukemia

Leukemia is a rare disease that affects the blood. Advances in treatment are made all the time; in some cases it can be cured, in all cases life can be prolonged.

Q Can leukemia run in families? My uncle died of leukemia and my father is now almost neurotic with worry.

A There are a few unusual hereditary diseases that are associated with an increased incidence of leukemia. These are mainly immunodeficiency diseases and those associated with an abnormal fragility of chromosomes. Both of these conditions are rare.

Q I have heard that X rays can cause leukemia. Is this really the case?

A Yes, this is true, but it is very unlikely that even if you have undergone X rays on many, many occasions will you be at an increased risk. People who spend their lives taking X rays have only a slightly increased risk of developing any form of leukemia.

In contrast, those who have been heavily exposed to radiation, such as the survivors of the Hiroshima atomic bomb that was dropped in 1945, have a greatly increased risk.

Q My best friend's brother has developed leukemia. Is this very serious?

A It is very sad, but the answer must be yes, it is serious. The outlook for lymphocytic leukemia is much better these days and in some cases a cure can result. However, the outlook with acute myeloid leukemia is not so good. It is always better to have the disease treated in centers where special facilities for treatment are available.

Q I have been told that leukemia is caused by a virus. Is there any truth in this?

A One form of leukemia, epidemic in Japan, the Caribbean, and the southeastern United States, has been shown to be caused by a particular virus. This is the Human T-cell leukemia virus type II (HTLC II).

Leukemias that occur in animals, such as feline leukemia in cats, have been known to be virus-induced for many years.

Leukemia is a cancer of the blood that can start in the bone marrow or the lymph system (see Cancer). Bone marrow is one of the places where blood cells are made: these may be red cells, which carry oxygen; white cells, which fight infection; or platelets, which form clots to seal injured blood vessels and prevent bleeding (see Blood).

There are four main types of leukemia, but the common factor in each is the proliferation of abnormal white blood cells. This abnormality usually begins in the bone marrow, where mutated, often immature white blood cells begin to multiply and spread throughout the body. Although leukemia sufferers have a huge number of immature white cells, or blasts, in their bodies, these cells are essentially nonfunctioning. Instead the blasts crowd out the red cells and platelets, and prevent healthy white cells forming. As a result, the leukemic sufferer is unable to fight off serious infections, becomes susceptible to anemia, and has a tendency to bleed easily.

The immature, abnormal white cells are called myelocytes, and leukemia that starts in the bone marrow is called myelocytic or myeloid leukemia. White blood cells called lymphocytes are made mainly in the lymph nodes, and some occur in the bone marrow (see Lymphocytes). Leukemia of the lymphatic system is known as lymphocytic leukemia (see Lymphatic system).

However, in both cases, the leukemic cells spread outside their place of origin, so that in lymphocytic leukemia abnormal lymphocytes can be found in the bone marrow and vice versa.

Incidence

Contrary to popular belief, leukemia is not a disease that is more common in children. Approximately 20,500 adults and 2,500 children are diagnosed each year with the disease, which causes 16,000 deaths annually. Nevertheless, the incidence of leukemia remains constant until the age of 75 at about 10 per 1,000,000 per year in the US; it then rises to 50 per 1,000,000 per year. Males are affected twice as much as females.

However, lymphocytic leukemia is much more common in children than in adults. It reaches a peak incidence of 50 per 1,000,000 children per year from two to four years old; then it falls, only to rise again in adults over 65.

Acute and chronic leukemias

Either type of leukemia may appear in acute or chronic form. In acute leukemia, the disease develops rapidly and the symptoms are severe and immediately apparent. Chronic leukemia develops much more slowly and the symptoms, which are similar to those of acute leukemia, may take years to appear, and may seem less severe.

The acute leukemias are a lot easier to treat than the chronic forms, and in some instances may be cured completely. The chronic leukemias tend to affect people in middle age, and are essentially incurable. However, because of their slow course and the gradual appearance of the symptoms, many people, particularly the

Normal blood cells (left). In leukemia the numbers of white cells, stained purple, are greatly increased (right).

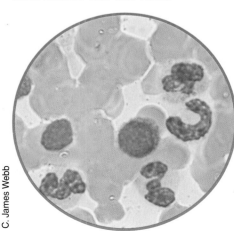
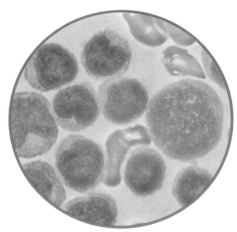

C. James Webb

aged, tend to die of illnesses that are unrelated to their condition.

What happens in acute leukemia

In a healthy individual, normal white blood cells cannot reproduce themselves, and after a life cycle of a few days or weeks are replaced by new cells. With leukemia two things go wrong. First abnormal white blood cells crowd out normal white blood cells, so that the latter are unable to fight infection. Second, they live for much longer than usual. This

A cross section of a vertebra (far left) with the bone marrow and blood vessels that supply it. The white blood cells are made in the bone marrow and then carried out of the bone in the blood vessels (inset). All the blood cells originate from the same stem cell (left), which is found in the bone marrow. In acute leukemia the white blood cells do not mature properly, the granulocytes never develop beyond the myelocyte stage, and the lymphocytes stop maturing at the lymphoblast stage. Both types of immature white blood cells have a tendency to live longer than normal.

means that eventually they accumulate to clog up the bone marrow and then spill into the blood to invade the lymph system, the liver (see Liver and liver diseases), and the spleen (see Spleen).

Cause

The acute leukemias originate from a single mutation in a white blood cell, which alters its genetic structure. There may be several causes for this. It is believed that a virus (see Viruses) similar to AIDS may be a cause. Another cause is atomic radiation; there was an enormous increase in cases after atomic bombs were dropped on Japan in 1945 (see Radiation sickness). Radiologists (doctors who handle X-ray equipment) also have a slightly higher risk of developing the condition.

Cases of chronic leukemia also increase following exposure to atomic radiation; chronic myeloid leukemia (of the bone marrow) is more common after prolonged exposure to benzene, a constituent of petroleum. Both chronic types occur in 15 new cases per 1,000,000 people per year in the US; both are fairly uncommon below the age of 20.

Chronic myeloid leukemia is als linked to a chromosome abnormality i which a piece is missing from chromo some number 22: the Philadelphia chro mosome. Abnormalities of chromosom number 21, the cause of Down's syn drome babies, are also linked to a highe incidence of myeloid leukemia (se Down's syndrome).

Symptoms

When the bone marrow teems with th abnormal leukemic cells, it cannot func tion properly and the patient become anemic through lack of red blood cell susceptible to infection because of lack c efficient white cells, and suffers fror excessive bleeding because the bloo cannot clot without platelets. Anemia ma be one of the earliest signs and sometime appears before any abnormal blood cell are found (see Anemia). Bleeding in od places like the gums, easy bruising, an heavy nosebleeds are also warning sign Infection occurs more commonly, resul ing in dental abscesses, sinusitis, or pne monia. Liver, spleen, and lymph nodes als enlarge; in leukemia the liver and splee

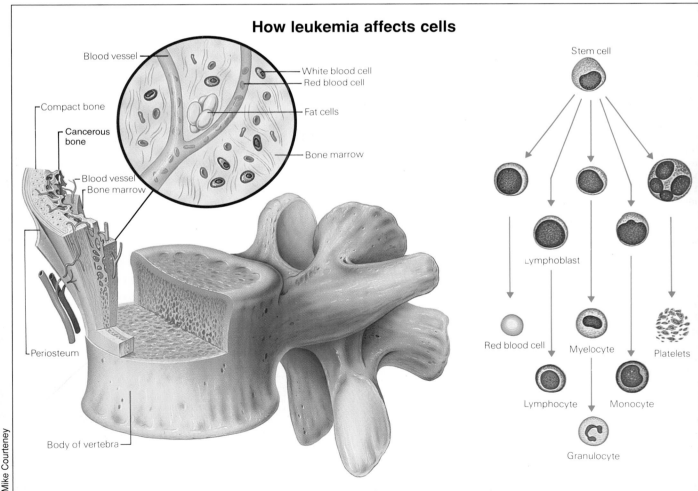

How leukemia affects cells

Blood vessel
White blood cell
Red blood cell
Compact bone
Cancerous bone
Fat cells
Blood vessel
Bone marrow
Bone marrow
Periosteum
Body of vertebra

Stem cell
Lymphoblast
Red blood cell
Myelocyte
Platelets
Lymphocyte
Monocyte
Granulocyte

Bone marrow puncture

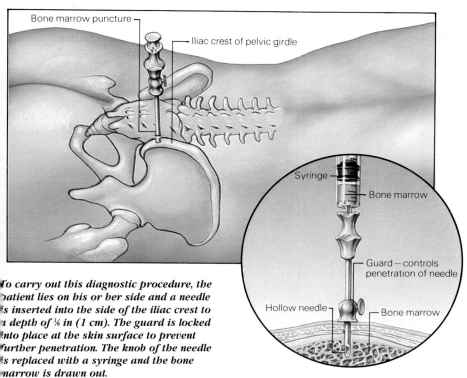

Bone marrow puncture

Iliac crest of pelvic girdle

Syringe

Bone marrow

Guard — controls penetration of needle

Hollow needle

Bone marrow

To carry out this diagnostic procedure, the patient lies on his or her side and a needle is inserted into the side of the iliac crest to a depth of ⅜ in (1 cm). The guard is locked into place at the skin surface to prevent further penetration. The knob of the needle is replaced with a syringe and the bone marrow is drawn out.

may drop down below the level of the ribs and can be felt on examination.

Diagnosis

Doctors diagnose the disease by examining a blood sample. Because red blood cells are made in the marrow, it is always abnormal to see immature red blood cells circulating. The diagnosis is sometimes made before such abnormal cells appear in the blood by taking a sample of bone marrow. This is done under local anesthetic by inserting a needle through the bone into the marrow cavity, often of the patient's breastbone or hip.

Treatment

Modern drugs can now cure lymphocytic leukemia, and life expectancy can be prolonged with myeloid leukemia (see Marrow and transplants). The most important treatment involves boosting the patient's bone marrow function until it normalizes itself.

Anticancer drugs, which are important, can initially make the patient's bone marrow function worse rather than better. Two types of drug treatment, called chemotherapy, may be given. The first drug kills all the white blood cells to get rid of the leukemic cells. When this hospital treatment is finished, the new white blood cells that develop in the bone marrow will be healthy. The second drug

keeps the cancer in remission (slows its progress) and can be taken at home.

Alternatively radiation treatment may suppress the reproduction of cells. A large dose destroys all blood cells, but a small dose affects only abnormal ones.

A more drastic treatment entails killing the patient's marrow and replacing it with a donor's graft. This eradicates any leukemic cells and the remaining normal blood cells that the patient had. This treatment, however, carries the risk that the patient will be attacked immunologically by the donor's cells, which perceive the patient's tissues as foreign. This can result in serious complications or even death (see Donors). Treating the donor's cells to remove these killer lymphocytes before giving them to the patient can prevent this serious complication.

Patients suffering from the symptoms of chronic leukemia can sometimes survive for years, and new drugs have greatly improved their quality of life. Progress in leukemia management has been exciting, as many patients can now expect to be long-term survivors.

It has been found that excessive doses of radiation stop the formation of all blood cells. Workers in nuclear energy plants must wear protective clothing.

Libido

Q Since recently having a baby, I have felt less like making love than before I was pregnant. Does this mean my libido is permanently diminished?

A No. It is quite common for the desire for sex to decrease after giving birth. Sometimes the lessening of desire is because of stress, sometimes it is due to postnatal depression.

If there is no improvement after a month or so, see your doctor, who may be able to advise you, or may send you to a specialist. Psychiatric counseling for such problems is increasingly helpful these days.

Q My husband nearly always feels like making love in the morning. At this time of the day I am rarely in the mood. What should I do?

A First suggest that morning lovemaking should be centered on the weekends, when you have the time to relax and enjoy it. Then, sometime during the week, initiate a lovemaking session yourself at night. In this way, your husband may well become an evening lover.

Q Is it my libido that lessens as I grow older, or just my ability to make love?

A Neither. It is your mistaken belief that your libido is decreasing that is to blame. This sort of anxiety can actually be translated into reality if you dwell on it long enough. Provided you are not bored with your partner, or your lovemaking, your desire for sex should continue at the same level into your late 50s or even longer.

Q Does being deprived of sex increase or decrease libido?

A The answer depends on the type of person and sometimes on the amount of guilt the person feels about sex. For those who have a guiltless attitude, the desire for sex increases with deprivation, unless they have chosen to lead a celibate life. For those with guilty feelings about sex, the desire tends to diminish with deprivation.

What matters about libido is not how high or low it is, but your attitude toward it. This is important because, to some extent, you can control the level of your sex drive.

Central to many of the theories of Sigmund Freud (the founder of psychoanalysis) about sex is the concept of libido. He saw it as a form of emotional energy, generated by the sex drive, which pushes us all through life. However, because the existence of such an energy cannot be proved, and because much human sexual activity is learned, libido is now generally used to mean sex drive.

What controls libido?

In both men and women, one particular hormone or chemical messenger, called testosterone, is responsible for our ability to experience sexual pleasure. It does so by creating the bodily conditions which enable sex to be enjoyed, including increased sensitivity of the genitals and a buildup of the response to sexual stimulation. Without the presence of this hormone, one cannot have sexual pleasure.

Humans, however, have considerable control over this chemical switch, as is proved by the many monks and nuns who have chosen to lead a life without sex. The brain partly controls the production of testosterone (see Hormones).

The growth of libido

Testosterone is present in the body in tiny amounts from infancy. In children this may lead to childhood masturbation and sexual

High libido is not exclusive to the young, but their need to form relationships may give the impression that it is.

play. Testosterone production begins t increase dramatically at the age of eight c nine in both sexes. Then, during adolecence, it levels off in girls but continues t increase in boys, so much so that by th time they reach adulthood, men are pr ducing about 10 times as much testo terone as women.

Strength of the libido

The strength of the sexual urge vari sharply, and is not merely a matter of th general testosterone level. In effect, th amount of the hormone circulating in th blood has little effect on either the se drive or behavior, so long as some testo terone is present.

Actual sexual desire and activity is, reality, almost entirely governed by th availability of a willing partner, togeth with the factors of mood, situation, and wish to indulge in sexual activity.

After sexual maturity is reached, su factors as pregnancy, alcohol, illness, ar stress can influence the strength of th sex drive. Apart from the fluctuatio that these may cause, the libido remai broadly constant. Some believe that middle age a decline in hormone produ

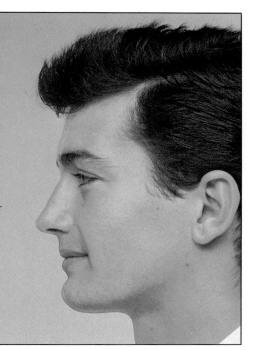

Libido: fact and fiction

Because sex preoccupies most of us at least some of the time, all too many theories have arisen about libido. Some are based only on conjecture, but a few are established facts

Fact
- Libido does not always fade with age
- Libido is lessened with tiredness, stress, alcohol, and drugs
- Women do have greater, and lesser, levels of libido at different stages of the menstrual cycle.
- Men show daily changes in libido

Fiction
- Libido is stronger in the morning
- Women are less libidinous than men
- Libido is affected by low sex hormone levels
- Introverted, shy people are always less libidinous than noisy extroverts

on weakens the libido; but this has not een proved. Most older people know hat if conscience and opportunity per-nit, a desire for sex is seldom lacking.

Some people believe that the libido is tronger in the morning than at night, articularly in men. There is little to sup-port this view. Both sexes dream fre-quently before waking, and in men this automatically produces an erection, whether the dream has sexual content or not. Some men may also feel aroused as a result of having a full bladder after sleep-ing, and like the erection caused by dreaming, imagine this as a sexual state (see Erection and ejaculation).

For women, sexual arousal is nearly always produced through the attentive-ness and competence of a lover, factors more associated with night than morning.

Both men and women show day to day differences in libido, but the precise caus-es of this are unknown. Changes in wom-ens' libido occur over the menstrual cycle, but researchers do not agree on when the peaks and troughs occur.

There is only a limited connection between libido and personality. Outgoing (extrovert) characters are generally more libidinous than inward-looking (introvert-ed) people, but the emotional sensitivity of introversion can actually assist the forma-tion of relationships.

Differences between the sexes

The most common question put to psy-chiatrists on libido is whether it is differ-ent in men and women. This is not an easy question since we are influenced by what society wants us to believe.

The only certainty is that women do indulge, statistically, in less sexual activity during their lifespans than men. It would be wrong to draw conclusions from this because women may have sex less often because they are expected to be more modest than men; because they have fears of unwanted pregnancy; and because they wish to be certain that they are being loved, not used, when having sex.

If the inclination exists, libido need not decline in middle age; in fact, it generally remains constant.

Lice

Q My daughter recently caught head lice at school. Although she was treated successfully—the doctor gave me a special shampoo—I am still worried in case the lice have spread undetected. Can someone with head lice get lice on other parts of the body?

A No. Of the three types of louse that live off humans—head, body, and pubic—the first two do not shift from their original environment because they have evolved in a way that means it would be impossible for them to survive in different conditions. The pubic louse may transfer to the hair of the eyelashes, eyebrows, underarms, or chest. The infestation by one kind of louse does not mean that an individual will be predisposed to contracting another type.

Q I love going to garage sales, but my mother keeps telling me that I could get lice from wearing old clothing. Is this really true?

A Lice will die if they cannot feed regularly and stay at body temperature. Therefore there is unlikely to be any risk of catching lice from clothing bought in a garage sale or secondhand store.

Q I would like to work on a farm but am a little worried about catching lice from the animals. Is this possible?

A It is very unlikely that humans would be at risk from the lice that live off animals; they would not be able to survive the change of environment. By the same token animals are unlikely to catch lice from humans. It has been found, however, that human body lice can live on pigs for a short time.

Q Are children with head lice kept out of school?

A There is no need for this once treatment has been given. If there is an infestation, school nurses will check each child regularly and insure that the necessary treatment will be given.

In the past, because of poverty and poor standards of hygiene, most people were infested with lice. Today, far fewer people harbor these parasites, but it is still possible, as always, for even the most fastidious people to become infested. Fortunately simple treatment is effective.

Lice are small, wingless, slow-moving, six-legged creatures that seldom exceed ⅛ in (3 mm) in length. They are unique, for insects, in that they possess seizing claws similar to those of crabs and lobsters. These claws enable lice to grip body hairs or the fibers of clothes. Lice have flattened bodies and are a grayish color with darker markings.

Appearance of lice

Head and body lice: The head and body lice, *Pediculus humanus capitis* and *Pediculus humanus humanus*, are similar in appearance, the only difference being that head lice are slightly smaller than body lice.

The features can be easily made out with the aid of a magnifying glass. The heads are longer than they are broad and carry a pair of simple pigmented eyes and a pair of five-segmented antennae. The thorax has fused segments and gives rise to the six legs with their gripping claws. The abdomen is long and heavy and has a series of distinct indentations along its edges.

The male is slightly smaller than the female. In the male the rear tip of the abdomen is rounded; in the female it is slightly forked.

Pubic lice: The pubic or crab louse, *Phthirus pubis*, is quite different in shape and, as the name implies, resembles a miniature seashore crab. The head is distinct, but the thorax and abdomen are fused into a single unit so that the whole body appears heart-shaped. The front two pairs of claws are weak and feeble, but the other two pairs are extremely powerful, more so than any of the claws of the head or body louse. These hind claws secure the parasite to pubic hairs at a par-

ticular site; here the creature remains fo[r] long periods, with its mouth parts burie[d] in the skin. These are withdrawn durin[g] molting. Pubic lice are seen as small, dirt[y] white, yellow, or grayish specks that ar[e]

Young children are particularly prone to catching head lice, so be prepared and check your child's scalp regularly (right). The itchy and inflamed reaction to louse bites on the arm (below).

C. James Webb/Bruce Coleman Ltd.

The three types of louse that live off humans—head (inset), pubic (above left), and body (above right)—have evolved in such a way that they require different living conditions for survival.

attached to the hairs. They live for about one month.

Of the many types of louse, only two main groups—*Pediculus humanus*, which includes the head and body louse, and *Phthirus pubis*, the pubic louse—live by infesting humans and sucking their blood. Fortunately lice can be dealt with quite easily, but the treatment varies because each type of louse requires different conditions for survival.

Effects of louse bites

Disorders caused directly by the bites of head and body lice are called pediculoses. The bites are usually painless but cause itching and may lead to dermatitis (inflammation of the skin). This inflammation is aggravated by scratching, and the result may be secondary infection of the skin with impetigo (see Impetigo) or boils (see Boils). Night biting causes loss of sleep in those infested.

In people who remain affected for years, the skin can become markedly altered and heavily bronzed by the deposition of pigment, which is tattooed by scratching. The skin can also become roughened and thickened. These changes are never found in people who acquire a brief infestation.

Only two major diseases are transmitted by lice: epidemic typhus (see Typhus) and relapsing fever. Neither of these conditions is at all likely to occur as a result of a mild infestation.

Head lice

The eggs of the head louse are laid in the hair close to the scalp and are secured to it by a cementlike substance. Each egg is about 0.04 in (1 mm) long and can be seen by the naked eye. After eight days or so the eggs hatch, and the lice begin to feed off the scalp by sucking blood.

Over a period of about nine days, the louse molts three times. At the end of this stage, the adult is fully formed and ready to reproduce. Each louse will then live for

about two more weeks, during which time the female will lay as many as 10 eggs every night.

The effects of head lice vary greatly from person to person. Some people experience only slight itching, while others may be driven to distraction by the itchiness of what may be a swollen and inflamed scalp. An itching scalp is the most obvious symptom of head lice, but under inspection it is possible to see the discarded egg casing, or nits, still cemented to the hair, and this will indicate that treatment is necessary.

Treating head lice

The safest way to deal with head lice is to use a special shampoo, preferably containing gamma-hexachlorocyclohexane (lindane, gamma-benzene hexachloride) or malathion, which can be applied directly to the head. It is never necessary to shave the head.

The shampoo should be spread onto the palm of the hand and worked well into the hair, avoiding the eyes. This should be repeated until the whole head is moist. It should then be left to dry naturally. Do not use a hair dryer because heat will weaken malathion and there is also a danger of igniting the lotion. The head should be washed 12 hours later (usually overnight) and the hair carefully combed out with a fine-toothed nit comb to remove any remaining eggs. Remember that these are usually attached close to the skin. Such a treatment will achieve an almost 100 percent cure rate.

It is now thought possible that some of the lotions that are intended to be left on the head for a longer period (i.e., 12 hours) contain chemicals that may be harmful, particularly to children. However, this suspicion has not yet been proven one way or the other. To be on the safe side, it is always best to consult a doctor before using any preparations, particularly those containing malathion.

Transference of head lice
Head lice transfer easily from head-to-head contact. Young children are more likely to be at risk, since they are often in close physical contact with each other when playing. School medical services are well aware that this is the case and should inform parents if an epidemic of lice occurs.

Brushing or combing children's hair with a fine-tooth comb before they go to bed may provide some protection, because adult lice that are injured in a comb cannot lay eggs. Keeping children's hair cut short may also provide some protection, but there is little else that can be done to safeguard them from a possible infestation.

Since lice are not killed by ordinary shampoo and water, cleanliness will provide no defense.

Body lice
Body lice occur less frequently than head lice. They need to feed regularly and to live in a constant temperature, so they will thrive under any conditions in which their human host changes clothes infrequently. They have therefore been associated with groups such as troops during wartime and prison populations, where conditions exist in which body lice can develop undisturbed—due to a lack of soap or washing facilities—and easily transfer from person to person.

The adult female louse lays her eggs in clothing, preferring the safety of the seams where the eggs will be undisturbed. Even if the clothes are removed at night, this may not bring about a change in temperature sufficient to kill the louse and its eggs, so the use of an insecticide is always advised.

Treatment of body lice
Malathion and BHT are highly effective. Follow the instructions on the lotion bottle with care. Lice will also be killed in extreme temperatures, so washing clothes in hot water (followed by careful ironing of all seams) will insure that the body lice are eliminated.

Diseases caused by body lice
The adult female louse can lay up to 250 eggs. This reproductive rate makes it very difficult to prevent the spread of body lice, and their numbers can reach epidemic proportions if the environment is suitable and they are left to reproduce unchecked. Their bites produce itchy inflammations that will alert the infested individual to their presence. Treatment should be sought without delay.

There are a number of louse-borne diseases, the most dangerous of which is typhus. This disease starts with flulike symptoms, followed by a serious fever and rash on the body. It is spread by excretions from the louse. Fortunately, however, the incidence of this disease is now much more rare than it used to be.

Pubic lice
Pubic lice, sometimes called crab lice or just crabs, are usually found living in the pubic hairs. As mentioned earlier, they look a little like miniature crabs.

Once again there is little that can be done to prevent the lice from being caught. If there is close contact with a person who has crabs—and since they infest the pubic area, this contact is likely to be sexual—they may well transfer themselves. For this reason, and because of its appearance, the pubic louse has been called the butterfly of love.

Many people are concerned about the possibility of picking up pubic lice in public toilets. The habits of the parasite already described, make this most unlikely. *Phthirus pubis* rarely leaves the body while it is still alive.

Life cycle and effects of pubic lice
Pubic lice thrive in warm conditions, and once a pubic louse has made its way onto the pubic hair, it will lay eggs in a similar way to the head louse. The eggs are cemented onto individual hairs and can be seen by the naked eye. A female pubic louse lays up to 50 eggs in her lifetime.

After a month the pubic lice hatch from their eggs and begin to feed off the human host. The symptoms vary from person to person and are usually at the worst and most irritating during the night. There may be inflammation of the pubic area in addition to an uncomfortable rash.

Pubic lice sometimes spread to the hair of the chest, armpits, eyebrows, and eyelashes, but they are never found on the hair of the head, because these hairs grow too close together.

Pubic lice do not carry sexually transmitted diseases but they are associated with them; so if pubic lice are present, it is best to have a checkup to make sure no other disease has been contracted. All sexual partners should be checked to see if they need treatment for the infestation.

Treatment
In dealing with pubic lice it is unnecessary to shave the affected area. Sometimes forceps are used to remove adult parasites, but this is often difficult because of their strong attachment to the hair. They can easily be disposed of, however, by the application of yellow oxide of mercury ointment, twice a day for a week.

If children are found to have pubic lice, it is likely that adult family members are also infested.

Because children tend to make close physical contact, they are susceptible to contracting head lice at school. Medicated shampoo provides a complete cure.

G. Baden/Zefa

Life expectancy

Q I smoke pretty heavily and am constantly being told to give up. Are the dangers of smoking exaggerated?

A No. It is estimated that well over 300,000 people die each year in the United States as a result of smoking-related diseases, and many of them are under the age of 65. For example, if you are currently smoking 25 cigarettes a day, you are 25 times more likely to contract lung cancer than a nonsmoker. However, if you give up smoking, this risk will diminish.

Q I am 16 and am thinking about choosing my future career. Are there any occupations I should avoid if I want to live longer?

A Most occupations have their own built-in stresses and risks, and how you react to them depends very much on your own personality and circumstances. According to life insurance companies, the highest risk occupations include deep-sea fishing and working on an oil rig.

Q My father is retiring next year, and I am worried that he may become depressed because he will no longer have a job to occupy him. Is there anything I can do?

A Retirement can present very real problems, especially to people who have led busy working lives and have had little time to develop other interests. Suggest to your father that he prepares for retirement before it actually happens by exploring a variety of hobbies and interests. Then when he stops working, the break will not be so sudden.

Q What can I do to live longer and keep healthy?

A More than ever survival is within our own hands. By not smoking, by drinking in moderation, eating sensibly, and getting plenty of exercise, you can give yourself every chance of resisting disease and living to an active old age.

People now live longer than their parents, grandparents, and great grandparents. Why has this happened, and what are the chances of further increases in life expectancy?

Sally and Richard Greenhill

Leading an active, fulfilling life and taking care of your health can help to increase your life expectancy.

A hundred years ago only six out of 10 babies born in Western countries survived into adulthood. A newborn baby boy had an average life expectancy of 48 years and a baby girl 50 years. Today this has risen to over 70 for men and over 78 for women.

The enormous improvement in longevity has been brought about by a number of factors, such as water purification, sewage disposal, better food and living conditions, improved medical care, and the virtual eradication of many infectious diseases (see Public health).

However, although more people are living longer, and there has been an enormous drop both in infant mortality and in all deaths between the ages of nine and 35, there has been no significant increase in life expectancy in recent years at the older end of the age scale. This is because, regardless of the advances in living standards and preventive medicine, it would appear that the body has a definitive life span.

Determining life expectancy

Life expectancy is made up of a variety of factors, but these can be summed up in two words: genetics and environment.

Environmental factors (surroundings and lifestyle) are, to some degree, within human control. Smoking is the most important of these factors. It has been estimated that a 25-year-old person who smokes two packs of cigarettes a day for the rest of his or her life will shorten their life by almost eight and a half years (see Smoking).

Atmospheric pollution is another health risk that could be controlled to some extent; by moving to the country from the city, for example (see Environment). Choice of occupation is a contributing factor in terms of fatal accidents and stress-related illnesses. Other factors include diet, exercise, and weight.

Genetic factors (those that are inherited and that determine physical makeup) are beyond human control (see Genetics).

The body runs on a clock that is counting down from the moment one reaches maturity. Each person's body clock is set differently; some people retain excellent mental functioning until they are well into their 80s, while others suffer from memory loss, which makes them incapable of looking after themselves. Some remain physically fit, even athletic, until later in life, while others develop arthritis and other conditions that impair movement.

A third, not quite so obvious, factor in life expectancy is simply how long a per-

LIFE EXPECTANCY

Children can be saved from death or serious injury if they are seated in the back of a car and wear specially designed seat belts.

son has lived. Life can be seen as a succession of hurdles: the more of them a person jumps, the more accurately life expectancy can be gauged. If a man lives beyond the age of 60, his chances of living well into old age are increased, because at around 60 the death rates from cancer and heart disease are at their peak. In other words, death and disease weed out the less fit, or less lucky, and those who pass 60 without succumbing to cancer or heart disease consequently have a relatively good life expectancy.

Discrepancies

The improvement in life expectancy is not shared by everyone. People living in developing countries have a much shorter life expectancy (about 40–55 years) than those living in Western countries (see Public health). There are also variations in life expectancy between countries of the developed world. For example, in the United States, 83 out of every 100 men who are 45 years old can expect to live to be 65. However, in Britain only 73 out of a comparable 100 men reach retirement age.

In the developed world, life expectancy can be affected by prenatal care (e.g., infant mortality), living conditions (e.g., neighborhood violence, and homicide), lifestyle (e.g., stress, and smoking), and access to quality medical care.

In both the developed and undeveloped world, however, life expectancy is still longer for women than men. In developed countries this is probably due to the fact that a huge number of men and not women smoked at the beginning of the 20th century. Today, women are just as likely to smoke as men, and this would account for the narrowing in the gap between male and female life expectancy. Lung cancer related to smoking is still the leading cause of cancer death in men, but there is now a rising mortality rate among women.

Outlook

If there is to be an improvement in life expectancy for everyone, more attention must be given to preventive measures that preserve health. For example, 80 percent of lung cancers could be prevented if no one smoked. The main preventive mea-

Improvements in living conditions for many people in Western countries have meant a great increase in life expectancy. Given good health, most grandparents can now expect to live to see their first grandchild— or even great-grandchild!

sures include: controls on environmental factors such as air, water, noise, and industry (see Pollution); better health education, including the key factors of diet and

exercise; and improved living conditions. In addition, advances in medical science (i.e., research into the screening and eradication of diseases) continue to be made.

Zefa

Ligaments

Like car doors, which have check-straps to prevent them from being opened too far and torn off their hinges, joints in the human body have ligaments to restrict movement.

Anatomy of ligaments

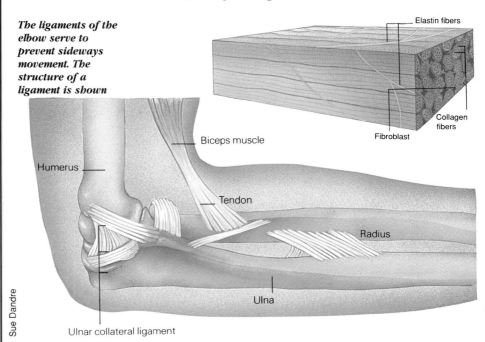

The ligaments of the elbow serve to prevent sideways movement. The structure of a ligament is shown

Labels: Elastin fibers; Collagen fibers; Fibroblast; Biceps muscle; Humerus; Tendon; Radius; Ulna; Ulnar collateral ligament

Sue Dandre

The bones at a joint are moved by muscles (see Muscles). These are joined to the bones by tendons, which cannot stretch (see Tendons). Ligaments, which can stretch very slightly, join the two bones that form the joint and keep them in place by restricting the amount of movement they can make. The bones would become dislocated very easily without ligaments.

Many people are unclear about the difference between ligaments and tendons. Although they are both made from the same materials, mostly tough fibrous collagen, their function and, to some extent, their appearance are different.

In a ligament bundles of collagen are arranged so that they form sheets of tough fibrous connective tissue. These sheets hold bones together properly at the joints to restrict any inappropriate movements of the bones. Ligaments also support internal organs in the abdomen. In tendons similar bundles are twisted together to form a cordlike structure or band of white inelastic collagenous tissue that runs between the ends of a muscle and the bones to which the muscle is attached. Tendons transfer the pull of a muscle to a bone.

Many ligaments become very closely associated with tendons when tendons are joined to bones near joints; sometimes tendons reinforce or even replace the ligaments that form the capsule (covering) of a joint.

Other locations

Ligaments are also found in the abdomen, where they hold in place organs such as the liver and uterus, while at the same time allowing the degree of movement necessary for adopting different postures and for the changes that accompany eating, digestion, and pregnancy. There are also ligaments made up of very fine fiber strands in the breasts. These support the breasts and prevent them from sagging.

People are not usually aware of the existence of ligaments until they injure one. A strained or torn ligament makes its presence felt in no uncertain way and can be just as painful as a broken bone.

Tensile forces

The pulling (tensile) forces applied to many ligaments are considerable and their slight elasticity would not, in itself, provide sufficient protection against tear-

LIGAMENTS

ing. An additional protective mechanism comes into play, however.

When a ligament is suddenly and excessively stretched, nerve endings in it are strongly stimulated. This results in nerve messages being sent to the appropriate muscles, which, on contraction, move the part (or even the whole body) in such a way as to relieve the pull on the ligament (see Reflexes). Unfortunately even this reflex mechanism is not always capable of preventing ligament damage. Some ligaments, such as those on the inner and outer side of the ankle that help to bind the foot onto the lower leg, are extremely susceptible to sudden stretching and tearing. This particularly affects women who wear shoes with high heels and narrow toes and twist their ankle.

Structure
The body's bones and internal organs are kept in place by connective tissue, which consists of cells and protein fibers gelled together; without it the whole framework would sag and collapse. Ligaments are one form of this tissue. The connective tissue in ligaments is made up mainly of a tough white protein called collagen, with some yellowish and more elastic protein called elastin. In most ligaments this tissue is arranged in sheets of fibers.

These fibers run in definite directions, depending on the type of movement they resist. In ligaments that are arranged in a cylindrical shape as a long cord, the fibers run longitudinally down the length of the cord and resist stretching along the length. Others, which help prevent joints from moving sideways, are arranged as a flat band of crisscross fibers that prevents movement through the band.

Between the fibers there are specialized cells called fibroblasts that are responsible for the creation of new collagen fibers and the repair of damaged ones. Between the fiber bundles there is a spongy tissue that carries blood and lymph vessels and provides space for the nerves to pass through.

Ligaments are attached to the bones they unite by fibers that penetrate the outer covering of the bone (the periosteum). The periosteum is supplied with nerves and blood vessels so that it can nourish the bone as well as provide an attachment for the ligaments and muscles (see Bones). The ligament and periosteum grow together so perfectly that the periosteum is often affected if a ligament should become injured.

Specialized ligaments
There are various types of joints in the body and specialized ligaments exist for each. Major joints like the knees, hips, elbows, fingers, and spinal joints are completely enclosed by a fibrous joint capsule containing synovial fluid to lubricate the joint (see Joints). Parts of this capsule are especially thickened for strength and are known as intrinsic (capsular) ligaments. There are also other ligaments inside and outside the joint capsule that play individual roles in restricting particular types of movement. These are known as extrinsic (accessory) ligaments.

Purpose
The variety of movements that the body can make depends on two things: the shape and design of the bone surfaces at the joint (the articulating bone surfaces), and the ligaments.

In some joints the bones are the most important factor. In the elbow joint the ulna (in the forearm) forms the lower half of the joint and is a hooklike shape that

allows only backward and forward movement, similar to a hinge (see Elbow).

Here the ligaments serve only to prevent side-to-side rocking, and a specialized ligament (the annular ligament) fits like a collar around the head of the radius (the outer bone in the forearm) to attach it to the ulna while still allowing rotation.

In the knee joint, however, the shapes of the bones offer no resistance to the movements of the joint. So, although the knee is also a hinge joint, it is controlled by specialized (cruciate) ligaments that prevent the knee from bending backward and help to lock the joint while a person is standing still (see Knee).

The muscles at the joints work in groups, some contracting while others relax, to enable the bones to move. The ligaments work in concert with these muscles, preventing them from making excessive movement.

Ligaments have no ability to contract, and they function as static and passive structures in the body. They can be stretched slightly by movement in the joint, and as this happens they gradually become tighter and tighter until no more movement is possible.

There are also ligaments that pass between two points on the same bone and remain unaffected by any movement.

The function of these ligaments is to protect or hold in position important structures such as blood vessels and the nerves.

Movement

Every joint in the body relies on some form of control by ligaments for its stability. Such control is particularly important where the bones themselves cannot restrict movement. The mobility of knees, hips, and shoulders all rely on the fact that the ligaments become progressively tighter at the extremes of each movement (see Movement).

Strains

The most common cause of pain and discomfort from ligaments is either a strain or a sprain. A strain, which is the least serious of the two, is caused by prolonged or violent stretching of the ligament. Many cases of pain in the lower back and hips are due to ligament strain that arises if the back muscles are allowed to become flabby and lose their tone. Ever since humans began to stand on two legs, many of the muscles and ligaments of the body, especially around the spine, have had to resist Earth's gravity by a continuous balancing act.

If faulty posture develops through habitual slumping in chairs or lack of exercise, the normal curves of the spine are increased, because the muscles are not taking the load sufficiently. Thus the ligaments are continually having to restrict excess movement, and eventually they stretch, leaving the joints less well

Each movement that a trained athlete makes depends on the interplay of joints, muscles, tendons, and ligaments. Shown below are the most important ligaments needed for actions involving (A) the shoulder, (B) the elbow, (C) the hip, and (D) the knee when Olympic-medal-winning athlete Daley Thompson goes into action.

protected and more prone to injury. Pain may start in the ligaments, the surrounding structures, or both (see Pain).

A strain is likely to be brought on by unaccustomed vigorous activity, such as lifting heavy boxes or skiing. The demands of the particular form of exercise often exceed the fitness of the muscles and ligaments, and they protest with pain when they are stretched.

Sprains

Sprains often occur in joints such as the ankle, shoulder, knee, and wrist following a fall or sudden blow. The joint is twisted or forced so quickly that the muscles do not have time to react and guard the joint against impact (see Sprains).

If it is a severe sprain, some of the ligament's fibers may be torn and the periosteum may be lifted from the bone underneath. This type of injury is extremely painful and is accompanied by inflammation and swelling (see Swellings). The most serious form of injury occurs if the ligament is completely separated from the bone or if it takes part of the bone with it. This is called an avulsion fracture (see Fractures).

Ruptures and tears

A ruptured ligament is one that has broken completely; a torn ligament results when some of the fibers twist and tear. Complete rupture of a ligament will produce an unstable joint. Surprisingly the

avulsion fracture, where the ligament remains intact but the whole of its attachment to the bone has been pulled off, is easier to deal with surgically than a complete rupture of the actual ligament. Such injuries most commonly occur at the ankle, knee, and finger joints. There is severe pain and often considerable bleeding under the skin, which can cause swelling in the joint.

Treatment

In an avulsion fracture an X ray will show a detached flake of bone near the point of the insertion of the ligament. This bony flake makes the reattachment of the ligament to the bone easier and makes for better healing than in the case of a torn ligament. Flakes can be put into place using stainless-steel wire or some other strong suture.

Torn ligaments will heal well in four to six weeks if they are held without tension. In young people with severe joint instability, such injuries are best treated by an operation. This must not be delayed due to the tendency for torn ligaments to shorten fairly quickly. Once this has happened it may then be impossible to bring the edges together by stitching.

After the operation the joint is immobilized, often in a cast, to insure that there is no pull on the ligament. This will usually be removed after three or four weeks so as to allow some exercising of the muscles, but wrapping the joint in an ace

bandage will be continued for several more weeks.

Most strains and sprains will heal by themselves with sufficient rest. The injured ligaments need to be protected from further strain by rest in bed or a supporting bandage. Ace bandages, if properly applied, are preferable because they give support and warmth without restricting circulation. If the sprain involves a limb, further support from a sling or crutch may be necessary.

After the initial injury some of the pain is caused by the pressure of the swelling. Cold compresses and massage toward the heart help to reduce the swelling and pain (see Pain management).

Ligaments have a very poor blood supply, are slow to heal completely, and can take several months to mend. The pain has usually disappeared long before this, but it is important not to use the joint too vigorously too soon. Gentle use promotes healing, however.

If a ligament is badly torn or ruptured from the bone, surgery will be necessary to reconnect it before it can heal and its function is restored. A new technique involves sewing the ligament together with special carbon-fiber thread, which is later absorbed into the body.

It is important to recognize that permanent instability at a joint may result if a severe ligament injury is not properly treated. When a ligament, such as one at the knee or ankle, is torn and the free edges are brought firmly together by stitching or other means, the scar tissue that forms between the edges is minimal and the tensile strength of the ligament will be slightly, if at all, impaired (see Scars). If, however, the ligament is allowed to heal slowly with a gap between the torn ends, this gap will fill with fibrous tissue that will inevitably stretch under tension. The result will be an incompetent ligament and a joint capable of undergoing the excess movement that caused the injury.

Another important practical point is that since ligaments require the cooperation of muscles to work correctly, the treatment of a severe ligamentous injury must not be allowed to interfere with the health of the relevant muscles. Therefore, treatment must insure that the torn ends of the ligament are so securely brought together that active exercises can be undertaken to strengthen the muscles. Such exercising must not, however, be started too soon and should be deferred until all acute pain has subsided.

It is important for patients with ligament strains and sprains to rest completely to avoid permanent damage of the affected joint. Tears and ruptures require surgery.

Oscar Burriel/Latin Stock/Science Photo Library

Lightning strikes

Q When there is lightning, my grandmother covers all the mirrors in the house. Is she sensible in doing this, or is she just following an old wives' tale?

A It used to be thought unlucky to see your own reflection in a mirror illuminated by lightning, but this is pure superstition. The light from lightning can be frightening because of its strange whiteness and anyone would look ghostly lit up by it, but there is no need to cover mirrors for safety reasons.

Q A friend told me that it would be safe to go out in lightning provided I wore rubber boots. Is this true?

A No. The voltage of lightning is so high that rubber soles give little or no protection. Shoes with metal spikes or studs positively encourage lightning to strike and should never be worn in a storm. Metal is one of the best lightning conductors. If you are caught outside in such shoes, take off your footwear while the storm lasts, and put it well away from you.

Q My father pulls out all the electrical plugs when there is lightning. Is this necessary?

A Lightning passing through a house can fuse electrical appliances, and in the past these might have caught fire. Today most wiring is so much safer that this cannot happen and there is no need to take out the plugs. Some people like to go through the ritual of precautions when there is a storm, because they are a little bit frightened and it reassures them.

Q Should you keep away from fireplaces when there is lightning?

A If you live in a tall house or a high apartment block with chimneys, it is sensible to keep away from the part that is most likely to conduct lightning during an electrical storm. Better still, get a lightning conductor. They are not costly and give complete protection to everyone inside.

A flash of lightning is what we see when the atmosphere discharges millions of volts of electricity. When this current travels to earth it can cause injuries, but these are easy to avoid if the right precautions are taken.

The actual force of an electrical current is measured in volts: one volt is the amount of force necessary to carry one unit of current (an amp) through one unit of resistance (an ohm).

Flashes of lightning can be up to 20 ft (6.1 m) in diameter and over 1 mile (1.6 km) long, so the voltage involved is of the order of thousands of millions, and the force of the current is in the region of 10,000–20,000 amps. When lightning reaches the earth, such high voltages can burn most objects in its path. When a human or an animal is struck by lightning, the result is either instantaneous death or shock with severe burns. Electrocution is the most common accident that is caused by lightning (see Electric shocks).

Conductors

Air is a poor conductor of electricity. The same is true of many solid objects on land such as tall buildings, but they may be caught up in the path of lightning. Water is an excellent conductor of electricity. Human beings and animals, being mostly composed of water, are good conductors, and if they are standing outside in an open space they are likely to be struck.

Forked lightning strikes more than one place and is highly dangerous.

LIGHTNING STRIKES

Although trees are tall they are relatively poor conductors unless they are wet; the lightning simply travels down them to earth. However, if a human being or an animal stands beside the trunk, the lightning will jump from the tree and earth down whoever is standing beside it.

The best conductors are water and metal. Tall buildings and ships have strips of copper at their highest points to act as conductors, grounding the current safely. Airplanes flying high in the clouds are rarely affected by lightning: it passes around their metal hulls.

Someone whose heart has stopped due to electrical shock may be revived if artificial respiration and cardiac massage are applied immediately. A conscious patient must be treated for shock and burns and taken to a hospital at once (see Shock).

Lightning can cause severe internal injuries; as the current passes through the body, it destroys some cells but leaves others unharmed. In the hospital the patient needs rest, sedation, treatment for burns, and careful observation of organs such as the liver and kidneys. Someone who has suffered only slight effects may be kept in the hospital for 24 hours.

Outlook

Most people who survive being struck by lightning nearly always make a complete recovery, but sometimes they carry burn scars and suffer some loss of efficiency in the general working of the body. The most dangerous period is the first few seconds after someone is struck, when the electrical shock may prevent the heart and lungs from working and so cause death.

An oak tree struck by lightning (right). Fires are started by either forked or streak lightning (below).

Dealing with lightning

What to do
- **In the pool:** Get out
- **Out of doors:** Find sheltered valleys away from trees. If in open country lie flat on the ground
- **In an open boat:** stay in the bottom of the craft, below the waterline
- **In a car:** drive on safely; no risk
- **At home:** no need to take out plugs, but if you have a rooftop television aerial, disconnect it from the set
- **Field sports:** take off spiked shoes that can act as conductors

What not to do
- Never stand under or near a tree
- Don't carry golf clubs; put them flat on the ground, well away from you
- Never shelter under a car; you would be part of the path to earth
- Avoid using the telephone; cables from overhead lines can conduct lightning
- If you are out of doors, don't put up a tent: the poles may act as conductors
- Don't go out in a small boat; you would be the best conductor for miles

Camera Press

Types of lightning

Forked lightning: cloud-to-ground, branches into several earth points near the ground. Most dangerous type of lightning because it strikes more than one place

Streak lightning: cloud-to-ground, earthing at a single point. Dangerous to be near the earthing point

Sheet lightning: cloud-to-cloud and not at all dangerous

Heat lightning: really streak lightning seen from a great distance, and appearing red because the whitish-blue light has been dispersed in transmission. Not dangerous

Limping

Mike Hill/Walking stick: John Bell of Croyden

Q I recently broke my leg, and although the cast has been off for several weeks, I still have a limp. Will it be permanent?

A No. When a bone is broken and set in plaster, the muscles around the break become weak through disuse. Gradually, as you get more exercise, the strength will return and the limp will disappear.

Q Sometimes when I am out walking I am forced to limp through a sudden weakness in one leg. Why is this?

A There could be several reasons, but one of the most likely is that there is something wrong with one of your knee joints. This makes it difficult to straighten the leg fully and means that the leg cannot support your weight properly and appears to be weak.

Q My son cut his foot playing football without his cleats on. The cut has healed, but he still has a limp. Why is this?

A His original limp took the weight off the cut, allowing it to heal and minimizing the pain. Your son has now got into the habit of limping, but this will gradually wear off. You should encourage him to put his full weight on the cut area occasionally, and tell him to practice walking without a limp.

Q My 10-year-old brother has had a limp for about a week. He is not in pain. Should he see the doctor?

A He should be seen by a doctor immediately and examined for signs of an abnormality in his hip joint. He could have a disease called Perthes' disease.

Q My father begins to limp after he has walked a short distance, and then he has to rest. Why is this?

A He probably has intermittent claudication, caused by a poor blood supply to the muscles of the leg. He should see his doctor immediately.

The uneven way of walking described as a limp can have numerous causes, so it is essential to consult a doctor if anyone in the family develops a limp.

A walking stick can help to counteract the tilting of a damaged hip joint.

The original medical term for limping was *claudication*. This is thought to derive from the name of the Roman Emperor Claudius, who was said to have had a limp. Today it is usually used to describe limping that is caused by poor circulation in one leg.

Causes

Because there are so many causes of limping, it is useful to divide them into two broad categories: those within a limb and those outside it.

The first class is the larger of the two and is headed by the most obvious cause—pain. Pain usually results from either an injury to the leg or foot, or from inflammation. Causes of inflammation include arthritis, which is inflammation in a joint, and infections of the leg and foot, such as boils (see Inflammation).

Deformity

Doctors use the word *deformity* to describe any abnormality of the shape of a limb, and this could, of course, include a leg that is too short or is bent in some unusual way. It can also apply to a joint, typically the knee joint, which can develop a sideways bend as a result of injury or as an effect of disease (see Knee).

Arterial disease

The main early effect of arterial disease is a narrowing of the arteries, so that the blood flow to the muscles is reduced (see Arteries and artery disease). This means that they are deprived of an adequate supply of glucose fuel and of the oxygen needed to use it. As a result lactic acid (a metabolite) accumulates in the muscles. Normally it is washed away in the bloodstream, but in this case it remains at the site of production and causes cramplike pains in the leg muscles.

The pain, which causes limping, develops when the leg is used for walking. The leg is normal when at rest, and the distance a patient can walk before he or she starts to limp varies with the severity of the arterial disease. For these reasons the ailment is called intermittent claudication. It is highly characteristic of arterial disease and must be taken seriously by both the doctor and the patient, principally because if the arteries in the legs are diseased, the arteries in the heart and brain are often diseased, also.

A similar, but distinct, condition called venous claudication can also cause limping. It is the result of extensive clotting (see Thrombosis) in the main drainage veins of the leg with almost complete blockage. There is a considerable rise in the pressure in the veins, and after a few minutes walking a bursting sensation is felt in the calf. This rapidly increases when walking continues until it becomes agonizing and prevents further exercise. The distinction between this and arterial claudication is important, because the medical management is quite different.

Another type of claudication causing limping is cauda equina claudication. The *cauda equina* (Latin for "horse's tail") is the leash of nerves that hangs down in the spinal canal below the termination of the spinal cord. A tumor in this region of the spinal canal will press on these nerves and cause sciatic pain in the leg and a limping gait.

Muscular disease

There are several muscular diseases that can cause limping. The most serious of these are muscular dystrophy (in which the muscles become weak and shrunken, see Muscular dystrophy) and myositis (in which the muscles become inflamed).

Previous injuries to muscles or tendons that may have left permanent scars, and hence permanent abnormality, should also be mentioned in this category.

In the past many thousands of people have suffered in this way as a result of the permanent partial paralysis of muscles caused by polio (anterior poliomyelitis). This disease of the motor nerves of the spinal cord commonly affected one or two leg muscles, usually on one side, and was a prolific cause of a severe and permanent limp (see Poliomyelitis). Fortunately, because of the work of the virologist Albert Sabin and the immunologist Jonas Salk, almost no new cases have occurred for many years in the developed countries (see Immunization).

Other causes of limping that originate in the lower limbs include:
- hip joint osteoarthritis
- hip joint fixation (where bones actually fuse together)
- hip joint dislocation, whether congenital or acquired
- muscular rheumatism
- muscular insufficiency with strength imbalance
- knee joint arthritis
- cartilage tear
- laxity of knee joint ligaments
- chondromalacia patellae
- rickets
- muscle compartment syndrome due to overdevelopment
- ankle joint disorders
- clubfoot and other foot deformities
- flatfoot
- gout
- bunions (hallux valgus)
- pain in the long bones of the foot (metatarsalgia)
- ingrown toenail
- wart on sole of the foot (see Verruca)
- limb amputation.

Outside the leg

There are several disorders of the spine (vertebral column) that can cause limping

---

The effect of a limp

A   B   C

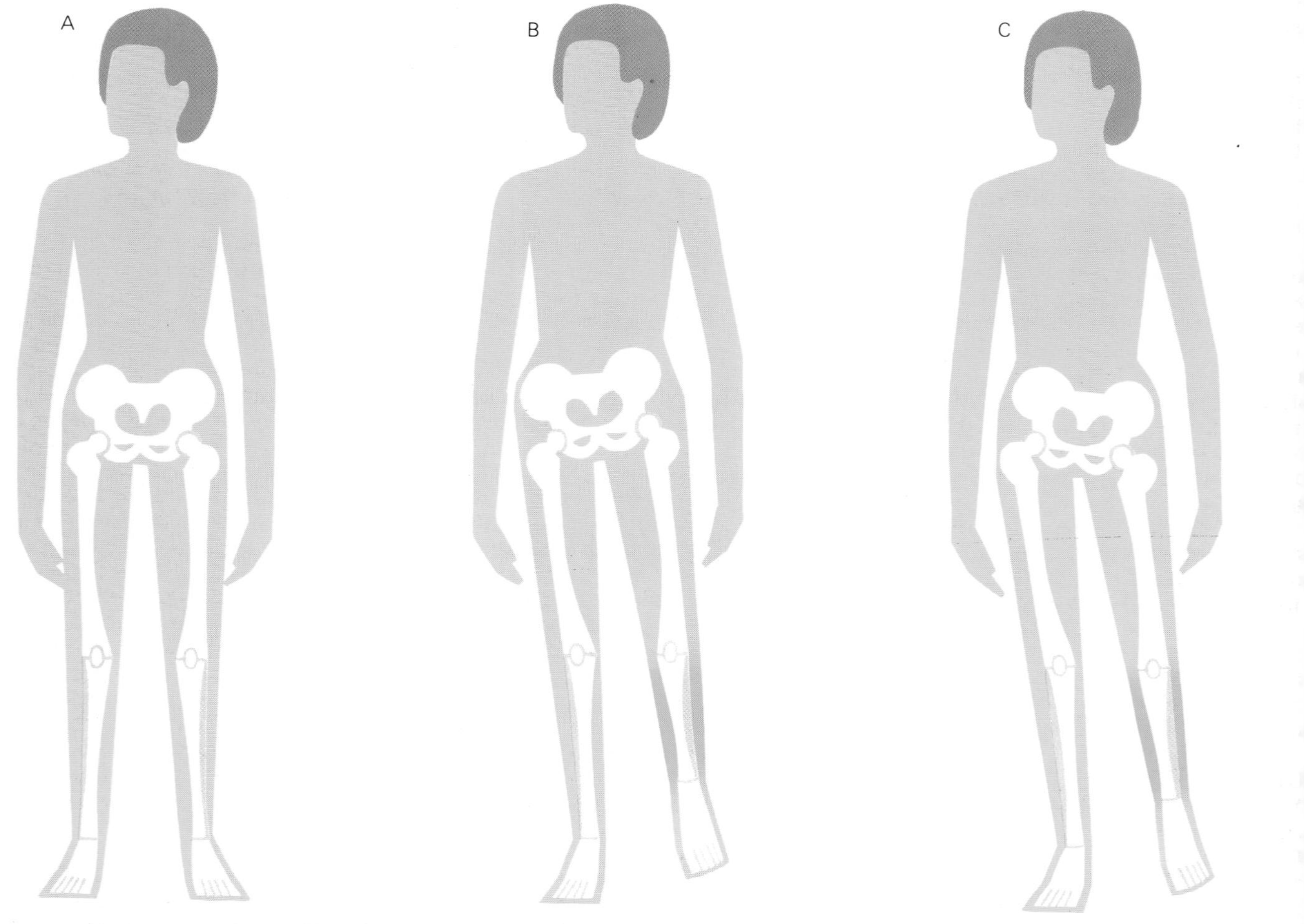

ng. These include scoliosis, the deformity n which the spine is twisted sideways nd the pelvis is often tilted (see coliosis); osteoporosis, with resulting eformity (see Osteoporosis); protrusion f an intervertebral disk, with sciatic pain see Sciatica); narrowing of the spinal anal (spinal stenosis) due to bone over-rowth, with resulting claudication; and cute lower back pain from any cause see Lower-back pain).

If it is not something inside the leg that s causing a patient to limp, a doctor will ook elsewhere, and the first possible ause on his or her list will be an abnor-nality of the nerve supply.

This could mean an abnormality of the erves themselves or an abnormality in he central nervous system—the brain or pinal cord—where all the commands hat travel down the nerves originate (see Nervous system).

One of the most common causes of mping in elderly people is a minor troke. A stroke is arterial failure (caused y arterial disease) in the brain. An area of rain tissue is deprived of its vital blood upply, and the resulting damage causes ome degree of paralysis to various egions of the body, including the legs see Stroke).

Most strokes are caused by blood clot-ing (see Thrombosis) in an artery sup-lying part of one side of the brain. Because each side of the brain controls he movement in the other side of the ody, such strokes commonly give rise to artial paralysis of most of the muscles n one side of the body only.

In some cases the motor damage, lthough one-sided, is so severe that valking is almost impossible; in others t s much less severe and may amount to o more than a minor weakness causing . limp. In every case attempts at walking hould be made, however difficult this nay be. Experience has shown that even vhen the normal nerve supply from the rain to the leg muscles is seriously dam-ged, alternative motor nerve pathways, ollectively called the extrapyramidal ystem can, to some extent, take over and llow walking. This will not occur, iowever, unless the effort is made. Jnfortunately the additional psychologi-al effects of a stroke often induce pes-imism and lack of motivation. In such ases even severe limping may be con-idered a major success.

Diagnosis

Asking a patient about his or her limp is rital when trying to establish its cause. 'he doctor has to know how long it has oeen present; if, for example, it has been oresent since infancy, a congenital cause night reasonably be expected.

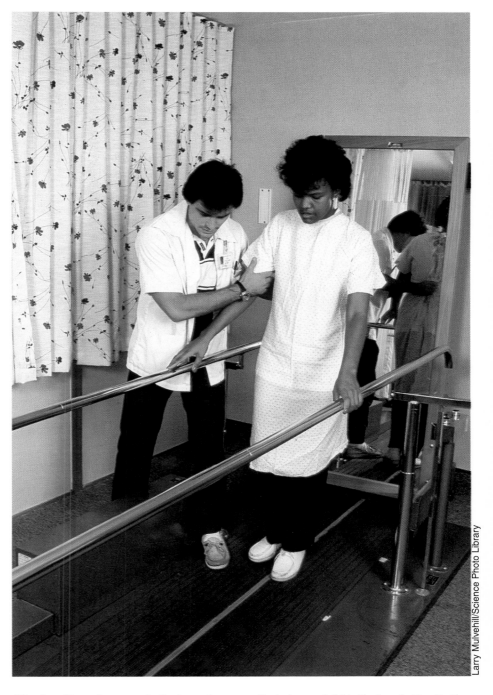

Larry Mulvehill/Science Photo Library

After breaking a leg, many patients need physical therapy (above) to help them relearn how to walk. It is usual to have a limp until the muscles around the break have returned to full strength. A limp may have various causes (far left), some of them not even directly involving the legs. In a normal pelvis (A), both sides are aligned and the hips are level. When the left foot is raised (B), the left side of the pelvis tilts upward as the weight is transferred to the left leg. But if the right hip is damaged (C), the pelvis tilts downward on the left side even when the left foot is raised, resulting in

a limp. A cane held in the hand opposite the affected hip can prevent the tilting of the pelvis and will largely overcome the limp. Other physical causes of a limp include: an injury to one or more of the leg muscles; a strain of the knee joint; a crack or fracture of the fibula (the thin leg bone alongside the tibia, or shinbone); a cut or sore on the sole of the foot; and even a spinal injury, such as a slipped disk pressing on a nerve that serves the leg. An arterial or circulatory disorder that affects the blood supply to the leg can also cause a limp, and a doctor should be consulted without delay.

Q My 18-month-old daughter is walking and seems to be getting around fine. But my mother noticed that her toes seem to be turned in, and she thinks I should take her to see an orthopedist. Is this really necessary?

A The foot condition you describe, called pigeon toes, is very common in young children. If the effect is mild and doesn't seem to be interfering with your daughter's getting around, then probably nothing needs to be done.

These mild abnormalities of gait often correct themselves as the child grows older. You should see a marked improvement, particularly when she is out of diapers, because it will be easier for her to move.

Q I have a friend who had cancer and had to take chemotherapy. Now his cancer is gone, but he limps badly, and he also seems to drag his toes and stumble often. Does this mean his cancer is coming back?

A Probably not. Some of the medicines used to treat cancer can damage the nerves. It sounds as though your friend has *foot drop,* a term that refers to not being able to lift the foot properly at the ankle. As a result his toes point downward and scrape along the ground, causing him to stumble.

Q My neighbor has very bad diabetes and has had a lot of trouble with his circulation, particularly in his legs. He limped badly for a long time and finally had to have his leg amputated below the knee. Now he hardly limps at all. How can this be?

A Limb replacement technology has become so sophisticated that, even though it is not as good as a healthy, natural limb, an artificial limb can be easier to get around on than a badly diseased natural limb.

In osteoporosis there is a loss of bone density. This often affects the thighbones and pelvis and it increases the risk of bone fractures, which can result in limping.

The doctor is also likely to ask the patient if the leg hurts, if it feels weak, or if the limp comes on after exertion, such as walking. Answers to these questions are almost bound to narrow the cause of the limp down to one of the categories described, and the examination can then be carried out.

Often the examination immediately indicates the cause of the limp. It is relatively easy to determine whether a patient is putting his or her foot on the ground for only a short time because it is painful; or to see that when a patient is standing, the pelvis is tilted, suggesting that one leg is shorter than the other.

An X ray of the leg, hip joint, and spine may help to determine the cause of the limp, but, in some cases, more searching investigation may be needed. Contrast X rays of the spinal canal (myelogram), in which a fluid opaque to X rays is injected into the cerebrospinal fluid surrounding the cord, or a computed tomography (CT) or magnetic resonance imaging (MRI) scan may be needed (see Scans).

The investigation of muscular causes of limping may call for sophisticated electrophysiological tests, such as the electromyogram (EMG) or nerve conduction tests.

Osteoarthritis

One of the most common causes of limping in middle-aged and elderly people is osteoarthritis of the hip joint (see Osteoarthritis). This is the result of years of wear and tear on the joint, and the ensuing pain and stiffness cause the sufferer to limp, as does the accompanying loss of movement in the joint. In a few cases there is a tendency for the head of the femur (the thighbone) to collapse.

This sort of limping can be minimized by the use of a walking stick—the stick is held in the hand opposite to the side affected, so that the tendency of the hip to dip is counteracted.

Treatment

Other treatments are governed by the severity of the disease and include drug therapy, physical therapy, and, in severe cases, a surgical operation to replace the damaged joint with an artificial one.

Intermittent claudication is also treated in a number of ways. The first advice to patients who smoke is always to stop smoking, since this is a proven cause of narrowing of the arteries (see Smoking). In cases of severe disablement surgery may be needed. The object of the surgery is to bypass the affected arteries with artificial segments or to actually widen those that are already in existence (see Arteries and artery disease).

Treatments for limping that result from other, miscellaneous causes, fall into place once the cause has been established. Natural healing will benefit a large number of injury and accident cases; and physical therapy may correct, in time, what nature cannot restore in the way of deformed or permanently damaged muscles or ligaments.

Special shoes or boots are effective where there is limping due to shortness of one leg. Calipers or braces, worn either occasionally or permanently, can give back use of a paralyzed or weakened limb, and due to the support they provide, can be comparatively comfortable to wear (see Calipers and braces).

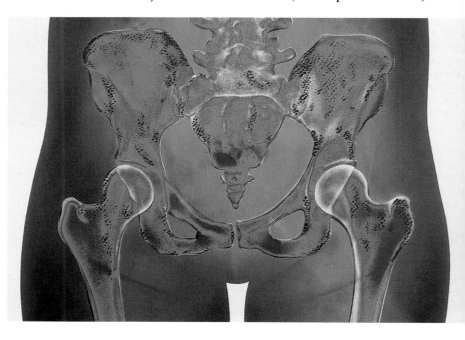

Liminents

Q Do liminents themselves do any good, or is the real benefit from the massage that goes with them?

A Most of the good is probably done by the massage. However, most liminents, even by themselves, do give a feeling of warmth and are also useful as counterirritants, making the patient feel better by soothing the inflamed area and drawing attention away from the pain.

Q Are there any conditions in which liminents should not be used?

A Yes, several. Liminents should not be used on any area where the skin is broken, say, by a scrape or a burn, because the active ingredients in the liniment may be absorbed and do harm internally. Also people who know they have sensitive skin or who are prone to eczema should consult their doctor before using liminents, because they may inflame the skin too much. Liminents should not be used as a base for massaging strains and sprains unless it is quite certain that there is no possibility of there being a fracture.

Q If someone has a fever, is it safe to give them a rubdown with a liniment that produces a feeling of heat?

A Yes, it is usually safe, but not really the best idea. Someone who is running a temperature is more likely to appreciate being allowed to rest rather than being massaged; he or she would generally prefer a feeling of warmth to come from a hot bath or an electric blanket.

Q Are liminents poisonous, and should I keep them away from my children?

A Liminents are intended to be used externally only and should never be taken orally. A few do have ingredients that could cause poisoning. In any case it is a vital home safety precaution to keep all medicines, external as well as internal, out of the reach of children (and animals).

A liniment is a liquid ointment applied to the outside of the body, often by means of massage, to soothe the pain of aching joints or ease a bronchial chest. Liminents can also act as counterirritants, reducing the pain of inflammation.

The word *liniment* comes from the Latin, meaning "to smear" or "anoint." A liniment is applied to the skin by gentle rubbing or massage. Liminents achieve their effects locally by their action on the skin and the nerve endings in it, rather than by being absorbed through the skin into the bloodstream, and having a general effect on the body.

Uses of liminents

In general liminents are used solely for their action on the skin. A notable exception is camphor liniment or ointment. Camphor liniment is principally used not for its effect on the skin, but because when it is smeared on the chest it gives off a vapor that, when it is inhaled by the patient, has a soothing and beneficial effect on bronchial symptoms. Menthol can be used in a similar way.

The initial effect is for the skin to be irritated by the substance that is being applied to it. In response the skin's blood vessels enlarge so that more blood can get to the area to fight off the threatened invasion by a foreign substance. This results in a typical inflammatory reaction, with the affected area becoming red and hot. Because of this, such liminents are called rubefacients (see Inflammation).

Providing a counterirritant

The sensations of burning and tingling are responsible for another use for preparations of this sort—as counterirritants. Their application over an internally inflamed part, such as an arthritic joint or a lung affected by pleurisy, effectively makes the pain in the joint or chest seem much less severe (see Pleurisy).

Local anesthesia

Stronger liminents can cause a temporary paralysis of the nerve endings in the skin and thereby act as a local anesthetic (see Anesthetics).

Such preparations may be a useful remedy for itching, though more sophisticated substances are more commonly used nowadays (see Itching). Very strong liminents, such as those made from the oil distilled from black mustard seeds, may even cause a blistering of the skin.

Liminents are most commonly and usefully applied for their soothing, counterirritant effect in painful conditions of muscles, ligaments, and joints and also as an aid in massage; their oily consistency

decreases friction on the skin and makes the rhythmical rubbing of the underlying tissues easier (see Massage). The liminents most commonly used for this purpose include saponis (soap) liniment, ethyl salicylate (oil of wintergreen) liniment, and terebinthinae (turpentine) liniment.

Sports injuries

An increasingly common use of liminents is for sports injuries. Sprained ligaments, pulled muscles, and inflamed tendons are all very common consequences of many games, and the prompt application of a liniment containing an anti-inflammatory drug may enable the player to continue and complete an important match. Such liminents often come in an aerosol spray pack for easy application.

Top tennis player Govan Ivanisevic receives treatment between sets for a pulled muscle. His coach is on hand throughout the match with a liniment to relieve the pain.

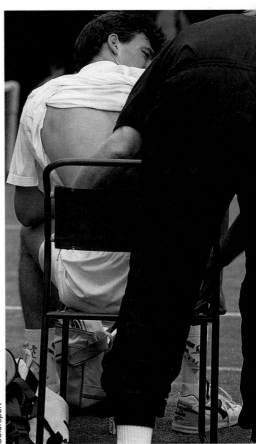

Colorsport

Liquid diet

Q If I put food through a food processor does it change the food value?

A Not really, because the calorific value remains the same. The blades of the food processor do, however, chop up fiber so it does not form bulk in the intestine. This can eventually lead to constipation, which is one of the inevitable hazards of liquid diets. However, a daily drink of prune juice usually relieves constipation.

Q Can I use a liquid diet to lose weight?

A Yes. You can obtain a liquid diet with a low calorific value, but it is a great deal easier and more pleasant to lose weight on a balanced diet containing plenty of fiber and roughage. You can still drink plenty of liquefied fruits and juices, but the roughage and fiber will prevent constipation.

Q My sister is going to have a colostomy. Will she have to live on a liquid diet?

A Colostomy patients usually return to a normal diet as soon as possible after the operation, which creates an artificial anus in the side of the abdomen. When this happens they defecate regularly with normal feces. Some patients find that certain foods do upset their bowel movements, but there is never any need for a liquid diet. Much more useful is a very careful analysis of the foods that help to keep the patient defecating regularly.

Q I like the liquid foods that you can buy at the drugstore, but can they really be used to replace a normal diet?

A It is important to read the description on the label for any such foods very carefully indeed. If they claim they can replace a normal diet, then they should do so, but only if taken in the required quantity. If you are going to rely on such foods for any length of time, you should check with your doctor.

During illness and convalescence a liquid diet can be a vital form of nourishment for a patient. There are other times when liquid diets can be beneficial, but any such diet must be nutritionally adequate and medically approved.

There are two situations in which a prolonged liquid diet may be appropriate. Doctors sometimes recommend that a patient be given nothing but liquids for a time for a specific reason, such as a throat infection; and people who are recovering from illness often feel so weak that they too can only take in liquids. However, whenever a liquid diet is followed for a prolonged period, it is vital that it contain all the nutrients needed by the patient.

There are other occasions when a liquid diet may be appropriate for a short period. This might be before an operation or following a tooth extraction. Because the diet will only be followed for a few days, there is no need to worry too much about the balance and calorie content of the diet. When a liquid diet has to be followed for a longer period of time, however, it is necessary to ask the advice of the nurse, doctor, or dietitian (see Diet).

All basic nutritionally adequate liquid diets must contain sufficient vitamins, minerals, fats, carbohydrates, and proteins that include the essential amino acids. This balance is especially important when healing is taking place, and most such diets include additional vitamin and

mineral supplements. As well as being balanced in its fat, carbohydrate, and protein content, it is important to check that the liquid diet contains sufficient calories. Sick people very often require up to 2,000 calories a day, especially if they are recovering from surgery or a high fever.

Types of diet

A pure liquid diet contains no large food particles so the food can be drunk from a cup or beaker. In some circumstances it can simply be poured down a nasogastric tube (a tube from the nose to the stomach), since it is completely fluid. Although it is only rarely necessary, a properly constituted, nutritionally adequate liquid diet can be continued indefinitely, since it contains all the nutritional elements needed for growth, repair, and body maintenance.

A pureed diet is semifluid. It is usually prepared with a food processor that chops the food into small particles, destroying roughage and reducing the fiber content.

A soft diet is a little nearer to an ordinary diet, but it still does not require chewing and is easily swallowed. It is ideal for tempting an invalid and is very easily digested.

Liquid diets in the hospital

A preoperative diet is totally different and is never used at home. It is designed to remove all food from the intestines in preparation for surgery, and it is neither nutritionally adequate nor intended to be used for any length of time.

In normal circumstances food is reduced to a pulp by chewing and is swallowed as a bolus or soft lump by the action of the throat. Even by the time the food is swallowed, the process of digestion has begun, and the bolus is pliable and moist (see Digestion). Liquid diets are used when swallowing a bolus is painful or difficult (see Throat).

When a patient has a severely fractured jaw, the bones are held in place by wiring the top teeth to the bottom teeth so that chewing becomes impossible. A liquid diet may have to be followed for several weeks until the fractured bones have united. Overweight people can also have their jaws wired, and in this case a low-calorie, but balanced diet is needed. Where the teeth are wired, the liquid must be totally free of large food particles so that simply washing out the mouth is sufficient for effective cleaning.

Where there is a cancer of the mouth or throat, or where there has been radiation to the throat or esophagus, then a liquid diet may have to be used for some months. A cancer can partially block the normal mechanism for swallowing, making solids stick and causing pain. A fluid diet slides down easily and provides the necessary nutrition. Where there has been radiation to tissue, it causes inflammation in the ordinary cells lining the esophagus. Hard foods will irritate the cell lining, whereas fluids or a puree diet enable food to pass into the stomach without damaging the esophagus.

In cases where there is paralysis of the swallowing muscles, solids may cause

Most fruit has a high vitamin C content and is a valuable addition to a liquid diet. When liquefied, as here, fruit is easy to absorb. Many vegetables, either raw or lightly cooked, can be treated this way, too. However, an invalid must have a diet properly balanced in its fat, protein, and carbohydrate content. If someone in your family needs a liquid diet, ask your doctor or a hospital dietitian for advice.

Tom Belshaw

Tom Belshaw

choking and a liquid diet becomes the only solution. When there is total paralysis of the swallowing muscles, feeding has to be through a nasogastric tube and a liquid diet must be used permanently.

Occasionally a liquid diet may be used in the treatment of inflammatory conditions of the intestines. Diverticulitis is inflammation of tiny pouches, or diverticulae, which can form in the large intestine; in the acute stages of this disorder, some doctors recommend a liquid diet. In effect this gives the intestines a rest and allows the inflammation to subside (see Diverticulitis).

Liquid diets at home

Liquid diets can be extremely helpful when coping with illness or convalescence at home.

Someone who has undergone a complicated tooth extraction may find chewing painful, and trapped particles of food can encourage infection. A liquid diet can be used for a time, and then gradually changed to a puree diet, and then a soft diet, as the ability to chew returns.

A viral infection that causes severe ulceration of the mouth can make eating extremely painful. A liquid diet can give the lining of the mouth the chance to heal more quickly.

Bouts of diarrhea and vomiting nearly always get worse, or continue for longer, if solid food is eaten too soon. After 24

hours on clear fluids, such as broth, Jell-O, water, or tea, the patient will probably be ready for a full liquid diet (usually sorbets, soups, and stews). Taken for the next 36 hours, this will hasten recovery without upsetting the stomach further.

Recovery from any illness is always helped by good nutrition. In the initial stages of convalescence, a liquid diet provides the extra calories required to give strength, without the need to eat huge meals. As the patient progresses more solid food can be introduced, and a puree diet can be followed by a soft food diet.

Fevers increase the body's requirement for energy and liquid. As a fever rises digestion is impaired, and so a liquid diet is appropriate since it provides both extra fluid and nourishment (see Fevers).

Patients with terminal illnesses who are being nursed at home or in hospices are often unable to take solid food. Small amounts of tasty liquid meals are appropriate in this situation, and will provide all the nutrition needed. This may not halt the progress of their disease, but it will help to make the patient more comfortable (see Hospices).

Problems

The chief danger of a liquid diet is that if it has not been recommended by a doctor, it may not contain the essential balance of ingredients. Checking with a doctor or dietitian can eliminate this risk.

A young convalescent may have very little appetite. Tasty enriched-milk drinks can be much more acceptable than plates of meat and vegetables, so long as the doctor agrees. Small, frequent portions are better than big meals.

Normally defecation occurs less often on a liquid diet and the reduced fiber content can lead to constipation. But because the diet is low residue, this is not uncomfortable. The condition can be helped by taking a daily quantity of prune juice. A vitamin C supplement may also be needed if vegetables are pureed, because an extra cooking needed to make them soft may destroy their vitamin C content.

If a patient loses weight on a liquid diet, this means either they are not getting enough calories or that the diet is not nutritionally adequate. Weight loss should always be reported to the doctor.

Coming off a liquid diet

Patients are never advised to switch straight from a liquid diet to solid food. From a pure liquid diet, they should pass to a liquefied diet, and then on to a soft diet before returning to normal food. This transition can be made over a period of days, depending on the advice of the doctor or dietitian. Once the condition for which the patient required the liquid diet has improved, then solids can slowly be reintroduced into the diet.

CLARKSTON